UNIVERSITY OF NORTH CAROLINA AT CHAPEL HILL

DEPARTMENT OF ROMANCE LANGUAGES

NORTH CAROLINA STUDIES
IN THE ROMANCE LANGUAGES AND LITERATURES

Founder: URBAN TIGNER HOLMES
Editor: STIRLING HAIG

Distributed by:

UNIVERSITY OF NORTH CAROLINA PRESS

CHAPEL HILL
North Carolina 27514
U.S.A.

NORTH CAROLINA STUDIES IN THE
ROMANCE LANGUAGES AND LITERATURES
Number 226

NOVEL LIVES:

THE FICTIONAL AUTOBIOGRAPHIES OF GUILLERMO CABRERA INFANTE AND MARIO VARGAS LLOSA

NOVEL LIVES:
THE FICTIONAL AUTOBIOGRAPHIES OF GUILLERMO CABRERA INFANTE AND MARIO VARGAS LLOSA

BY

ROSEMARY GEISDORFER FEAL

CHAPEL HILL

NORTH CAROLINA STUDIES IN THE ROMANCE
LANGUAGES AND LITERATURES
U.N.C. DEPARTMENT OF ROMANCE LANGUAGES

1986

Library of Congress Cataloging in Publication Data

Feal, Rosemary Geisdorfer.
  Novel lives.

  (North Carolina studies in the Romance languages and literatures; no. 226.)
  Bibliography: p. 170.
  1. Cabrera Infante, G. (Guillermo), 1929-   . Habana para un infante difunto.   2. Vargas Llosa, Mario, 1936-   . Tía Julia y el escribidor.   3. Fiction, Autobiographic — History and criticism.   I. Title. II. Series.
PQ7389.C233H334   1986 ·   863   86-2561

ISBN 0-8078-9230-0

© 1986. Department of Romance Languages. The University of North Carolina
  at Chapel Hill.

ISBN 0-8078-9230-0

IMPRESO EN ESPAÑA

PRINTED IN SPAIN

DEPÓSITO LEGAL: V. 807 - 1986   I.S.B.N. 84-599-1359-7

ARTES GRÁFICAS SOLER, S. A. - LA OLIVERETA, 28 - 46018 VALENCIA - 1986

CONTENTS

ACKNOWLEDGMENTS

I wish to express my gratitude to those who read and commented on this study at its various stages: Mireya Camurati, Henry Richards, Jorge Guitart, and above all, my husband, Carlos. I also owe a great intellectual debt to the participants in the NEMLA sessions on autobiography and fiction in Hispanic literature in 1984 and 1985, especially to Sharon Magnarelli and Jonathan Tittler. My thanks extend to Stirling Haig and the NCSRLL Editorial Board and to the readers who evaluated my study. I gratefully acknowledge the financial assistance provided by Canisius College in support of my research. A portion of Chapter I appeared in a slightly different version in *Folio,* Number 16 (December 1984), pp. 36-49. Finally, I dedicate this book to my family, whose encouragement and support have been invaluable.

ROSEMARY GEISDORFER FEAL
Buffalo, New York

PREFACE

Many of the novels of the "boom" in Spanish American literature explore such fantastic topics as the return to primordial civilization, the force of witchcraft and magic, and the existence of the living and dead on the same plane; at the same time, the authors of the "boom" have experimented with the creation of a new literary language through such techniques as the distortion of chronology, the confusion of narrative voices and point of view, and the use of linguistic word games and puns. The literary works of the "boom" hold universal appeal not only because of their ground-breaking innovations in prose style, but also because of their exploration of Spanish America as a theme and as a symbol.

The first-person self-conscious autobiographical novel is not generally associated with the "boom" in the literature of Spanish America, nor is it a widely cultivated mode in Hispanic letters as a whole when compared, for instance, with the literatures of France or England. In general terms, autobiographical writing in Spanish America has followed two traditions: historical or political memoirs, and religious confessions. With a few notable exceptions — Domingo Faustino Sarmiento in the first group, Sor Juana Inés de la Cruz in the second — historical or religious autobiographers have not achieved status as great writers.

On the other hand, many outstanding Spanish American novels from the earliest writings to recent works have been called autobiographical, but only in the vaguest sense of the term. Critics are often quick to call autobiographical fiction a work in which the protagonist and his circumstances bear some resemblance to the author's life. If autobiography is viewed more narrowly as involving a conscious intention on an author's part to re-create himself as character, then few of the so-called autobiographical novels of Spanish America may legitimately be classified under that genre heading.

It is interesting to note, then, the appearance within a two-year span of two legitimate autobiographical novels by major Spanish American writers. *La Habana para un infante difunto* (1979) by Guillermo Cabrera Infante and *La tía Julia y el escribidor* (1977) by Mario Vargas Llosa steer away from those fantastic topics culti-vated in the early novels of the "boom" and instead turn inward to a richer territory of the imagination: the exploration of the self as writer, as man, and as character. Cabrera Infante and Vargas Llosa remain at the forefront of this literary mode in modern Hispanic letters, but they do not stand alone: we may include in the ranks of self-conscious autobiographers other writers — some young, some established — from both Latin America and Spain, in particular José Donoso, Mempo Giardinelli, Juan Goytisolo and Carmen Martín Gaite.

In this study, I will undertake an analysis of the rhetorical devices that serve to characterize Cabrera Infante's and Vargas Llosa's auto-biographical novels, and second, I will examine the works as they relate to the discovery and creation of the self within the overall context of fiction. To lay the foundation for the discussion of these novels as autobiographical writing, a preliminary theoretical in-troduction to the genre is in order. While I do not propose to review all the literature on autobiography, I will trace the major lines of recent critical thought to show their applicability to the study of the two novels in question. It is my intention, then, to provide an analysis of the autobiographical mode in modern Hispanic letters as typified by *La Habana* and *La tía Julia* while offering a thorough discussion of these two novels within the overall context of their authors' literary production.

THEORETICAL INTRODUCTION

> What is the past, after all, but a vast sheet of darkness in which a few moments pricked apparently at random, shine?
>
> JOHN UPDIKE, "The Astronomer"

The subject of autobiography has received much critical attention recently as a consequence of the current tendency in literary studies toward redefining the concept of genre. More than the story of one's life written by oneself, autobiography has come to be seen as synonymous with the exploration of the self through writing, a literary endeavor that takes on certain structural features characteristic of the autobiographical mode but often shared simultaneously with other textual forms. To explore Guillermo Cabrera Infante's and Mario Vargas Llosa's use of literary autobiography, a discussion of the theory of autobiography is essential. I will examine a variety of approaches to autobiography in an attempt to situate *La Habana para un infante difunto* and *La tía Julia y el escribidor* in the context of the modern autobiographical novel.

Efforts to define the term "autobiography" have given rise to many conflicting theories on the nature of this literary form. Using what might be called a prescriptive approach, one group of writers distinguishes certain elements whose presence is mandatory in any work to be labeled autobiographical. Other critics put few restrictions on the notion of autobiography and accordingly accept a wide spectrum of works into the autobiographical mode.

For Philippe Lejeune, who in his early writings offers a highly limited definition of the term, it is the exact correspondence of the name within the text to the name on the cover of the book that constitutes the autobiographical pact between author, character, and reader. Conversely, Lejeune maintains that the name of the character and that of the author cannot be identical in a work labeled fiction, for the author who affirms his identity as the narrator of the text to whom he gives his own name writes autobiography, whether or not the literary version of his life is in agreement with historical reality. However, a protagonist who does not bear the same name as the author on the cover cannot be the subject of an autobiography no matter how closely he resembles the author, since no pact, no affirmation of identity, has been executed. For Lejeune, then, legitimate autobiography reflects a conscious act on the author's part to sign his name to the story of his own life while assigning that same name to the figure within the text. Lejeune holds that the autobiographical vocation and the desire for anonymity are mutually exclusive and therefore cannot coexist within the same person. [1]

Lejeune makes reference to that gray area of autobiography into which Cabrera Infante's *La Habana para un infante difunto* seems to fall: the case marked by the use of the first person singular in the text and the apparent identification of the author with a narrator who lacks a name in the text. According to Lejeune, it is the reader who must determine if the work in question is autobiography, contingent on the author's having reached a "novelistic pact" or an "autobiographical pact" in writing his story. A novelistic pact, however, can never be made if a character and his creator share the same name. [2] Whereas Lejeune asserts that autobiography has no degrees, he leaves in shadow a large terrain of writings in which no overt pact is discernible.

Lejeune re-examines his own critical stance on this question in "Le Pacte autobiographique (bis)," in which he remarks that he based his initial "all or nothing" approach to autobiography on linguistic and formalistic criteria. Lejeune recognizes here that different readings of the same text are admissible, and that the "contract" may be subject to interpretation. The paradoxical nature of autobiography leads the author to affirm that no essential difference between the autobiographical novel and the autobiography per se

---

[1] Philippe Lejeune, *Le Pacte autobiographique* (Paris: Éditions du Seuil, 1975), pp. 14-38.

[2] Lejeune, *Le Pacte,* pp. 28-31.

is detectable on the internal level of the text. [3] In recognizing that the literary autobiographical novel encroaches on the domain of the "real" autobiography, Lejeune removes some of his previous restrictions on the nature of the pact.

In *Je est un autre,* Lejeune progresses beyond his limited conception of first-person autobiography to focus instead on the multiple manifestations of the *I* as another. Departing from his narrow "autobiographical pact" Lejeune finally arrives at an all-encompassing approach to autobiography. In so doing, he is able to include into the autobiographical mode a wide variety of works, such as third-person narratives, tape recorded interviews, biographies, testimonial writings, and so forth. If we accept along with Lejeune the illusory nature of every autobiographical *I* — always a mask, a figure split in two — we may then search for textual expression of the self not only in proper names and pronouns, but also in encoded and implicit forms. Lejeune claims that autobiography of any type harbors "the tension between the impossible unity and the intolerable division" and thus illustrates "the fundamental break that turns the speaking subject into a fugitive." [4] Lejeune's critical trajectory typifies the evolution of autobiographical theory in general; the circle may soon be complete when all works are once again considered to be autobiographies in that they inherently contain traces and reflections of their authors' life, personality, or fantasies.

Of those critics who link specific structural traits to the style of autobiography, Jean Rousset, in his study of the first person in the novel, provides a detailed analysis of the possible variations within the genre. The interior autobiographical monologue is characterized by a present *I* who contemplates within himself his double of the past and tells the story of that past *I*. A simple memoir novel, on the other hand, must be retrospective, detached from the present, and follow a chronological order beginning with the birth of the self. The *énoncé* "je conte mon histoire" ('I tell my story') defines pure autobiography and sets the stage for a central protagonist who as-

---

[3] Lejeune, "Le Pacte autobiographique (bis)," in *L'Autobiographie en Espagne: Actes du IIe Colloque International de la Baume-les-Aix,* Études Hispaniques 5 (Aix-en-Provence: Université de Provence, 1982), pp. 12-16.

[4] Lejeune, *Je est un autre: L'autobiographie de la littérature aux médias* (Paris: Éditions du Seuil, 1980), p. 38 (translation mine).

sumes the function of narrator both of his own experiences and those of the other characters who serve as his satellites. Conceived in this fashion, autobiography represents the literary variant of the mirror and the *mise en scène* of self-love incarnated in the narrator. This focus on the self in the text in turn upsets the balance of the actors: one is subject while the rest are objects. For Rousset, this inherent injustice in the narrative order creates a type of monarchic system wherein the subject of the text, the narrator, rules over the subordinate characters — his subjects within the text. [5]

Rousset maintains, along with Lejeune, that the textual *I* who attempts to tell his story creates much confusion in modern narrations, due to a semantic instability of the pronouns *I* and *he* which in turn causes the subject *I* to question his own power as a narrative voice ("Suis-je bien celui qui parle?"). [6] The *I* in modern letters is undergoing a crisis at the same time that the unity and stability of narrative persons are called into question. This observation of Rousset's may certainly be applied to the first major novels of Cabrera Infante and Vargas Llosa, in which the narrative voices become intermingled and at times indistinguishable, as well as to their autobiographical works *La Habana para un infante difunto* and *La tía Julia y el escribidor*.

Another critic who delimits certain structural traits of autobiography is Elizabeth Bruss, who argues that while autobiography has no being or features outside of the social and literary conventions that create and maintain it, a generic identity may be formulated on the basis of several rules to be satisfied by the text and its surrounding context. The autobiographer undertakes a dual role in that he is "the source of the subject matter and the source for the structure to be found in his text." [7] In his writings, the autobiographer reports events

---

[5] Jean Rousset, *Narcisse romancier: Essai sur la première personne dans le roman* (Paris: Librairie José Corti, 1973), pp. 17, 20, 23, 33, 109-110.

[6] Rousset, pp. 35-36.

[7] Elizabeth W. Bruss, *Autobiographical Acts: The Changing Situation of a Literary Genre* (Baltimore: Johns Hopkins Univ. Press, 1976), p. 10. To use French structuralist terminology, we may say that the autobiographer is both the *sujet de l'énoncé* and the *sujet de l'énonciation*. Throughout this study, the term *énoncé* will refer to what is being told (the story), while the term *énonciation* will refer to the act of narrating or telling (the discourse). See especially Émile Benveniste, *Problèmes de linguistique générale* (Paris: Gallimard, 1966), who distinguishes between *histoire* and *discours,* and Seymour Chatman, *Story*

that in reality have taken place or that have the potential for being real; that is, a "truth value" is assigned to autobiography regardless of how private the experiences described may be. Above all, the autobiographer purports to believe in his own story as he tells it, whether or not his report can be discredited. The author's adherence to these rules may be publicly verified by the readers, according to Bruss, and while any and all of these rules may be broken, the pact between author and reader concerning their validity lays the foundation for true autobiography. [8] For Bruss, then, extra-textual criteria play an important role in determining the sincerity of a writer's autobiographic intention, and like Rousset, she places importance on the reader's judgments of and reactions to the text.

Adherence to truth as the major requirement for producing an authentic autobiography is also cited by John N. Morris in his study *Versions of the Self*. Morris states that the writer must in his language and his design be faithful to the truth of his experience. While recognizing that the reader cannot very well ascertain the truth value, Morris says it is the text itself that convinces the reader of the author's sincerity. Morris remarks that "in achieving this success, what counts is the autobiographer's manner — his way with language, and his sense of form. His manner has to do not only with how he tells his truth; it is itself that truth." [9] According to Morris' theory, it is therefore possible for the autobiographer, through his style, to convince the reader of the authenticity of the report, even when the account given in the text contains errors and deliberate suppressions of significant data.

Ultimately, it is once again the reader who must be convinced that the author is telling the truth in his story. The fabricator of tales who has mastered a convincing style stands a greater chance of achieving success in an autobiographical endeavor than does the "sincere" but inept writer who sets out to tell the true story of his life. But, as Gérard Genette remarks, "the verbal 'imitation' of nonverbal

---

and Discourse: Narrative Structure in Fiction and Film (Ithaca: Cornell Univ. Press, 1978), who discusses this terminology in English.

   [8] Bruss, pp. 6-12.

   [9] John N. Morris, *Versions of the Self: Studies in English Autobiography from John Bunyan to John Stuart Mill* (New York: Basic Books, 1966), p. 213.

events is simply a utopia of illusion," [10] which may explain why many literary autobiographers explore a variety of means of self-expression.

If some critics discern those marking features that signal the presence of "true" autobiography, the next group of writers perceives few limitations in the re-creation and expression of the self and accordingly accepts a much wider range of works into the autobiographical mode. James Olney has collected numerous critical studies of autobiography, many of which lend support to his contention that *bios* is a "*process* ever moving towards the ineluctable present of 'is' that gathers up into its own creative image all that 'was becoming' . . . ." [11] It is through the act of writing that the self and the life assume a form or image, and thus the autobiographer's narrative can have no real ending since the actualization of the self is seen as an open-ended process. [12]

The re-creation of the self in autobiography is often compared to the act of painting a self-portrait. [13] For William Howarth, the author-artist-model alternately poses and paints: that is, he arranges the composition to resemble life, but as an artful invention that defines, restricts, and shapes that life. [14] James Olney carries Rousset's mirror metaphor a step further in stating that through the act of writing "the self and the life, complexly intertwined and entangled, take on a certain form, assume a particular shape and image, and endlessly reflect that image back and forth between themselves as between two mirrors." [15] The mirror that reflects can also deform, as Cabrera Infante will show in the concluding chapter of *La Habana para un infante difunto,* leading us perhaps to the ultimate distorted mirror image: the *esperpento,* Valle-Inclán's term for the esthetic deforma-

---

[10] Gérard Genette, *Narrative Discourse: An Essay in Method,* trans. Jane E. Lewin (Ithaca: Cornell Univ. Press, 1980), p. 169.

[11] James Olney, "Some Versions of Memory/Some Versions of *Bios:* The Ontology of Autobiography," in *Autobiography: Essays Theoretical and Critical,* ed. Olney (Princeton: Princeton Univ. Press, 1980), p. 240.

[12] Olney, "Autobiography and the Cultural Moment: A Thematic, Historical, and Bibliographical Introduction," in *Autobiography,* ed. Olney, p. 25.

[13] For a psychoanalytic study of the manifestation of the self in modern art, see Mary Mathews Gedo, *Picasso: Art as Autobiography* (Chicago: Univ. of Chicago Press, 1980).

[14] William L. Howarth, "Some Principles of Autobiography," in *Autobiography,* ed. Olney, pp. 85-86.

[15] Olney, "Autobiography and the Cultural Moment," p. 22.

tion of reality comparable to the manner in which a concave mirror alters physical reality. [16]

The quest for the true self through writing gives rise to many variants within the autobiographical mode, forms which critics divide into several categories. According to William Spengemann, Saint Augustine's tripartite *Confessions* provides three models for all subsequent autobiographers who struggle with the problem of self-knowledge. In the first model, an autobiographer surveys past actions from an immobile point either above or beyond those experiences (historical self-recollection). This mode rests on the conviction that the retrospective narrator can see his life from a fixed point outside it. In this sense the narrator (present self) functions like God in the universe. In the second model, the autobiographer moves inquisitively through memories and draws conclusions (philosophical self-exploration). The narrator's voice follows the protagonist's voice in time, but the two can be reconciled only in the narrator's memory, also subject to the temporal factor. This second mode analyzes the memory and its relation to eternity and time in an attempt to discover some link with the absolute. In the final model, the autobiographer performs a series of symbolic actions through which the self can be realized (poetic self-expression). This third mode of confession evolves from Saint Augustine's struggle (and failure) to fix memory in time, and to follow its movement to a point where all movement ceases. [17]

For Spengemann, the defining quality of all autobiographical writing is the underlying notion of an absolute self that transcends and thus justifies all conditional experience. Thus, autobiography can lack certain features which other critics consider to be essential, such as a consistent viewpoint in the present, the assignment of the author's name to the narrator and protagonist, and even the assignment of the same name to both narrator and protagonist. The major concern that Spengemann identifies, that is, the autobiographer's

---

[16] See Ramón del Valle-Inclán, *Luces de Bohemia,* 4th ed. (Madrid: Espasa-Calpe, 1973), Scene xii, p. 106.

[17] William C. Spengemann, *The Forms of Autobiography: Episodes in the History of a Literary Genre* (New Haven: Yale Univ. Press, 1980), pp. 4-9, 19, 27-32. Paul Jay finds fault with Spengemann's attempt to link disparate works under a heading of genre. See *Being in the Text* (Ithaca: Cornell Univ. Press, 1984), p. 17.

efforts toward the discovery and realization of an absolute self through writing, may also be found at the core of fictional works. It is not the inclusion of autobiographical data in a text that constitutes autobiography; rather, the author's intent to explore the self forms the essence of the autobiographical act, and this may be carried out in fictional texts as well. Spengemann maintains that an accurate recollection that does not evoke a "conviction of self" creates a barrier between author and reader and thus alienates the writer from autobiographical truth, whereas lies can bear truth value if they generate those feelings which are the ground of the true being. Spengemann does not probe the issue of how to ascertain authorial intent, but it is clear that fiction and autobiography become more indistinct when this problematic question of explicit intent is used as the basic criterion for distinguishing between these modes. To further complicate the matter, this critic asserts that "for those who have accepted Hawthorne's conclusion, that the self is continually reshaped by efforts to explain, discover, or express it, autobiography in the Augustinian sense is no longer possible." [18]

The desire to fix lost time forever by recalling the past underlies all autobiographical writings, according to Georges Gusdorf. The author's purpose is to shed light on his past in order to give form to his being in time; autobiography thus becomes man's struggle to "reassemble himself in his own likeness at a certain moment of his history." [19] For Gusdorf, this autobiographical drama turns into a tragedy of sorts: the creator becomes entangled in a match with his shadow, his opponent, the self he can never fully grasp. [20]

The self-interpretation that the writer performs when recalling his past leads to the problem of truth in autobiography. Jean Starobinski points out a paradox common to memoirs, biographies, and autobiographies: the *I* of the narrative may be assumed by a nonentity, and therefore an author is free to engage in fictive invention. This *I* without a true referent cannot be distinguished linguistically from the *I* of a so-called sincere autobiographical narrative. [21]

---

[18] Spengemann, pp. 120, 71, 132, 167.

[19] Georges Gusdorf, "Conditions and Limits of Autobiography," trans. Olney, in *Autobiography,* ed. Olney, p. 43.

[20] Gusdorf, pp. 37, 43-45, 48.

[21] Jean Starobinski, "The Style of Autobiography," trans. Seymour Chatman, in *Literary Style: A Symposium,* ed. Chatman (New York: Oxford Univ. Press, 1971), p. 286.

Even when an author's sincere quest for truth is verifiable, the version of himself that he creates in his text often rivals the most extravagant fictional heroes. Patricia M. Spacks remarks that the act of turning lives into words rescues the life from confusion and imposes an orderly and revealing pattern belonging to literature or myth. But the autobiographer must face the question of reliability, a problem that twentieth-century writers often deal with by focusing on their works' status as artifact. [22] Factuality ceases to be the standard of judgment when an author places more emphasis on the literary shaping of his life's material than on the external public reality that makes up his life.

Literary autobiographies often are most effectively studied as artistic objects in their own right since the *I* subject has been transformed into the *I* object. According to John Pilling, a special allegiance arises from this transformation, involving the author and the reader, for both of whom the object (and objectification) transcends the subject. [23] The *I* has the appearance of a universal, but in fact is employed to express radical singularity in autobiography. [24] In fiction, the grammatical marker *I* is empty because it lacks an extra-textual referent, whereas the *I* of autobiography is theoretically filled up by the work's subject. [25]

The *I* with a true referent nevertheless encounters numerous obstacles when attempting the autobiographical act. If autobiography is the story of one's own life, and life encompasses the span from birth to death, then the very opening and closure of autobiography — "I was born," "I died" — cannot be uttered legitimately by the author himself. Louis Marin posits that "I was born," always a quotation of another person ("on m'a dit que je naquis") which is held to be true, represents a "textual interruption," which makes autobiography a "machination of writing." Citing another person forces the autobiographer to interrupt the story of his own life before

---

[22] Patricia Meyer Spacks, *Imagining a Self: Autobiography and Novel in Eighteenth-Century England* (Cambridge: Harvard Univ. Press, 1976), pp. 21, 42.

[23] John Pilling, *Autobiography and Imagination: Studies in Self-Scrutiny* (London: Routledge and Kegan Paul, 1981), p. 119.

[24] William Earle, *The Autobiographical Consciousness* (Chicago: Quadrangle Books, 1972), p. 15.

[25] Lionel Grossman, "The Innocent Art of Confession and Reverie," *Daedalus*, 107 (1978), 62.

it has truly commenced, and the resulting fragmentation takes the form of "a tissue perforated by these interruptions," which Marin calls "micro-births" and "micro-deaths." [26] However, it should be pointed out that the only fact an autobiographer may unequivocally state concerning his birth is precisely that he was born: any other details about the circumstances of his birth must emanate from what others have told him.

If autobiography, then, cannot legitimately begin with the writer's recollection of the circumstances of his own birth, neither can it finish with his death, except as a metaphor, an invention, or a machination. Autobiography does not follow the life span or *bios* from birth to death; many critics view the genre as an exploration of what one has been, a regression from maturity to birth. [27] The life recorded necessarily ends at a specific point (the author's present or *temps de l'énonciation*) and is therefore a "dead" text that constitutes a suicide note, in Roger Rosenblatt's terms. [28] Since death is not a possible autobiographical closure, the author must end his text on another stasis, such as the author's arrival at his vocation, or leave it open, "to be continued." [29] A third possibility — that a work begin where it ends — is suggested by Steven Kellman in his analysis of the "self-begetting novel," [30] a sub-genre under which many autobiographical texts may be classified.

The author's need to formulate his life with words and the impossibility of this task partially account for the self-consciousness that characterizes autobiographical writing. The autobiographer continually shows himself at work, or as Elizabeth Bruss remarks:

> there must always be something which is just outside the autobiographer's immediate field of vision, something he can reach only by turning his text back upon itself to ex-

---

[26] Louis Marin, "The Autobiographical Interruption: About Stendhal's *Life of Henry Brulard*," *Modern Language Notes*, 93 (1978), 603.

[27] See Georges May, *L'Autobiographie* (Paris: Presses Universitaires de France, 1979), pp. 166-67.

[28] Roger Rosenblatt, "Black Autobiography: Life as the Death Weapon," in *Autobiography*, ed. Olney, p. 178.

[29] Robert Kellogg and Robert Scholes, *The Nature of Narrative* (New York: Oxford Univ. Press, 1966), pp. 214-15.

[30] Steven G. Kellman, *The Self-Begetting Novel* (New York: Columbia Univ. Press, 1980), p. 3. Cabrera Infante's *La Habana* fits especially well into Kellman's scheme.

amine the vantage point rather than the view. Thus an autobiography typically calls attention to its own devices, to the progress it is making in unfolding its tale, to its successes and even more often its failures to capture and communicate its subject. [31]

This is perhaps the fundamental difference between biography and autobiography: the self-conscious narrator, object and subject of the text, cannot possibly recount his life in the same manner as a biographer unfolds the life of another.

The autobiographer, conscious of his enormous task, seeks particular narrative strategies that allow him to transmit the density of his life experiences. Stephen A. Shapiro points out that these strategies must be used to simulate, to give the illusion of a life being lived or re-created, something a biographer also strives to achieve. Autobiography transforms its subject into object through the metamorphic mirror of imagination and memory, in an attempt to align the private self with the public face. Shapiro, therefore, sees autobiography as emerging from "a desire to understand and integrate one's selves through the process of objectifying," a process which involves both verbal expression, recollection, and discovery. [32]

To accomplish his task, the autobiographer often eschews the historical mode to employ techniques associated with literary writing and, as we shall see, especially with fiction. What Northrop Frye calls the confessional mode, a form of prose fiction, rests on "a creative, and therefore fictional, impulse to select only those events and experiences in the writer's life that go to build up an integrated pattern." [33] A coherent text thus emerges when the autobiographer imposes a pattern, establishes certain stages in his life, and "defines, implicitly or explicitly, a certain consistency of relationship between the self and the outside world." [34] This process of selecting and

---

[31] Bruss, p. 164.

[32] Stephen A. Shapiro, "The Dark Continent of Literature: Autobiography," *Comparative Literature Studies*, 5 (1968), 438, 444-47. Spacks also comments that the autobiographer must reconcile some form of the person he presents to the world with an acceptable rendition of his private self-image (pp. 87-88).

[33] Northrop Frye, *Anatomy of Criticism: Four Essays* (1957; rpt. New York: Atheneum, 1968), p. 307.

[34] Roy Pascal, *Design and Truth in Autobiography* (Cambridge: Harvard Univ. Press, 1960), p. 9.

ordering inevitably leads to the formulation of a version of the self, rather than a re-creation of the entirety of one's being within textual boundaries. [35] The version rendered can even be that of a divided self, as Christine Downing remarks, since the author struggles with an awareness of something within radically different from the conscious ego. [36]

Seen from another perspective, the division within may be attributed to the author's self-consciousness in writing his autobiography; concerned with both the events of his life and the effect he is making, he cannot maintain total involvement in even the deepest experiences he reports. [37] Louis Renza postulates that the self-consciousness implied in writing about one's own existence leads to a denial of life as one's own, to the "autobiographical split" that occurs when *I* becomes *he*. Renza questions the autobiographer's use of the *I*: "how can he keep using the first-person pronoun, his sense of self-referential, without its becoming in the course of writing something other than strictly his own self-referential sign — a de facto third-person pronoun?" [38]

A possible result of the autobiographer's acute self-consciousness is that his text may take the form of a work-in-progress, or *poioumenon,* which Alastair Fowler sees as an ideal vehicle for treating the relation of art to life. A narrative of this type is usually discontinuous, with "frequent references to the process of composition" and the "self-conscious highlighting of the style," more often than not with self-deprecating irony. [39] In a similar vein, Robert Spires analyzes the structural traits of Hispanic metafiction to show that "the act

[35] Pilling, p. 119, among others, refers to autobiographies as "versions of the self," also the title of Morris' study.

[36] Christine Downing, "Re-Visioning Autobiography: The Bequest of Freud and Jung," *Soundings,* 60 (1977), 213.

[37] Bruss, p. 122.

[38] Louis A. Renza, "The Veto of the Imagination: A Theory of Autobiography," in *Autobiography,* ed. Olney, pp. 278-79. Renza sees autobiography as "an attempt to signify the autobiographer's non-textual identity or 'interiority' " (p. 276). This "split" when *I* becomes *he* brings to mind Rimbaud's statement "Je est un autre," the title of Lejeune's recent study.

[39] Alastair Fowler, *Kinds of Literature: An Introduction to the Theory of Genres and Modes* (Cambridge: Harvard Univ. Press, 1982), pp. 123-24.

of narrating is real" while "the product or what is narrated is always a fiction." [40]

It has become readily apparent that the majority of the critics writing about autobiography in recent years agree that the conscious shaping of the events of one's life or of the unconscious self leads to the use of devices normally associated with fiction. As early as 1937, E. Stuart Bates declared that there is no dividing line between autobiography and fiction, an opinion widely held in modern criticism. [41] Alfred Kazin, for example, believes that autobiography as narrative cannot borrow techniques from fiction without actually becoming fiction; Georges May states that autobiography is so modeled on fiction that external criteria are needed to distinguish between them; Louis Renza notes that autobiography self-consciously borrows from the methodology of fiction; Robert Kellogg and Robert Scholes claim that an autobiographer heads toward fiction as he selects and arranges his life's events; and Patricia Spacks observes that twentieth-century autobiographies deliberately adopt techniques of the novel. [42] Renza's statement on the subject underscores the impossibility of genre distinction on the level of the text: "*any* first-person narrative-of-a-life that necessarily seems to represent the author's own mental experiences at the time of writing could be termed autobiographical and/or fictive." [43] Paul Jay makes a convincing argument for the impossibility of distinguishing autobiography from fiction: "For if by 'fictional' we mean 'made up,' 'created,' or 'imagined' — something, that is, which is literary and not 'real' — then we have merely defined the ontological status of any text, autobiographical or not." [44]

Autobiography may be viewed as a variant of fiction insofar as mechanisms of historical writing cannot effectively retrieve and re-

---

[40] Robert C. Spires, *Beyond the Metafictional Mode: Directions in the Modern Spanish Novel* (Lexington: Kentucky Univ. Press, 1984), p. 76.

[41] E. Stuart Bates, *Inside Out: An Introduction to Autobiography* (New York: Sheridan House, 1937), p. 9. Also see Paul de Man, "Autobiography as De-Facement," *Modern Language Notes*, 94 (1979), 921.

[42] Alfred Kazin, "Autobiography as Narrative," *Michigan Quarterly Review*, 3 (1964), 211-12; May, p. 178; Renza, p. 269; Kellogg and Scholes, p. 258; Spacks, p. 300.

[43] Renza, p. 272. See also Pilling, who states that autobiography has become a highly elastic term liberally applied to any kind of writing having to do with the author's life (p. 1).

[44] Jay, p. 16.

produce original fact or experience pertaining to the self. An autobiography therefore reads like a novel written in the present with one's
past life as subject. [45] Bertil Romberg's study on narrative techniques
offers some relevant commentary on the devices of what he terms
the fictional autobiographical first-person novel, in which the main
character surveys his life or describes particularly exciting parts of it.
This structure allows the author to "take advantage of the primitive
but remarkably persistent demand that the novel-reader in general
makes of a narrative: namely, that it shall give an illusion of reality
and truth." [46] Like Pilling, Romberg claims that autobiographers need
to invoke the reader and consequently, they often appeal to a second
person, a *you,* when attempting to convey the essence of their *I*.

For Romberg, the simplest yet most illusionistic narrative device
in the first-person novel consists of the author's giving to the fictional
narrator the profession of writer. [47] This presents serious complexities
if the writer-protagonist in the text remains nameless, or pseudonymous, as in the case of the narrator of Cabrera Infante's *La Habana para un infante difunto*. But, on the other hand, the author's
outright use of his name in the text — for example, in Vargas Llosa's
La tía Julia y el escribidor — does not guarantee autobiographical
authenticity or even intention. In the course of this study, I will
discuss the importance of the lack of a name for the narrator of *La
Habana* and Vargas Llosa's deceptive assignment of his name to the
protagonist of *La tía Julia*.

Intent has been suggested here as a basis for determining the
autobiographical validity of a work, a concept that mandates exam-
ining criteria beyond the scope of the text in question. Some critics
have suggested that the intention of autobiography speaks clearly,
even through fiction techniques, and therefore influences the manner
in which a book is to be read and interpreted. [48] Others insist that

---

[45] Burton Pike, "Time in Autobiography," *Comparative Literature,* 28 (1976),
337.

[46] Bertil Romberg, *Studies in the Narrative Technique of the First-Person
Novel,* trans. Michael Taylor and Harold H. Borland (Lund, Sweden: Almquist
and Wiksell, 1962), pp. 58-59.

[47] Romberg, p. 94.

[48] See, for example, Barrett J. Mandel, "Full of Life Now," in *Autobiography,* ed. Olney, p. 53.

any reader can instinctively tell the difference between autobiographical fiction and non-fictional autobiography, since both factuality
and intention affect narrative stance. [49] As a rule, modern criticism
tends to disallow the distinction between autobiography and the
novel, and rather speaks of a fusion of genres and modes in literature,
and of the hybrid autobiographical novel. Spacks remarks on this
dilemma shared by writers and critics alike:

> Twentieth-century autobiographies deliberately adopt the
> techniques of novels. Twentieth-century novelists write
> thinly veiled autobiography, call it a novel, then complain if
> readers suspect some direct self-revelation. Or they write
> real novels and complain; readers still believe them to be
> autobiography. The multiplying confusions of genre are en-
> couraged and publicized, becoming part of the general con-
> fusion of our times. [50]

This brief survey of some critical thinking on autobiography
highlights the impossibility — or rather, the futility — of arriving at
a precise definition of autobiography. Nor would this definition be
requisite to interpret the two works I have chosen as the primary
focus of this study. By applying relevant critical theory to these texts,
I propose not to classify them in strict categories of "novel" or
"autobiography," but rather to reveal the forms which the self takes
when re-created in writing. It matters little whether "Varguitas" of
La tía Julia acts and speaks in the image of Mario Vargas Llosa as
a youth; what demands our interest is the manner in which Vargas
Llosa gives literary existence to himself as character. The emergence
and development of the textual *I* (or *he,* the other) shall be the
primary focus of the discussion of *La Habana* and *La tía Julia* in an
effort to explore the interrelationship between autobiography and
fiction. Through this exploration of representative texts, I also wish
to come closer to uncovering some specifically Hispanic traits of
autobiography and to situating Cabrera Infante and Vargas Llosa
within the tradition of the Hispanic confessional mode. Finally, it

---

[49] For example, Spacks, p. 311.
[50] Spacks, p. 300. See also de Man, p. 921, on autobiography as a figure
of reading.

is my hope that the discussion of *La Habana* and *La tía Julia* in relation to Cabrera Infante's and Vargas Llosa's other works will shed more light on the vital link between the authors' autobiographical novels and the remainder of their literary production.

CHAPTER I

THE STRUCTURE OF AUTOBIOGRAPHY IN GUILLERMO CABRERA INFANTE'S *LA HABANA PARA UN INFANTE DIFUNTO*

Some of the questions that are pertinent to our discussion of the nature of autobiography have also interested Guillermo Cabrera Infante, whose preoccupation with language and its function in literature is reflected in the following questions he poses: "¿Quién escribe? ¿Quién habla en un poema? ¿Quién narra en una novela? ¿Quién es ese yo de las autobiografías?"[1] This last question is particularly appropriate, for the fundamental enigma in Cabrera Infante's *La Habana para un infante difunto* is precisely the identity of the *yo*. How may we attempt to solve this problem of identity? If, as some have stated, autobiography and fiction are indistinguishable at the interior textual level, then perhaps some external criteria should be applied to determine autobiographical intent. These criteria fall into two broad categories: the particulars of an author's life, and his reflections on his own writing as autobiography. I will not attempt to relate directly the known facts of Cabrera Infante's life to *La Habana*; rather, I will explore some of the author's remarks in order to situate this work in the autobiographical mode.[2] After a

---

[1] Guillermo Cabrera Infante, "La voz detrás de la voz," *Exorcismos de esti(l)o* (Barcelona: Seix Barral, 1976), p. 143.

[2] The correspondence, however, between the author's life and his text can be verified quite easily by consulting the chronology written by Cabrera entitled "Orígenes," in Julio Ortega et al., *Guillermo Cabrera Infante* (Madrid: Espiral/Fundamentos, 1974), pp. 5-18, which narrates his life from 1924 to 1965.

The short entries are often capsules of the events later elaborated in *La Habana,* as illustrated by the following:

brief exposition on Cabrera Infante's comments, I will turn to the *I* in the text, the figure that, with or without a true referent, stands independent of its creator and assumes its own identity.

In "La voz detrás de la voz," a short reflection on the narrative voice, Cabrera recognizes the autonomy — or even the dichotomy — of the *I* within the text:

> ¿Quién es ese ventrílocuo oculto que habla en este mismo momento por mi boca —o más bien por mis dedos?
>
> La pluma, por supuesto, a primera vista o de primera mano anoche. O la máquina de escribir ahora en la mañana. Una segunda mirada sonora, escuchar otra vez ese silencio nos revelará —a mí en este instante; a ti, lector, enseguida— que esa voz inaudita, ese escribano invisible es el lenguaje.
>
> Pero la última duda es también la primera —¿de qué voz original es el lenguaje el eco? [3]

For Cabrera, language itself forms the essence of all literature; it undergoes a type of personification as it turns into a ventriloquist, a voice, an echo. Language appears to supplant its own source: whose voice does language reecho? Cabrera Infante has affirmed: "No hay escritores, sólo existen libros," [4] a statement that harmonizes

---

1941
Deja detrás una niñez pobre pero feliz . . . para encontrar una igualmente pobre, pero infeliz adolescencia.

1949
Muy breve (y de nuevo desastroso) encuentro con una trotacalles negra.

1950
Primera experiencia sexual con éxito con una mujer adulta. Para su sorpresa eternamente divertida, ella es la antigua Muchacha Más Bella del Bachillerato (ahora casada), quien insiste en hacer el amor oyendo *El Mar,* de Debussy: un disco prestado en un tocadiscos también prestado. (pp. 9-12)

These vignettes correspond respectively to three chapters in *La Habana:* "La casa de las transfiguraciones"; "Mi último fracaso"; "La muchacha más linda del mundo." It is also of interest to note that Cabrera has written this chronology in the third-person singular.

[3] Cabrera Infante, *Exorcismos,* p. 143.

[4] Interview with Isabel Álvarez-Borland, "Viaje verbal a La Habana, ¡Ah Vana!," *Hispamérica,* 11 (April 1982), 68. Cabrera Infante has on numerous occasions denounced French structuralist critics even though his views on language and literature bear similarities to the ideas expressed by them.

with a structuralist approach to texts. The writer does not speak through his text; rather, words speak through the writer, or through his instruments (pen and paper, typewriter). Appropriately, then, when asked what literary creation means to him, Cabrera responds with Hamlet's "palabras, palabras, palabras." [5]

To create his text, the author must work with words, and Cabrera transforms language into a seemingly plastic material to be molded and shaped on the blank page: "Para mí la literatura es un juego, un juego complicado, mental y concreto a la vez, que actúa sobre un plano físico, la página, y los diversos planos mentales de la memoria, la imaginación, el pensamiento . . . . " [6] Cabrera has expressed the belief, both in his fiction and in interviews, that literature is essentially a game of words: "Literature can and must be a game . . . . " [7] Unlike Vargas Llosa, who writes to "exorcise his demons," Cabrera Infante writes to amuse himself; if, therefore, the reader is able to participate in the author's puns and games, then the amusement is mutual. Cabrera maintains that "a writer writes for himself and then he publishes for others." [8]

Literature is essentially language for Cabrera, but he does not see clear dividing lines between literary genres: "Nunca pienso en términos concretos de novela, o de cuento o de crónica, ensayo, artículo o lo que sea. Jamás pienso en términos de géneros, pienso en términos de literatura." [9] His definition of a novel parallels his clas-

---

[5] Interview with Cabrera Infante in *Siete voces,* ed. Rita Guibert (Mexico: Alfred A. Knopf, 1972), p. 417.

[6] Interview with Cabrera Infante in *Siete voces,* ed. Guibert, p. 418. Some specific examples of this belief may be cited in Cabrera's *Tres tristes tigres* (Barcelona: Seix Barral, 1970), such as the construction of reversible words ("azar/raza"); the formation of a circular star of David in large print; the use of increasingly smaller type to illustrate disappearance; and the many graphic illustrations found in the section "Rompecabeza" (pp. 205-24).

Further page references to this edition of *TTT* will be given parenthetically in the text.

[7] "Guillermo Cabrera Infante: Man of Three Islands," comp. William L. Siemens, *Review,* 28 (January-April 1981), 9. The author also remarks on the therapeutic effect of writing: "Continúo escribiendo para divertirme y aspiro a entretener. . . . Hubo días en que esa tarea de escribir dos o tres páginas me salvó de la depresión." Interview with Sharon Magnarelli, "21 en el 21: Una entrevista de larga distancia con Guillermo Cabrera Infante," *Prismal/Cabral,* No. 5 (Fall 1979), p. 40.

[8] "GCI: Three Islands," comp. Siemens, p. 9.

[9] Interview with Cabrera Infante in *Siete voces,* ed. Guibert, p. 417.

sifying literature as "words, words, words": "Te dan trescientas páginas en blanco y tú tienes que llenarlas. Nada puede ser más difícil." [10] Writing, then, first and foremost involves the author's struggle to fill the blank page with words. The emerging text responds not to a predesigned model, but rather forges its own generic pattern as it is shaped and reshaped until the work becomes in the reader's hands "signos negros congelados en blanco papel." [11]

Reference has been made to the reader as a secondary participant in the author's literary games, a theme that will require particular attention in the analysis of Cabrera's autobiographical novel, *La Habana para un infante difunto*. For Cabrera, there exists no ideal reader except himself: "The ideal reader is impossible. He would be so much like me that it would be impossible to distinguish between the reader and me, the writer." [12] Besides, in his attempt to decipher the coded text, the reader becomes a translator, because for Cabrera, "toda lectura es una forma de traducción. Escribir es traducir del lenguaje a la escritura. No hay diferencia entre una traducción y una lectura, excepto en el tiempo que toman una y otra." [13] With these remarks, Cabrera Infante already shows an acute awareness of the complexities involved in the author-text-reader relationship. In *La Habana* Cabrera focuses on the echo he refers to in "La voz detrás de la voz" as he listens to himself composing his own portrait with language and then offers commentary on the consequences of the self-conscious mode he is employing. He clearly perceives that the voice within the text is not the author's, that literature, especially autobiography, rather than transform the word into flesh, changes flesh into mere words.

When asked if the characters of *Tres tristes tigres* were real, Cabrera responded: "No hay, no puede haber, personajes reales en un libro de ficción. Me inclino a pensar que aun en las biografías hay una distancia entre el personaje biografiado, la escritura y la subsiguiente lectura que carga de irrealidad a los documentos más rea-

---

[10] Rosa María Pereda, "Habla Cabrera Infante: una larga entrevista que es una poética," *Guillermo Cabrera Infante,* Escritores de todos los tiempos (Madrid: EDAF, 1978), pp. 123-24. Cabrera attributes this definition to "an anonymous Cuban writer."

[11] Álvarez-Borland, "Viaje verbal," p. 64.

[12] "GCI: Three Islands," comp. Siemens, p. 9.

[13] Pereda, "Habla CI," p. 110.

les." [14] To write biography, the story of another, is to create a type of fiction, according to Cabrera. In parallel fashion, to write the story of one's own self also entails a degree of fictive invention.

Most of *TTT* is written in the first person, a narrative technique that has led to speculation that the novel is autobiographical. Cabrera remarks:

> Muchas veces he lamentado que el libro estuviera escrito en primera persona, porque hay demasiados lectores que tienden a identificar a este o aquel personaje con el autor . . . . Como otros escritores antes que yo, he combatido esta asociación de una voz gramatical con la persona del escritor . . . [15]

Cabrera himself has called *TTT* a "gallery of voices," since the *I* used throughout the novel is multi-referential. But the *I* can confuse the reader who searches for the person implicit in the personal pronoun, as Cabrera recognizes with some misgivings. In the final analysis, however, the author points to the mechanisms of writing and their consequences with respect to *TTT*: "las parodias no las improvisó Bustrófedon sino que las inventé yo: yo soy el autor de esas imitaciones escritas: Bustrófedon nunca existió, es un personaje, otra invención. En una palabra, Bustrófedon soy yo." [16]

Cabrera manifests his need for a textual disguise if he is to re-create himself through writing: "Cuando escriba un libro realmente autobiográfico me cuidaré, para ficcionalizar mi persona como ficcionalicé a mi alter ego crítico, de escribirlo en tercera persona del singular o del plural tal vez." [17] The difficulties of writing autobiography in the third person may have proved insurmountable, however, since Cabrera does eventually embrace the first-person singular in *La Habana*, the same grammatical person he employed successfully in *TTT*.

The possibility that references to a real name within a literary text may actually serve to obscure an identity is mentioned by Cabrera in regard to the characters of *TTT*:

[14] Interview with Cabrera Infante in *Siete voces*, ed. Guibert, p. 423.
[15] Interview with Cabrera Infante in *Siete voces*, ed. Guibert, pp. 427-28.
[16] Magnarelli, "21 en el 21," p. 34.
[17] Interview with Cabrera Infante in *Siete voces*, ed. Guibert, p. 428.

> Poe se incluyó en varias narraciones con su nombre, pero en circunstancias ficticias; yo he incluido a algunos viejos amigos habaneros con sus nombres, apellido y dirección propios, pero sus apellidos funcionan en el libro como seudónimos, es decir, como nombres falsos . . . . [18]

Cabrera's assertion adds to the complexity of Lejeune's theories. For Cabrera, a pseudonym need not take the form of a false name, but can be a character's or author's name without a "true" referent. In the latter case, it would be similar to the empty grammatical marker *I* of fiction. Even if Cabrera Infante is making reference to real people in *TTT,* either through the use of their names or ones that sound similar, they nevertheless become characters of fiction as they take their place on the pages of the novel. Whereas Lejeune asserts that a pseudonym in the text invalidates an autobiographical pact, he does not discuss the many variants of the false name, the *nom de plume,* the textual "alter ego"; in short, he excludes what might be termed the "autobiographical deception," the inclusion of one's own name as a textual disguise.

The autobiographical split which occurs when *I* becomes *he* is evident in Cabrera's writing long before the publication of *La Habana.* The author himself alludes to this psychological game in his discussion of the evolution of his critical pseudonym, G. Caín, with which he signed his weekly movie reviews in the Cuban magazine *Carteles,* later collected under the title *Un oficio del siglo XX.* Cabrera discovers his own name as a source of amusement in his early exercises of criticism and witticism: or, in the author's words, "I was ready to start playing dirty games with myself alone and stop molesting the children of Sánchez." [19] His affinity for word games is transformed into an attraction to "dirty games," a process that leads to the auto-eroticism of *La Habana* and to the relationship between autobiography and pornography.

Cabrera's explanation of Caín's literary origins provides some clues to the way in which he perceives the self in literature, and deserves to be examined briefly:

---

[18] Interview with Cabrera Infante in *Siete voces,* ed. Guibert, p. 424.

[19] "GCI: Three Islands," comp. Siemens, p. 10. Perhaps this reference to Oscar Lewis' work points to those down-trodden characters that populated Cabrera's first fiction, a collection of short stories entitled *Así en la paz como en la guerra* (1960).

> It is an uncanny game of the self and the alter ego, which should be taken as an *altar* ego. By simply reducing my given name to the initial *G* and taking the first syllables of my middle and last names I raised Cain, who began as an alter ego and ended as my shadow marching before me in some kind of mad parade of charades. [20]

The game of disguises turns into a type of masquerade in which identities become confused and entangled. Cabrera thus illustrates Georges Gusdorf's idea that autobiography is essentially a struggle with one's own shadow, an opponent, a Cain. [21] The logical outcome of this struggle with the textual self is implied in the name Cabrera devised for his pseudonymous character:

> But I became Abel to Cain .... The book *[Un oficio del siglo XX]* was the terrain — or rather the theater — of this fratricidal fight, but even the book had changed during the fracas. It was no longer a collection of film criticism or movie reviews, but had become a work of fiction. It was not a novel, because the main characters — there were several in the book ... including myself, a false biographer — had been real. [22]

By adding an extensive prologue to his essays on film in *Un oficio,* Cabrera creates a sequence of what might be called "The Adventures of Caín"; he reveals Caín's pseudonymous identity (and therefore kills him), but at the same time he revives the character in a fictional setting, thus breathing autonomy into his former shadow or alter ego.

Cabrera Infante becomes a false biographer of a fictional character who had emerged from his own pseudonym. The textual games multiply under these circumstances, and one has great difficulty assigning *Un oficio* to a particular genre. Cabrera himself ponders the hybrid nature of *Un oficio:* "So now we had a frail collection of criticism, a faked biography and almost a novel. If I had to choose

---

[20] "GCI: Three Islands," comp. Siemens, p. 10.

[21] Georges Gusdorf, p. 48.

[22] "GCI: Three Islands," comp. Siemens, p. 10. Cabrera reverses the biblical roles of slayer and victim when he claims Abel killed Cain "with kindness." The interchange of identities brings to mind Unamuno's *Abel Sánchez:* "si Caín no mata a Abel habría sido éste el que habría acabado matando a su hermano" in *Obras completas,* II (Madrid: Escelicer, 1967), 710.

among these categories now I would choose the novel." [23] This confirms some notions set forth in theoretical writings on autobiography: that the act of incorporating fictional techniques in autobiography (or in critical essays, or in a "fake biography," etc.) transports the text through the looking-glass into the terrain of invention, imagination, and the novel.

To trace the line from Caín to the narrator of *La Habana,* a brief examination of Cabrera's prologue and epilogue to *Un oficio* is in order. In the first place, Cabrera Infante signs his own name to the pieces of fiction he attaches to his critical essays, thereby acknowledging that it is indeed he who has "raised Cain." But, much like Unamuno's Augusto Pérez in *Niebla,* Caín as character declares his independence and pressures his creator into complying with his wishes: "¿Sería mucho decir, decir que este prólogo se debe no tanto a la insistencia de G. Caín en que lo escribiera como a mi resistencia a complacerlo?" [24] The author-character relation comes to light as Cabrera insists: "siempre ha habido el mismo violento intercambio que entre el verdugo y su víctima . . ." (p. 13). In his re-creation of his pseudonymous character, Cabrera enters into the autobiographical struggle; he readily accepts his role as aggressor toward his Caín, for in this entanglement of the self and the other, there is no escaping a "violent interchange."

In the epilogue of *Un oficio* Caín comes to visit the author and, in an Unamunian gesture, requests his own epitaph from the character named Cabrera. Cabrera symbolically buries the character he created by revealing Caín's lack of identity, while at the same time, he immortalizes Caín as a fictive entity and, in that sense, destines Caín to outlive his creator. Cabrera becomes the critic's critic and, in so doing, administers the death sentence to Caín as the world knew him in *Carteles.* In other words, he ascribes a consciousness to the figure of Caín that alters his textual being: no longer a pseudonym for Cabrera Infante, Caín has been reclaimed by his creator who engages in a struggle to differentiate the voice from the echo.

---

[23] "GCI: Three Islands," comp. Siemens, p. 10.

[24] Cabrera Infante, *Un oficio del siglo XX* (Barcelona: Seix Barral, 1973), p. 13. Further page references to this edition of *Un oficio* will be given parenthetically in the text. All citations are in italics in the original.

The discussion of names acquires particular importance when one takes into account that the narrator of *La Habana* never claims to be "Guillermo Cabrera Infante," but instead gives clues in the form of pseudonyms, partial names, translated names, etc. It is therefore significant that Caín is born of Cabrera's own name: he is his literary flesh and blood. Cabrera himself accords special meaning to the use of a name, as he remarks of his original Caín: "His criticism had been published without any fictional connections, and he had a name. To name a thing is to bring it into reality . . . ." [25] Just as Cabrera gives Caín a form of his name, he wills him to die in *Un oficio* along with the discarded pseudonym: "Creo que nadie mejor que yo para despedir a Caín: si le vi nacer, bien puedo verlo morir. Caín, como los grandes buques, se hunde con su nombre" (p. 468).

But this death, this fratricide, is also seen as a suicide: "Como era hombre cabal . . . ha decidido suicidarse en el silencio: Caín muere para que viva su alter ego . . ." (p. 469). As indicated earlier, the autobiographical split produces a struggle when the *I* confronts the *he;* Cabrera willingly takes on this confrontation and converts it into a textual game in *Un oficio.* For Cabrera Infante, it seems that only one facet of the multi-referential *I* can be allowed to survive. Yet the very denial of the other's existence in the text (Caín is dead, long live Caín) provides this other with an ineradicable identity on the page. Perhaps Cabrera longs for that same destiny: to fix himself on the blank page, to translate his own being into words. *La Habana* reveals precisely the futility of this autobiographical intent: the failure of words to create a textual self outside the realm of fiction.

La Habana opens with a confusion of the narrative person that runs throughout Cabrera's works in general: "Subí, subimos, la que era para mí entonces suntuosa escalera." [26] The first-person singular is immediately changed to the plural; whereas the initial emphasis falls on the narrator's singularity, the subsequent use of a *we* evokes other voices in the text. Or perhaps the *we* calls into play the role

---

[25] "GCI: Three Islands," comp. Siemens, p. 10.

[26] Cabrera Infante, *La Habana para un infante difunto* (Barcelona: Seix Barral, 1979), p. 11. Further page references to this edition of *La Habana* will be given parenthetically in the text.

of the reader, the outsider drawn in by an *I* who seeks to blur its identity.[27]

Cabrera not only presents the problem of the narrative person and its referent in the first line of *La Habana,* but also introduces the temporal problem that permeates the entire autobiographical text. By stating "Subí, subimos, la que era para mí entonces suntuosa escalera," the narrator is contrasting the story time or *temps de l'énoncé* ("Subí, subimos") and the discourse time *(temps de l'énonciation),* signalled by the reference to a descriptive past *(entonces),* formulated from the perspective of the narrator's present. The emphasis on discourse time implies that the narrator's present will overshadow his past, and that the search for the past self will lead invariably to the fictive present. One of the principles of autobiography becomes evident in this introductory line of *La Habana:* that the historical past cannot escape the commentary and analysis that the autobiographer writing his text interjects. As Elizabeth Bruss notes, the autobiographer shows himself at work, and thereby reveals the machinery that controls recollection and memory; the narrator's self-consciousness distracts him from complete involvement in his own past experiences and leads him to examine the vantage point *(temps de l'énonciation)* rather than the view *(temps de l'énoncé).*

That Cabrera's first line of *La Habana* should harbor a basic autobiographical dilemma — to tell one's story of the past from the stance of the present — is indicative of the struggle that takes place throughout the some seven-hundred pages of the work. Another difficulty inherent in autobiographical writing is that of linking textual and extra-textual identity, an endeavor that can culminate in the type of word play Cabrera Infante has employed with his pseudonymous character Caín. This search for an identity, crucial to all autobiography, manifests itself in *La Habana* through a variety of narrative strategies. The first of these appears in the initial sentence of the text in which the narrative persons *I* and *we* compete to be the subject. A second conflict among the competing textual voices

---

[27] See Émile Benveniste, pp. 234-35, who sees the *we* as a vehicle for softening the strong imposition of the *I. La Habana* contains other instances of this juxtaposition of *I* and *we.* This occurs, for example, in the case of object pronouns: "Esa puerta siempre cerrada . . . me, nos, forzaba hacia el balcón . . ." (p. 15).

manifests itself in the opposition of the subject of the discourse to the subject of the story, implicit in the expression "la que era para mí entonces." The *yo* which continually asserts itself nevertheless points to an absence, since the first-person singular pronoun may refer to several different textual voices and ultimately cannot be attributed to a true referent outside the text. [28]

The opening line of *La Habana,* which I am interpreting here as an initiation into the autobiographical search, could just as well be found on the first page of a novel with no autobiographical intent. Since it should be fairly evident that the dividing lines between fiction and autobiography have become blurred to a great degree, then other criteria are imperative to determine the genre or mode to which a text belongs. Clearly, the hybrid nomenclatures "autobiographical novel" or "fictive autobiography," though appropriate, evade the problem at hand. At the same time, certain criteria, such as historical accuracy within the text, may be considered invalid means of approaching the question of genre. In addition, I have set forth the widely held tenet that to write of oneself is to create a fiction, and therefore, literary autobiography properly belongs to the terrain of the novel. What, then, permits a reading of *La Habana* as an autobiographical text? In this regard, it is instructive to consider *TTT,* a work which also treats similar themes: the narrator(s)' adventures in the city of Havana, the discovery of the pleasures and disappointments of youth, and so forth. In fact, *TTT* has been convincingly interpreted along the lines of the traditional autobiographical novel by Julio Matas, who remarks: "el libro es autobiografía en cuanto transposición de la memoria o de una serie de memorias que el autor recompone, en última instancia, con la

---

[28] In her discussion of the first-person pronoun in *TTT,* Sharon Magnarelli points to the absence that comes about as a result of the multi-referential *I*: "The first person dominates the novel and implicates the absence insofar as the narrator talks about a past self which no longer exists (even on a fictitious level) and insofar as the narrator which speaks at any individual moment emphasizes the absence of all those other *I*'s which are potential in the novel . . . ." "The 'Writerly' in *Tres tristes tigres,*" in *The Analysis of Hispanic Texts: Current Trends in Methodology,* Proc. of the Second York College Colloquium on Hispanic Texts, 23 April 1976, ed. Lisa E. Davis and Isabel C. Tarán (New York: Bilingual Press/Editorial Bilingüe, 1976), p. 332.

libertad del inventor de ficciones y con un propósito puramente estético." [29]

While Matas' words may also be applied to *La Habana,* perhaps the fundamental difference between one text and the other lies in the intention of the author. On the internal level of the text, this difference can be discerned to a degree through the use of the narrative persons, as I shall explore further. Outside the text, one may choose to place credence in an author's statements concerning the nature of his work, even though Cabrera's word games may serve to mislead more than to enlighten. Nevertheless, I believe Cabrera's references to *La Habana* clarify in part its classification here as autobiography presented as fiction, and at least reveal the author's conscious intentions in writing this work.

In 1977 Cabrera indicated that he was undertaking an autobiographical project: "ahora estoy haciendo autobiografía, pero confío que el lector inteligente (el lector que uno siempre espera) sepa apreciar dónde el mero relato autobiográfico se hace literatura." [30] Cabrera provides a page from the manuscript to which he refers ("de título oculto") in the body of this written interview and dates it London, 1975-1978, the same dates given on the last page of *La Habana.* This fragment corresponds to the episode in which Margarita prepares the narrator a drink of the same name in *La Habana* — clearly the autobiography to which Cabrera is referring here. However, the author admonishes readers to exercise caution in approaching this book as autobiography and reminds them that the narrator and the author are different persons. Cabrera Infante himself recognizes a basic principle of autobiography: that the events of a life assume literary and consequently fictive qualities as they are encoded in language.

In reference to the classification of *La Habana* as novel, the author remarks: "no hay forma de llamarla de otro modo: sería amnesia llamarla memoria, sería olvido llamarla recuerdos, sería alejarla de mí si la llamo autobiografía . . . ." [31] This comment accurately describes the process of writing autobiography, for in order to cast

[29] Julio Matas, "Guillermo Cabrera Infante: Autobiografía y novela," in *La cuestión del género literario: Casos de las letras hispánicas* (Madrid: Gredos, 1979), p. 217.

[30] Pereda, "Habla CI," p. 100.

[31] Álvarez-Borland, "Viaje verbal," p. 55.

out a version of the self, an author must indeed face the impossibility
of bridging the gap between life and text. As a self-conscious writer,
Cabrera enters into the autobiographical exploration with a clear
perception of the nature of this narrative act. He implies that this
book must be read primarily as a literary work in its own right,
and only secondarily as an autobiographical attempt. [32] In other words,
the transposition of the *I* subject into the *I* as object takes precedence
over the identification of a possible extra-textual referent for the
subject. When speaking of the *I* in *La Habana,* then, it is to be
treated as a fictitious entity in the sense that, as Cabrera points out,
the narrator and the author inevitably are different persons. At the
same time, the author has acknowledged his autobiographical intention in writing this work, which allows for an interpretation of
La Habana as an attempt — albeit through parody — to re-create the
self in literature.

The exploration of the self in *La Habana* commences at a precise
stage: the transition from childhood to adolescence, and from the
country to the urban world of Havana: "con mi acceso a la casa
marcada Zulueta 408 había dado un paso trascendental en mi vida:
había dejado la niñez para entrar en la adolescencia." The narrator
summarizes: "ese día preciso terminó mi niñez" (p. 12). Burton Pike
remarks that "much literary autobiographical writing . . . has a tendency to become fixated on childhood and adolescence, and to lose
luminosity with adulthood, if it gets that far." [33] Indeed, *La Habana*
(as well as Vargas Llosa's *La tía Julia y el escribidor*) is a chronicle
of adolescence that winds its way toward adulthood. Pike sees the
focus on pre-adult experiences in autobiography as a screening device
to express what the mature consciousness might reject, and as a
means of blocking the passage of time that leads toward death.
Literary autobiography takes the form of "a novel written in the
present, with one's past life as its subject," which would be an appropriate description of *La Habana.* [34]

In the opening pages of *La Habana,* Cabrera relates the death
of his childhood and the birth of the self as adolescent, a sequence

---

[32] See John Pilling, p. 119, who proposes that all autobiography should be
read in this manner.

[33] Burton Pike, p. 333.

[34] Pike, p. 337. See also pp. 334-35.

of events which illustrates Louis Marin's notion of the autobiographical text as a series of micro-deaths and micro-births. Since autobiographical narration for Marin consists of a "machination of writing" in order to say "I was born" and "I died" (the landmarks of *bios*), then similacrums of birth and death must appear in the text. [35] The autobiographer cannot witness his own birth, but he can invent an experience for himself that would symbolize that event. The narrator of *La Habana* invents a birthday and a birthplace for himself when he tells of his emergence as an adolescent in the city of Havana: "yo puedo decir con exactitud que el 25 de julio de 1941 comenzó mi adolescencia" (p. 12). *La Habana* metaphorically fulfills an often proposed requisite for autobiographical writing: that the narrator trace his life from birth to death. Cabrera "begins at the beginning," so to speak, but it is an initiation of his own choosing and emerges from his recollection of events surrounding his *re*birth as an urban adolescent.

The ascent into adolescence is assigned an exact date in time, but it is also depicted symbolically in space: "Era la primera vez que subía una escalera .... Este es mi recuerdo inaugural de La Habana: ir subiendo unas escaleras con escalones de mármol" (p. 11). The step from childhood to puberty, taken on this staircase, is the narrator's first recollection of his life in the city and the starting point for the *bios* in this text. Since climbing stairs often has a sexual meaning in dreams, the narrator's claim that he became an adolescent as he ascended the staircase of Zulueta 408 seems most appropriate. [36] Havana provides the backdrop for the narrator's search for himself, a search that more often than not involves the world of the erotic. Cabrera begins his autobiographical narration with

---

[35] See "Theoretical Introduction," note 26. Further evidence of micro-births and deaths throughout *La Habana* may be cited. For example, the narrator refers to his symbolic baptism amidst the lights of the city: "todavía recuerdo ese primer baño de luces, ese bautizo, la radiación amarilla que nos envolvía ..." (p. 21).

[36] See, for example, Ángel Garma, *The Psychoanalysis of Dreams* (New York: Dell Publishing, 1966), pp. 84-85. This interpretation is further supported by the sexual symbolism of the first page of the work: "Enfrento ... un pasillo largo, un túnel estrecho, un corredor como no había visto antes ..." (p. 11). Clearly, this "pasillo largo" may be seen as representing the vagina, and thus also constitutes one more example of birth imagery in the opening pages of the text.

multiple erotic imagery, and, as we will see, ends the work with the ultimate sexual union: losing himself inside a woman.

An autobiographer, in re-creating his past, must relive it through writing. Yet this narrator states that he does not wish to relive his adolescence, the main time frame of *La Habana*: "una etapa de mi vida que no desearía volver a vivir — y sin embargo hay tanto que recordar de ella" (p. 13). The autobiographical quest often encompasses this paradox: or, as Stephen Shapiro notes, "autobiography emerges from a desire to understand and integrate one's selves through the process of objectifying, which involves not only expression but ... discovery." [37] Perhaps the way to come to terms with one's past self is to revive that self in literature and simultaneously cast it out, a form of "exorcism" Vargas Llosa also embraces. The text demands that the subject become object, and in this manner the author can produce a version of himself by fictionalizing it, as in the case of Cabrera Infante's Caín.

A basic structural element of this autobiographical novel consists of negation as a means of assertion. The narrator continually makes reference to what his story is not about, or should not be about and, in so doing, includes the very recollection he seeks to delete. An example of this is found early in the narration: "Pero no es de la vida negativa que quiero escribir ... sino de la poca vida positiva que contuvieron esos años de mi adolescencia ..." (p. 15). The use of the term *negativa* coupled with the limiting adjective *poca* preceding *vida positiva* produces not a vision of discovered happiness in the urban setting, but one of pain and disillusion. Another basic feature of Cabrera's autobiographical style may be called self-editing. The autobiographer must write his story from the perspective of his present vantage point, or the *temps de l'énonciation,* which in turn casts its shadow over the *temps de l'énoncé,* or story time. Self-editing in *La Habana* usually takes the form of the narrator's correcting his own story once he has committed it to paper. For example, in describing the conditions of life in his first residence in Havana, the narrator focuses on what he recognizes as his own errors: "Por lo menos en el cuarto del solar (estoy adelantándome lingüísticamente: en mi vocabulario todavía no existía la palabra solar: ya me he ade-

see
p. 36

---

[37] Stephen A. Shapiro, p. 447.

lantado antes, pero era la introducción, mientras que ahora estamos in medias res) dormíamos en dos camas" (p. 25).

The self-editing here follows two different paths. In the first instance, the narrator corrects the account of his arrival in Havana by pointing to the erroneous use of the word *solar,* a term not yet in the vocabulary of the past self who functions as subject of the story. The duality of the figure of the autobiographer-narrator stands out clearly: the self who remembers is not the self remembered. By halting the narration (the textual interruption that Marin considers basic to all autobiography), the focus is shifted from what is said to the manner in which it is told (the *énonciation*). Needless to say, this is a device consciously employed by the autobiographer. If the commentary provided by the narrator in the present were suppressed, the remaining text would not be an analysis of the past self (autobiography), but merely a memoir, fictional or otherwise. We may say that commentary and self-editing give rise to the autobiographical exploration itself, as the voice of the present interprets the voice of the past.

This editing technique goes to a deeper level when the narrator not only corrects the account of his past, but also comments on the writing process itself: "ya me he adelantado antes, pero era la introducción." In effect, he is stating: I couldn't have *said* that word *then* because I didn't know it, nor should I have *written* that word *now.*" The narrator shows his awareness of the machinery at work during the creation of the autobiographical text. His story exists both as a mental image and as a series of linguistic symbols on paper; both are subject to the scrutiny and commentary of their narrator. Once the curtain is lifted to show the wizard at work, he can no longer create a one-dimensional version of his life: he knows he must also give an account of the way he uses the machinery of autobiography to produce his text.

Further examples of this editing of the autobiographical text may be cited. For example, the narrator haltingly relates what seems to be a verbal account of a recollection, complete with immediate self-correction: "El verano anterior — no, ese mismo verano del 41, antes de abandonar para siempre el pueblo . . ." (p. 41). Self-staging on the pages of a text thus involves elaborate commentary from the protagonist-director, who continuously halts the production in a Pirandellian manner. The autobiographical text assumes the form of a tissue perforated by interruptions, in Louis Marin's terms, or a syncopated work-in-progress hiccupping its way back to the beginning.

The narrator's comments on his own devices in unravelling his life story often center on the role of memory, the link between the *sujet de l'énonciation* and the *sujet de l'énoncé*. In the process of "correcting" himself within the text, the narrator creates what might be called a recollection of a recollection in which the act of remembering takes precedence over the event recalled. But Cabrera allows further liberties to the role of memory in autobiography in the following observation: "Ese domingo de velaciones y revelaciones (tuvo que ser domingo y si no lo fue el recuerdo declara el día festivo) ..." (p. 29). As he decodes his past, the narrator may discover that a recollection is in fact inaccurate, and reserves for himself the right to revise it. Thus, autobiography becomes an exercise in rewriting one's past, and the narrator shows awareness of this process when he states: "tengo que ser fiel a mi memoria aunque ella me traicione ..." (p. 278). As he bows to this imperative, a new story emerges: the tale develops into the narrator's fictive invention as he rewrites or translates his memories. Autobiography inevitably becomes a twice-told tale.

As the narrator of *La Habana* performs the role of editor of his own story he encounters several technical difficulties, such as those mentioned above, and he may turn the methods used to confront those difficulties into effective textual strategies. Another device which originates in this process is the treatment of time and space in this work, a topic that also fascinated Cabrera in *TTT*. If *TTT* may be called a novel about space and velocity, *La Habana* may be seen as a treatise on time and memory, as the author himself has affirmed. [38] In this sense, *TTT* constitutes a preliminary study for the problems Cabrera confronts in *La Habana*. In *TTT*, Cué dramatizes the temporal-spatial relation: "Cué tenía esa obsesión del tiempo. Quiero decir que buscaba el tiempo en el espacio ..." (p. 296). Significantly, Cué is a writer as well as an actor, and thus his efforts to transform time into space have particular bearing on the literary craft:

See p. 37

---

[38] Remarks by Cabrera Infante at Cornell University, Ithaca, New York, 25 February 1982.

> Cuando Cué hablaba del tiempo y del espacio y recorría todo
> aquel espacio en todo nuestro tiempo pensé que era para
> divertirnos y ahora lo sé: era así: era para hacer una cosa
> diversa, otra cosa, y mientras corríamos por el espacio con-
> seguía eludir lo que siempre evitó, creo, que era recorrer
> otro espacio fuera del tiempo —o más claro—, recordar.
> (p. 297)

The writer who seeks to escape his own memories cannot undertake an autobiographical endeavor. Cué's flight through space becomes a flight through — and from — time. Sharon Magnarelli summarizes Cué's failure: "Cué, who had been a writer, considered
himself incapable of writing because he had no sense of history
(implying time) and thus turned to speed to transform time into
space . . . ." [39]

While *TTT* does not serve as Cabrera's forum for playing out
the variations on time and memory, it contains the roots for this
undertaking in *La Habana,* especially in the words of Silvestre. He
contrasts his feelings on memory with Cué's:

> Lo opuesto a mí, porque me gusta acordarme de las cosas
> más que vivirlas o vivir las cosas sabiendo que nunca se
> pierden porque . . . puedo vivirlas de nuevo al recordarlas y
> sería bueno que el verbo grabar (un disco, una cinta) fuera
> el mismo que en inglés, recordar también, porque eso es lo
> que es, que es lo opuesto de lo que es Arsenio Cué. (p. 297)

Yet this gallery of voices in *TTT* does not permit Silvestre to
utilize his faculties of recall to their fullest. The autobiographical
act remains for the narrator of *La Habana* who takes up many of
the concerns expressed through the voices of Cué and Silvestre in
TTT, and who truly prefers to remember — that is, record — his
past.

The relation between time, space, and memory, an underlying
theme in *TTT,* receives full treatment in *La Habana.* Cabrera has
stated his intentions in this regard:

> For me the city was what the jungle had been for other
> authors. My wish is that in *La Habana para un infante di-
> funto* and *Cuerpos divinos* it will cease to be topography,

---

[39] Magnarelli "The 'Writerly,' " p. 329.

as it is in *Three Trapped Tigers,* to be transformed into topology — that is, the science that deals with spatial relationships, and even with the possible transformation of space into time. [40]

In *La Habana,* this desire to integrate space and time appears early: "Aunque Monte 822 fue un intermedio, un interregno, proseguí allí el aprendizaje del amor, que había empezado en el pueblo con una prima de ojos verdes legendarios en la familia — pero ésa es otra historia y pertenece a otro lugar" (p. 46). The concept of space *(lugar)* is coupled with that of time *(historia).* The other story occurs in another time, and its "place" is not in this tale. The notion of space, then, may refer to a geographical situation (the setting for the action) or to the textual space which the story occupies. When the narrator indicates that the story he will not tell (inclusion by deletion) belongs to another place, he is not only referring to a geographical space but to another text, another written version of an oral tale or of a recollection.

In addition to geographical and textual space, memory is tied to physical space, to the "heavenly bodies" the narrator-explorer discovers: "esa espalda estará siempre en mi memoria . . . y solamente hay otra que recuerde con tanto fervor al verla por primera vez desnuda — pero ese recuerdo pertenece a otro tiempo, otro lugar y será revivido en otra parte, en otro libro" (p. 184). Memory takes shape on the page, and the text then becomes a way of remembering, a tangible storage bank for the tales of the past. Time cannot alter a memory preserved in this manner: "los años la desfiguraron pero no pueden envejecer el recuerdo . . ." (p. 184).

The narrator relies on his memory to transport himself into the past and re-create lost time. At the same time, he grapples with the problem of which story to tell and by the apparent act of negation, includes stories that he claims belong to another place or space. In the same manner the narrator highlights what is hidden of his past self by revealing only fragments, and thus teases the reader with incomplete references: "Dejábamos Monte 822 (significativamente en el mes de abril aunque la significación sea absolutamente personal) para volver al primer punto, la primera parada . . ." (p. 55). Why

---

[40] "GCI: Three Islands," comp. Siemens, p. 11.

should this remark on a personal experience be included if the narrator is reluctant to divulge its significance? In so doing, the autobiographer asserts that there are memories too personal to share and that the exploration of the self in writing can never be complete.

When he refuses to reveal the meaning of certain references, the narrator relegates these to the realm of the forgotten: "Nos volvimos a ver esa semana, cita que no cuento porque es privada y además está olvidada . . ." (p. 259). Here, "private" is equivalent to "forgotten" or even "repressed," but the act of recall and especially of recreation within the text can rescue past events from oblivion. Or, as the narrator summarizes in *La Habana:* "sólo se recuerda lo que está olvidado" (p. 504). The autobiographer must relinquish his most intimate, personal memories to the public domain lest he forget them. In Cabrera Infante, this textual exhibitionism leads to a predilection for the pornographic mode, a style not at all at odds with the nature of the autobiographer's task.

If on the one hand the narrator consciously conceals certain past events and their meaning, on the other he displays awareness of having repressed some memories:

> No recuerdo cuál de mis amigos en el pueblo —no creo que fuera Nano— me instruyó en el arte de la masturbación . . . . Creo significativa esta falla en mi memoria. ¿Por qué no recuerdo a mi iniciador en el placer solitario, que debió ser importante por la importancia que adquirió en mi vida la masturbación? (pp. 63-64)

Once again the autobiographer digresses from his story to comment on how to deal with the problems of telling that story. In this case, the failure of memory, pointed out by the narrator himself, acquires as much weight in the text as the actual events of the past he attempts to recount.

That recollections must be communicated through language creates special technical problems for autobiographers. In *La Habana,* a major difficulty encountered by the narrator consists in "translating" his memories from the naive language of a country childhood into the street-smart dialect of an urban adolescence. The narrator remarks on his ever-expanding vocabulary: "Esta era una verdadera belleza, con un cuerpo menos curvilíneo (ésa es otra palabra que aprendí en La Habana, donde tuve que aprender tantas, tanto que el español se

me hizo exótico) era más escultural (otra palabra nueva) . . ." (p. 82).
The *advertencia* by "GCI" that opens *TTT* presents a similar linguistic dilemma:

> El libro está en cubano. Es decir, escrito en los diferentes
> dialectos del español que se hablan en Cuba y la escritura
> no es más que un intento de atrapar la voz humana al
> vuelo . . . . Las distintas formas del cubano se funden o creo
> que se funden en un solo lenguaje literario. Sin embargo,
> predomina como un acento el habla de los habaneros y en
> particular la jerga nocturna, que, como en todas las grandes
> ciudades, tiende a ser un idioma secreto. (p. 9) [In italics
> in the original.]

For those unfamiliar with Havana slang, reading *TTT* becomes
an exercise in translation. But as Magnarelli points out:

> any endeavor to re-create, to transcribe, or to translate the
> past or speech is inevitably destined to a certain degree of
> failure. Language, then, fails to communicate and fails to
> represent, as shown by the characters' persistent necessity
> to explain what they mean and by the misunderstandings
> emanating from the words. [41]

The reader of *TTT* is forced to become "writer" in order to find
meaning in the novel, according to Magnarelli. Language in *TTT,*
rather than a conduit of communication, forms a barrier, and the
many voices of the novel that confuse what they remember with what
they have imagined eventually stop trying to transmit a message. [42]

The secret language that characterizes *TTT* is decoded and demythified in *La Habana,* in which the author continually furnishes
explanations, clarifications and justifications. This demythified language
is nonetheless mandated in *La Habana* since words are supposedly
being employed to re-create a form of "reality": the past self. The
narrator's search for a language adequate to the task of transmitting
his recollections leads him to the "exotic Spanish" that he had adopted

---

[41] Magnarelli, "The 'Writerly,' " p. 329. I have corrected a printing error
in the original.

[42] Jonathan Tittler, "Cabrera Infante's Novels: From the Failure of Language to the Language of Failure," Presentation at Cornell Univ., Ithaca, New
York, 25 February 1982. I quote from the unpublished paper with permission
of the author.

in Havana, as he tries not only to recapture lost time in autobiography, but also to evoke lost words from past worlds.

The identity of the *yo* in *La Habana para un infante difunto* lies at the center of the work and constitutes its primary enigma. As I have indicated, Philippe Lejeune establishes as an absolute condition for the classification of a work as autobiography the correspondence between the narrator's name and the author's name on the book's cover. If this autobiographical pact, as he calls it, is not explicitly executed, then the work falls into that gray area of anonymity or pseudonymity. Whereas the name "Guillermo Cabrera Infante" does not appear in the text, the narrator nevertheless provides some references to his name and thus to his identity. He reports, for example: "Un día me llamó [Delia] y me encantó cómo pronunció mi nombre detestable, destacando el inevitable diminutivo como una intimidad" (p. 83). Here, Delia is said to pronounce the narrator's name, a name he hates and therefore suppresses in his account. But the apparent act of omission is in reality one of commission: by making reference to his name without actually giving it, the narrator draws attention to it, and to its absence in the work.

If the assignment of the author's name to the narrator affirms identity in autobiography, as Lejeune contends, then the narrator's continuous search for a name in *La Habana* may be seen as an essential feature of its autobiographical structure. The hints at a name in *La Habana* reveal the narrator's attempts to secure a name, literally to make a name for himself. Autobiography thus becomes the medium through which an author employs his name in a text and then makes this name a symbol of his identity (*le nom propre* must become *le propre nom,* to use Marin's terminology).

An early example of the importance of the name as symbol in *La Habana* is the narrator's use of his initials to signal his affections for a girl:

> Mi amor anónimo tenía tanta necesidad de expresarse que tomé a la naturaleza por testigo: en un viaje que hicimos al pueblo vecino de Cuatro Caminos, a casa de unos parientes de mi padre, me las arreglé, siguiendo seguramente alguna película que vi con Nila, romántica y aburrida, para cortar las iniciales de Ester y las mías en un árbol del patio . . . . [43]
> (p. 47)

---

[43] The use of initials also appears in *TTT,* where "GCI" is a character who signs the *Advertencia* and a letter to Silvestre.

The adolescent's feelings toward Ester, described by the narrator as "anonymous," achieve their form and identity in the symbols carved on a tree. In telling this story, the narrator might have performed another type of engraving of his initials — his identity — on the page, but instead leaves a blank in the text where his specific initials belong.

The narrator maintains anonymity in *La Habana,* a situation that befits the social context about which he writes. To give one's name is to surrender a part of one's being, and thus the girls whom the narrator encounters also guard their identities:

> era endemoniadamente complicado preguntarle el nombre a una muchacha entonces, que era como pedirle prestado una propiedad, algo impropio, y excepto las muchachas del bachillerato . . . no sabía el nombre, nunca lo supe, de la mayor parte de las muchachas de quienes estuve enamorado . . . .
> (p. 186)

These nameless girls receive descriptors such as "la muchacha del cine Radiocine" or "la prieta del caballo" (p. 187). Intimacy cannot be established with these girls who withhold their names from the narrator, and he must keep his distance from the objects of his desire. This situation may be related to the narrator's first sexual encounters with prostitutes whose real names he never knew: "nunca supe su nombre, ni siquiera su seudónimo putesco . . ." (p. 331). Women from both ends of society — the correct young ladies who refuse to identify themselves, and the ones who only give their "professional" pseudonyms — remain nameless and loveless for the narrator. In parallel form, the omission of the narrator's name marks a significant absence in the text of *La Habana*: the intimate relationship between the autobiographer, his work, and ultimately his readers can never be totally consummated as long as the autobiographical pact is avoided.

The narrator's unwillingness to reveal his name stands in marked contrast to the eagerness of an acquaintance to give hers, as demonstrated in the following dialogue: [44]

---

[44] The inclusion of dialogues in autobiography is clearly a device that reveals the impossibility of reproducing past events exactly as they occurred. Any dialogue, such as this one which runs on for several pages, must be at least a partial fiction, since conversations of this sort cannot be recalled verbatim. See Bertil Romberg, p. 97.

—¿Y por qué tan formal? —dijo Virginia—. Trátame de
tú. Mi nombre es Carmen Virginia Rodríguez Mettee, pero
todo el mundo me llama Virginia.
Yo le dije mi nombre.
—Me gusta —me dijo.
—Yo lo encuentro odioso —le dije—, pero es una tara.
—¿Cómo?
—Lo heredé de mi padre. (p. 269)

Virginia is willing to give her four-part name to the narrator who, in
reporting his response, alludes to the name he spoke instead of reproducing it. The narrator, like Cabrera, bears his father's name, but
considers it a defect, a hateful name imposed on him against his will. [45]
This point is brought out later in *La Habana* when Margarita offers
the narrator a drink of that same name: "Yo odiaría tomar una bebida
que tuviera mi nombre, aunque por otra parte yo no escogí mi nombre,
me fue impuesto y lo detesto" (p. 605).

The narrator never declares himself to be the individual whose
name is on the cover of *La Habana,* but continuously provides clues
that could justify such a conclusion. In the process, he passes from
anonymity into pseudonymity, as seen in the following example:

Julieta conoció a Pablo Perera, pianista aficionado a los muchachos, y ella decidió, como no era Virginia, que si Pablo
quería ser concertista debía llamarse Paul y a Pablo le sonó
eufónico su nuevo nombre, Paul Perera. (Es curioso que Julieta no intentara cambiar mi nombre o afrancesarlo: resul-
taría cómico que me hubiera convencido de llamarme Guy).
(p. 393)

The name Guy (pronounced like *Gui* in Spanish) may be taken as a
shortened form of Guillermo, which in turn suggests that the narrator's unspoken name is the same as the author's. The narrator begins
to employ his professional pseudonym for private matters: "y yo le
repetí mi nombre. Para que no lo olvidara le di en realidad mi

---

[45] The first entry in Cabrera's "Orígenes" confirms this:

1929

22 de abril: Nace en Gibara, pequeña ciudad en la costa norte de la
provincia cubana de Oriente. Segundo hijo y primer varón de Guillermo Cabrera, periodista y tipógrafo, y Zoila Infante, una belleza
comunista. (p. 5)

seudónimo. Siempre he sentido que mi verdadero nombre, largo y farragoso, es además olvidable" (p. 540). This scene occurs at a time when the narrator declares he is working for the Cuban literary magazine *Carteles*; thus, it would be logical to conclude that this pseudonym is G. Caín, the same one that Cabrera Infante used to sign his cinematographic columns in that publication.

In *La Habana,* a parallel to the narrator's disguise of his identity through the use of pseudonyms arises in his relationship with Violeta del Valle (Margarita Pérez), who remarks as she and the narrator make their first visit to a *posada*:

> Tú me has dado tu seudónimo —por razones de seguridad sexual le había dado el nombre con que firmaba mis escritos, pero había además el problema de mi nombre, tan largo, con el que nunca había estado de acuerdo mi cuerpo, pero ¿y ella? —y yo te he dado mi nombre de actriz. (p. 569)

Both despised their given names, and had adopted pseudonyms by which the external world knew them (he as a writer, she as an actress). It is only in the intimacy of a sexual relationship that they are able to come as close to revealing their identities and discarding their masks as their insecurities will allow. On another level, however, the narrator never lifts the mask of his *yo*; he conceals his identity from the reader and refuses to enter into an autobiographical pact by avoiding the mention of his name in the text when it would have been appropriate to do so.

The narrator discovers, then, that he is not alone in playing name games, and also comes to know that Margarita has doubly tricked him. When he guesses that her real first name is not Margarita, she refuses to tell him the true one ("Mis padres no tenían idea de lo que marca un nombre," p. 586), which causes the narrator to reflect:

> Hasta ahora era yo el que había hecho los cambios de nombres . . . pero éste era mi primer encuentro con el enmascaramiento por los nombres: cubrir un estigma. Aunque yo mismo usaba a menudo un seudónimo (había llegado a usar en realidad cinco) pasarían unos años antes de encontrarme con gente que se cambiaba de nombre como de traje —sobre todo mujeres. (p. 587)

The *burlador* always runs the risk of being *burlado,* as this modern Don Juan discovers. The multiple false names in *La Habana* serve to conceal the real beings behind them, and also render futile the task of discerning if the characters have a referent outside the context of autobiography as fiction.

Margarita hides her true identity from the narrator by disguising her name, but she also initially conceals her true physical form by refusing to allow him to see her scarred chest, the result of burns suffered when she was a child. The missing breast, Margarita's deformity, represents the part of herself that she cannot share with her lover: "Pero eso significa que no me verás nunca desnuda, que hay una parte de mi cuerpo que no podrás tocar jamás, que estoy, como se dice, medio vedada para ti" (p. 578). In turn, the narrator has expressed reluctance to share his defect (*tara*), his given name, with others. But Margarita finally does allow the narrator to see her scars, and at that moment they reach a level of intimacy never before possible.

The narrator, however, never achieves this same level of intimacy with his autobiographical text and subsequently with his readers: he refuses to uncover his name in print. The narrator's identity remains enigmatic, elusive, and incomplete. Cabrera remarked that *La Habana* "involves my erotic relationship with words," but this relationship fails to reach consummation. The author is doubly correct when he asserts: "There is in the work a sort of ode to masturbation, a declaration that the narrator has only fulfilled himself erotically as a masturbator . . . ." [46] As he shies away from an autobiographical pact, the narrator fails to transcend his anonymous and solitary existence to emerge as the man behind the mask. On another level, the text itself is a homage to the joys of self-genesis. [47] In his attempt to forge an identity for himself — sexual and linguistic — the autobiographer engages in a game of self-amusement or self-stimulation. Or, to use Cabrera's term from *Tres tristes tigres,* the narrator employs his text to *masturhablarse.*

---

[46] "GCI: Three Islands," comp. Siemens, p. 11.

[47] Steven Kellman's comments on this subject apply particularly well to *La Habana*: "In the self-begetting narrative, the hero forges his identity as novelist and through a novel. . . . Sex preoccupies the self-begetting novel's lonely and aging hero, who somehow succeeds in giving birth to twins — self and novel," p. 8.

Despite the intimacy the narrator reaches with Margarita, their relationship eventually collapses when she decides to leave Havana for Venezuela, and he refuses to accompany her. The narrator states that he never plans to leave Havana: "La Habana no sólo era mi fin y mi principio sino mi medio . . ." (p. 661). In their last telephone conversation, he speaks his final words to her: "Que te vaya bien, dondequiera que vayas, con quienquiera que estés, santificado sea tu nombre, cualquiera que éste sea," and remarks to himself, "sabía la importancia que ella le daba a sus nombres" (p. 668). In acknowledging that he cannot tell her real name, the narrator attempts to negate the intimate relationship they were finally able to develop together.

The alienation that the two former lovers undergo is further reflected in this name game when Margarita sends the narrator a telegram from Venezuela: "EL TIEMPO Y LA DISTANCIA ME HACEN COMPRENDER QUE TE HE PERDIDO" signed "VIOLETA DEL VALLE" (p. 668). This retreat to her stage name also marks her break with the narrator, a turn of events he now recognizes: "Evidentemente era el final de Margarita, ahora perdida en el seudonombre risible" (p. 669). When the narrator's wife bears him a daughter, he remarks that the child's green eyes strangely enough resemble Margarita's: "eran los ojos de Margarita, de Violeta del Valle, de como se llamara esa mujer que había estado tan cerca — ella había estado dentro de mí, no yo dentro de ella — y ahora estaba tan lejos" (p. 674). The distance that separates Margarita and the narrator is both spatial and emotional. When he refers to her as "como se llamara esa mujer," he recognizes the process of alienation that has turned her back into one more nameless woman he was never able to know totally, a lover who belongs to his past. Like the pseudonym Caín, Margarita has gone down with her name.

If the narrator only hints at his name in the pages of the text, perhaps the true reference to his identity can be found in the title of the book, *La Habana para un infante difunto*. This "infante difunto" clearly refers to Cabrera Infante's past self, as many critics, as well as the author, have pointed out. Roger Rosenblatt has insisted on this aspect of autobiographical rhetoric: since the past self, subject of the narration, cannot be retrieved, "the life recorded is the life

complete to a specific point, and is therefore as good as dead." [48]
Emir Rodríguez Monegal states: "El infante ha muerto pero el narrador que hace su crónica sólo tiene palabras para cubrir esa ausen-
cia." [49] But the void created by the absence of a name in the text
cannot be completely filled by the pun contained in the title. Cabrera
has employed this same play on Ravel's *Pavane pour une infante
défunte* elsewhere in *La Habana*: "pues a mi nombre respondió ella
[a woman he met] con su número de teléfono para infantes enfer-
mos" (p. 523), a reference to the children's hospital where this
woman works. At another point in the narration, friends Branly and
Olga are making puns based on musical compositions: "El otro,
Ravel, compositor de valses y boleros, compuso *La pavana para un
gracioso difunto*" (p. 238). And in *Tres tristes tigres,* this title again
appears in a parody on Carpentier, "El ocaso": "Debe leerse en el
tiempo que dura la audición de *Pavane pour une infante défuncte*
[sic], a treinta y tres revoluciones por minuto" (p. 241). Thus, the
title of *La Habana* may be considered a variation on one of Cabrera's themes, and the *infante* fades into the maze of word games
that Cabrera sees as the basis of literature. The question still remains:
whose is the voice behind the voice? In autobiography, that underlying voice theoretically must be assigned to a real person, but the
figure in the text is transformed into a character of fiction, here an
infante difunto who is incapable of directly revealing his past or
present identity.

These parodies of the title found in the text of *La Habana* constitute one example of Cabrera's self-conscious style that characterizes
this work and also *TTT.* In *La Habana,* however, these parodies
take on additional significance within the context of the autobiographical mode, as they reflect the narrator's awareness of the self as
writer. Cabrera says of *La Habana para un infante difunto*: "The
book is to be read for fun, but for those who care to search for them
there is a series of literary allusions." [50] The most obvious of these
allusions are to works by Cabrera Infante himself, thereby revealing

---

[48] Roger Rosenblatt sees autobiography as an "extended suicide note,"
p. 178.

[49] Emir Rodríguez Monegal, "Cabrera Infante: La novela como autobiografía
total," *Revista Iberoamericana,* 47 (July-December 1981), 271.

[50] "GCI: Three Islands," comp. Siemens, p. 11.

an acute level of self-consciousness and self-parody. I have mentioned several instances of the narrator's versions of the title *La Habana para un infante difunto.* In addition, one may point to a series of alliterations and tongue-twisters beginning with the consonant *t*, a pattern evocative of Cabrera's *Tres tristes tigres.* For example, the narrator and friends Rine Leal and Matías Montes decide to leave Zulueta 408 for the adventure of night life in Havana: "Ya tarde en la noche el trío en tragos trastabilló más que caminó por el precario borde de La Habana Vieja (era difícil guardar el equilibrio en esa zona ese día) que era la calle Zulueta . . ." (p. 326). This "trío en tragos" could have easily been found among the pages of *TTT,* and the "precarious border" may perhaps be interpreted as the frontier between two texts: *Tres tristes tigres* (fiction) begins where the personal stories of Zulueta 408 (autobiography) end, where the night becomes a cloak of anonymity for the revelling threesome. Cabrera shows that it is indeed very difficult to keep one's balance when walking the tightrope between autobiography and fiction.

A second alliteration that brings to mind the title *Tres tristes tigres* may be cited: "le oí su larga litanía literaria [that of the narrator's mentor Antonio Ortega], que es lo que eran nuestras conversaciones y salí de su casa, atravesando el barrio de Colón, caído en desgracia, por Amistad para buscar Virtudes y encontrar tras tres trotes mi meta, el Rex Cinema" (p. 218). "Tras tres trotes" the narrator finds a movie theater, which he calls his goal (*meta*). Since the narrator, like Cabrera, takes up film criticism as an early career, the *meta* refers not only to his immediate destination, but also to his future métier.[51] Once again, this process is linked to the city of Havana: topography serves as the vehicle for the narrator who puns his way across town to the Rex Cinema. The allusion to *TTT* serves another purpose: Cabrera's main profession turns out to be fiction writing, not film criticism, so that he can truly say that he does achieve his goal and discover his vocation "tras tres trotes," that is,

---

[51] The pattern of including references within one text to titles of others is not exclusive to *La Habana.* In *TTT,* the titles of Cabrera's collected cinematographic criticism, *Un oficio del siglo XX,* may be found. The remark is made by the musician Ribot (Ribaut, Eribó), who comments on his job as a publicity agent: "Tampoco era un artista ni un artesano. Era un *profesional* . . . y me hallaba refugiado en la tierra de nadie, en el foso que era mi oficio del siglo xx . . ." (pp. 47-48).

through his first major novel, *Tres tristes tigres*. In *La Habana,* Cabrera also embeds other titles of his own works, such as the following references to *Vista del amanecer en el trópico*: "Ahora la veía bien, no impedido por la noche sino ayudado por el amanecer en el trópico . . ." (p. 435), and to *Exorcismos de esti(l)o:* "entonces estar vestida o desvestida así no era más que una reacción al calor de la tarde, exorcizando el estío" (p. 391). The autobiographical clues the narrator plants, then, go beyond the scope of one text to touch his works as a whole: perhaps the only way for this author to perform the autobiographical act consists of writing about writing, employing the word to evoke other words.

The self-consciousness I have discussed in relation to the hidden titles in *La Habana* differs greatly from the development in the text of the narrator's career as a writer. The instances cited above reveal an awareness of the self as writer that goes beyond the work in question: Cabrera Infante, in overriding the narrator's voice, creates an ironic text that plays the narrator against his creator. [52] The autobiographical split which occurs when *I* becomes *he* manifests itself in these instances of coded extra-textual references. To tell his story, an autobiographer cannot totally abandon his present self to assume the role of the narrator of his past. Thus, he becomes an ever-present shadow in the text who wedges an ironic distance between the *sujet de l'énoncé* and the *sujet de l'énonciation*. On the inner textual level, the narrator relates his initiation into the literary world in a schematic manner. He limits his remarks to events that also had a bearing on other aspects of his personality which he stresses in *La Habana,* particularly his sexual life. For example, the cultural society *Nuestro Tiempo,* founded by Cabrera's friend Carlos Franqui, receives little treatment except as a vehicle for gathering the intellectual group at the narrator's home in Zulueta 408 (pp. 169-70). In the context of *La Habana,* this early intellectual endeavor stands out not as a turning

---

[52] Ardis Nelson comments: "From the reader's perspective the writer pops in and out, receding ever again behind his typewriter ribbon. Meanwhile, the narrator, unaware of the intrusions, continues his story. While the writer must keep out of sight to satisfy minimally the conventions of fiction, his jack-in-the-box appearances provide distance, detachment and irony for the reader." *Cabrera Infante in the Menippean Tradition* (Newark, Delaware: Juan de la Cuesta, 1983), p. 104.

point in the narrator's search for a vocation, but as a meeting point for his friends, including the girl who is to become his first wife.

The narrator also makes mention of his first attempt at writing a short story: "Ese día yo venía de casa de mi mentor, aquel que había aceptado mi primer cuento (que era una burda parodia seria) y prometió publicarlo" (p. 215). His mentor, Antonio Ortega, introduces him to many great works of literature, which the narrator enumerates and annotates briefly. This account constitutes one of the few discussions of the literary craft in *La Habana*; unlike Mario Vargas Llosa, Cabrera does not place great emphasis on the actual emergence of the self as writer in his autobiographical text. When milestones in Cabrera's literary career, such as his work at *Carteles*, receive mention, it is only as asides and within the greater context of the narrator's personal relationships with the people around him. In other words, Cabrera Infante utilizes the text itself — primarily through meta-commentary — as the medium for expressing his involvement with the writing process, while other autobiographers choose to focus on their experiences with fictional creation in order to communicate their identity as author. Raymond Federman's words on the nature of "surfiction" may explain Cabrera Infante's strategy in *La Habana*: "while pretending to be telling the story of his life ... the fiction writer can at the same time tell the story of the story he is telling, the story of the language he is manipulating, the story of the fiction he is inventing, and even the story of the anguish (or joy, or disgust, or exhilaration) he is feeling while telling his story." [53]

A rhetorical device that ties in with the autobiographer's self-conscious writing style is the use of the narratee, Gerald Prince's term for the fictional creation to whom the narrator purportedly addresses himself. [54] Autobiography, which follows along the lines of literary confessions, must be told to someone else. In *La Habana*,

---

[53] Raymond Federman, Intro., *Surfiction: Fiction Now... and Tomorrow,* ed. Federman, 2nd ed. (Chicago: Swallow Press, 1981), p. 12.

[54] Gerald Prince, "Introduction to the Study of the Narratee," in *Reader-Response Criticism: From Formalism to Post-Structuralism,* ed. Jane P. Tompkins (Baltimore: Johns Hopkins Univ. Press, 1980), p. 7. See also Seymour Chatman's section on the narratee in *Story and Discourse* pp. 253-262. In the *Rhetoric of Fiction* (Chicago: Univ. of Chicago Press, 1961), Wayne Booth identifies an "implied reader" who functions as a work's ideal interpreter (p. 138). In my discussion here, the focus is primarily on the figure of a reader inscribed in the text, and not the "ideal reader" an implied author constructs.

it is the figure of the reader(s) to whom the narrator speaks directly. Prince observes that the most obvious role of the narratee consists in serving as a relay between the author and the reader or the narrator and the reader. [55] Cabrera himself has admitted as excessive the use of commentary, explanations, and justifications in *La Habana,* a characteristic I have linked to the style of autobiography. The narratee therefore becomes the necessary outlet for all the meta-narration that takes place in a text of this sort. Thus, the continuous process of stressing how to tell a story while actually telling it is complemented by the use of a narratee, as seen in the following: "(Debo intercalar aquí que tuve cuidado, al ver a Etelvina desnuda en la cama, de cerrar la puerta a mis espaldas . . . Etelvina era para mí el mal y además estaba muerta, ¿recuerdan?)" (p. 77). The parenthetical remark, directed to *ustedes,* contains a type of correctional device ("debo intercalar") to clarify the passage for those who may not have followed the story as the narrator would want.

One type of narratee in *La Habana* consists in a "poor" reader-in-the-text who supposedly requires hyper-explanations and is often the recipient of the narrator's scorn, as seen here: "Estoy siendo irónico, ya lo habrán notado, pero de verás [sic] que estábamos adheridos el uno a la otra, bailando sin movernos . . ." (p. 433). The narrator uses the narratee in order to make comments on his own style, to justify or even to criticize his writing. The narratee may also take the form of a neutral audience to whom the narrator appeals: "¿Me perdonarán la hipérbole? Tienen que perdonármela: de joven uno siempre es excesivo y si ella no era la muchacha más linda del mundo, por lo menos me lo parecía" (p. 333).

At times, the narrator attributes to his narratees the function of intuitive readers-in-the-text who perceive gaps or pose pertinent questions. When he inquires of a girl he sees on the street "Cuánto?", without having first announced that he was dealing with a prostitute, he anticipates the surprise that his rash question would cause for the narratee who has been following his story: "Ustedes se preguntarán cómo había sabido yo que era una puta sólo por su porte y pregunta. Pero es que ustedes no la tienen a ella delante como yo la tenía" (p. 328). Similarly, he creates situations in which his nar-

---

[55] Prince, pp. 20-21.

ratee can predict the outcome before it is told: "Para sorpresa de nadie (no mía entonces, no tuya lector, ahora) no volví a verla: cuando solté su brazo se separó de mí para siempre" (pp. 222-23).

The use of the narratee in *La Habana* is sometimes carried to comic extremes, as in the following question that opens the section "Falsos amores con una ballerina": "¿Alguno de ustedes, señoras y señores, ha intentado hacerle el amor (a la francesa) a una ballerina fuera de escena?" (p. 417). This query does not invite an earnest answer, but rather serves to call attention to the story, to awaken interest in the narrator's plight. This device has been employed successfully by Cabrera in *TTT*, which opens with the similar line: "*Showtime!* Señoras y señores. *Ladies and gentlemen*" (p. 15). The show continues in *La Habana* where the narrator acts as an exhibitionist before his audience, whom he addresses in the confessional mode with the pronoun *you.*

The technique of self-editing, basic to the structure of this autobiography, also touches upon the role of the narratee. Under the pretext of sparing the narratee another episode in a series of sexual encounters, the narrator cuts short his tale in the following instance: "No hay cosa más parecida a un coito que otro coito — por lo que dispensaré al lector de la repetición. Solamente añadiré que estuvimos mucho tiempo en el cuarto de la posada y que no pasamos el tiempo hablando . . ." (p. 477). One characteristic of pornography, as we will see later, consists of variations on a theme that increasingly seem alike, leading to a monotonous style. The narrator is cognizant of this when he spares the narratee another erotic description. Thus, the other voice in the text, the *you* whom the narrator addresses, is used as a device to force him into self-consciousness and self-censure.[56] Three indeed is a crowd in this text; when the third party accepts the narrator's invitation to observe the proceedings, the curtain is hastily drawn. The invocation of a narratee may be

---

[56] Examples of the narratee forcing the narrator into self-editing may be found in *TTT*: "pero fue el recuerdo total porque en uno o dos segundos recordé todas las tardes de mi vida (por supuesto que no las voy a enumerar, lector . . .)" (p. 304). Robert M. Adams defines this pose well: "Ever since Baudelaire blamed his bored reader for seeking vicarious stimulation in his verses, that second game of attacking the reader as a vampire has underlain (at least potentially) the first one of attracting him as a client." *Bad Mouth: Fugitive Papers on the Dark Side* (Berkeley: Univ. of California Press, 1977), p. 9.

considered a textual interruption of sorts that halts the flow of the story and causes the focus to shift from the *énoncé* to the *énonciation*. [57] At the same time, the narratee performs the important function of "defining more clearly the narrator himself." [58] And by inscribing an audience for himself in the text, the narrator of *La Habana* avoids having to perform his autobiographical act to an empty house. But as Robert Spires points out, the textual dramatization of a narratee highlights the distinction between the reader outside the boundaries of the work and the imbedded reader. [59] It then becomes apparent that the solitary autobiographer of *La Habana* may only be addressing the phantoms of his own linguistic creation.

In touching on several of the devices Cabrera Infante employs in his autobiographical work *La Habana,* I have stressed that the real text centers on the predicament of how to tell one's own life story. The self-consciousness that characterizes autobiography in general leads to the basic dichotomy analyzed here in terms of the *temps de l'énoncé* and the *temps de l'énonciation*. This problem of time in autobiography is neatly contained in these words spoken by the narrator of *La Habana:* "pero ese recuerdo pertenece al futuro y ahora hablo del presente, es decir del pasado" (p. 236). The subject of the discourse thus endeavors to upstage the subject of the story: with his intruding presence, the mature self overtakes the weak, distant voice of the *infante difunto*. Cabrera seems to affirm, along with Rimbaud, that "*je est un autre,*" and the autobiographical narration constitutes an attempt to repossess that otro *yo,* to state *ese otro soy yo*. But is it? This is precisely the paradox that the self-begetting *La Habana* sets up for us: the search for a name, an identity, a pronoun with a referent outside of fiction, leads to ab-

---

[57] Susan R. Suleiman's Introduction to *The Reader in the Text*: *Essays on Audience and Interpretation* (Princeton: Princeton Univ. Press, 1980) contains a pertinent observation on the role of the "inscribed audience":

> As for texts that are heavily discursive (in Benveniste's sense), they constitute a rich lode for the semiotician, who can study the function of literary or cultural allusions, the use of deictics ("here," "now," etc.), the role of explanations and definitions formulated by the narrator. All are indexes of readability and all are intimately linked to the inscribed audience, to whom the allusions and explanations are addressed and who must be situated in relation to the deictics. (p. 15)

[58] Chatman, p. 261.
[59] Spires, pp. 16, 53.

sence (of a referent for the *I*), to negation (of the story being told), or to deletion (of crucial information).

The autobiographical text is thus constructed around a void that the title only partially fills in its mention of the *infante difunto*. It is also a text about failures, but these are said to belong to the past: "La iniciación había sido un fracaso del presente pero un triunfo del recuerdo" (p. 325). Here, *presente* functions as above ("hablo del presente, es decir del pasado"): the capacity of memory permits the narrator to reconstruct — rewrite — his defeats and disillusions of adolescence.

I have given emphasis to the structure of the autobiographical mode as manifested in Cabrera Infante's text, stressing in particular the functions of discourse, memory, and identity. To comprehend the scope of *La Habana* as autobiography some further considerations are now necessary and shall be examined in Chapter II.

CHAPTER II

LA HABANA PARA UN INFANTE DIFUNTO: FICTION, FILM, PORNOGRAPHY

The preceding discussion of the rhetorical devices employed in Guillermo Cabrera Infante's *La Habana para un infante difunto* primarily focused on the narrative problems the autobiographer faces when determining how to go about telling his story and the ways in which those difficulties may be transformed into textual strategies. When the work is examined as a finished literary portrait, however, the problematic question of genre resurfaces. Literary autobiographies, like *La Habana,* cross over arbitrary genre boundaries and are often presented under many guises, such as historical accounts, religious confessions, picaresque narratives, the *Künstlerroman,* and even pornographic writing. My analysis of *La Habana* would not be complete, then, without a discussion of the text as a novelistic portrait in its own right, and an attempt to situate it in the general mode of "sexual fiction." [1] A reading of this type is suggested by the critic Matías Montes-Huidobro, himself a character in *La Habana,* who calls the work "una novela confesional ... con capítulos episódicos que tienen como unidad narrativa las experiencias sexuales de su protagonista." Despite its autobiographical nature, Montes suggests that *La Habana* should be analyzed with the following in mind: " 'Todo parecido con persona real viva o muerta (incluyendo el narrador) es pura coincidencia.' " [2]

---

[1] This term is the title of a study by Maurice Charney, *Sexual Fiction,* New Accents (New York: Methuen, 1981).

[2] Matías Montes-Huidobro, Rev. of *La Habana, Chasqui,* 8 (May 1979), 90.

In *La Habana,* much of the narrator's sexual initiation is linked to the movie theaters he frequents as a young man. The movies assume an important function in *La Habana,* both as a medium of entertainment and as a setting for the narrator's off-screen adventures. Cabrera Infante shares this interest in the cinema as a literary topic with other contemporary Spanish American writers, particularly with Manuel Puig.[3] The golden age of Hollywood coincided with these novelists' youth, and this common cultural base may account for the prevalence of the movie theme in their works. In *La Habana para un infante difunto,* the city has been identified as a symbolic birthplace for the narrator, and the movie theater also fulfills a similar function. The narrator recounts his initiation into the world of film:

> Poco después volví al cine con mi madre ... esta amante del cine que me llevó al teatro del pueblo a los veintinueve días de nacido, creándome un cordón umbilical con el cine, casi naciendo yo con una pantalla de plata en la boca, alienada por el lienzo de sombras cinescas, ella fiel esposa capaz de ser infiel a mi padre con el espectro proyectado de Franchot Tone, de Charles Boyer, de Paul Henreid —ahora íbamos los dos, como en los días primeros, como en la época de cine o sardina, rumbo a la cueva órfica. (pp. 211-12)

Several important aspects of the narrator's psychological development are revealed here. The narrator's mother took him to the movies when he was a newborn baby unable to recognize his surroundings or comprehend the experience of viewing a film. The narrator considers that this early exposure has created a bond with the cinema comparable to the umbilical cord, his original connection with the woman who holds him as a baby in the darkened womb-like theater.

Christian Metz proposes that a movie spectator is capable of following the unfolding of a film because he has already known the experience of the mirror and can therefore "constitute a world of

---

[3] For a study of the relationship between film and text in Puig, see Frances Wyers, "Manuel Puig at the Movies," *Hispanic Review,* 49 (1981), 163-81. Phyllis Mitchell takes a comparative approach in "The Reel against the Real: Cinema in the Novels of Guillermo Cabrera Infante and Manuel Puig," *Latin American Literary Review,* 6 (Fall-Winter 1977), 22-29. Ardis L. Nelson provides a detailed analysis of cinematographic and novelistic techniques in Cabrera Infante's first major work in her "*Tres tristes tigres* y el cine," *Kentucky Romance Quarterly,* 29 (1982), 391-404.

objects without having first to recognise himself within it." Between six and eighteen months of age, a young child goes through the mirror stage, which consists of the mother's holding him up in her arms to the reflecting glass: Metz remarks that "the child sees itself as an other, and beside an other" and "identifies with itself as object." [4] Film functions symbolically as mirror, as Metz points out, but a mirror that works like clear glass in that the spectator's body is not reflected on screen. [5] In *La Habana*, the narrator's cinematographic experiences begin prior to the mirror stage — or during the phase of primitive undifferentiation of the ego and the non-ego. Thus, for the young baby film may serve as a type of incomprehensible, metaphoric mirror experience. This means that the narrator who is exposed to the cinema as a month-old baby undergoes the experience in a manner fundamentally different from an adult's perception of the event.

No kidding!

(Repetition)

The autobiographic text may also be said to function as a mirror in which the narrator contemplates himself as another, and in the process of writing transforms the *I* into a *he*. Or, as Leyla Perrone-Moisés remarks on the narrator of *La Habana*: "idéalisé dans son paradis perdu, cet adolescent reste fixé ('éternel,' dit-il) dans le miroir narcissique." [6] Narcissus of course contemplates his reflected image as if it belonged to another, much the same way as the writing self relates to the written self in an autobiographical text.

The narrator's early bond with the cinema runs parallel to his attachment to his mother, for whom the movies represent much more than a mere diversion. The narrator imagines that as a child, he escaped with his mother into a fantastic world where she was unfaithful to her husband with the images of her movie heroes on the screen. In

---

[4] Christian Metz, *The Imaginary Signifier: Psychoanalysis and the Cinema*, trans. Celia Britton, Annwyl Williams, Ben Brewster and Alfred Guzzetti (Bloomington: Indiana Univ. Press, 1982), pp. 45-46. Metz bases his analysis on Jacques Lacan's explanation of the mirror stage. See Lacan, "Le Stade du miroir comme formateur de la fonction du Je," in *Écrits I*, Collection Points (Paris: Éditions du Seuil, 1966), pp. 89-97.

[5] Mitchell's remarks are appropriate here: "The characters look into the cinema much as they would look into a mirror. In fact, they sometimes make the mistake of thinking that the film is really a mirror," p. 28. Thus, the confusion of artifice and reality may occur in spectators of any age.

[6] Leyla Perrone-Moisés, "L'Enfant dans la glace ou Don Juan en Amérique latine," *Cahiers Confrontation*, No. 6 (1981), p. 51.

remembering their early excursions, then, the narrator reconstructs a scenario in which he and his mother (turned furtive lover) took refuge in the world of darkness and fantasy the movie theater provided.[7] Later, this intimate attachment that joins the child and his mother as film spectators will be severed in the same place it was fostered, that is, the movie theater.

Zoila Infante's zeal for the cinema leads her to offer her son a choice between food or a movie: "ya en el pueblo de niño ella tenía un refrán que proponía olvidar la comida por el alimento visual de una película y decía, para que escogiéramos: '¿Cine o sardina?' En La Habana iba mucho con mi madre al cine, lo que presentaba problemas típicos más que edípicos" (p. 192). By denying the oedipal aspect of his relationship with his mother, the narrator naturally calls attention to the very feelings he seeks to mask. The narrator, as I have indicated, envisions himself to be his mother's accomplice in her secret rendezvous with her movie idols. As the young boy enters adolescence, he seeks to break this close attachment to his mother who still accompanies him to the movies, usually without the narrator's father. We are told of only one instance when his father joins mother and son to see a film: "fui al Universal . . . con un amigo, con mi madre y además con mi padre que no iba nunca al cine" (p. 192).

The oedipal theme is restated when the narrator gives his account of what may be seen as his physical and emotional separation from his mother at the movies: "Esa noche en el cine Universal me di cuenta de que no veía de tan lejos y a mediados de la película, para asombro de mi madre, me levanté y dije: 'No veo nada.' Ella se alarmó pensando que me había atacado una ceguera súbita, Edipo tropical" (p. 193). These associations with Oedipus come about when the narrator finds himself with his mother in the darkness of the

---

[7] The complexities of the cinema's deeper significance increase when we take into account Metz's idea that the spectator at the movies resembles the child witnessing the primal scene. He notes the following similarities: the darkness surrounding the onlooker; the keyhole effect of the aperture of the screen; the spectator's solitude in the cinema; the filmic spectacle's ignorance of the audience; the segregation of spaces between the spectator and the film; the entering and exiting of the clientele in the dark in the middle of the action. Metz concludes that "the cinematic signifier is not only 'psychoanalytic'; it is more precisely Oedipal in type" (pp. 63-65).

movie theater. Since blindness was the punishment that Oedipus inflicted on himself, it symbolically represents the castigation for a son's incestuous desires. We may say that the narrator thus seeks to escape both the incestuous relationship and its corresponding punishment as he leaves his mother's side and takes a seat next to a young woman whom he walks home after the show. His mother waits for him outside the movie theater, and on his return, furiously scolds her wayward son for disappearing from the family circle:

> Pensé que la próxima acción de mi madre no sería verbal sino que me abofetaría en plena cara en plena calle —mejor dicho, en plena plaza. No podía alegar mis derechos porque con mi madre yo no tenía ninguno. Ni siquiera legalmente podía reclamar mis derechos porque no había cumplido dieciocho años todavía y entonces los derechos de la persona comenzaban a los veintiuno. Opté por el silencio, imitando a la noche y a mi padre. (p. 201)

The narrator's mother appears as a fear-inspiring figure to the young adolescent who is discovering a secret world outside parental boundaries. The movie theater becomes the backdrop for the narrator's erotic discovery of the opposite sex, a process he furtively began in the rooming houses Monte 822 and Zulueta 408, the settings for the first chapter, "La casa de las transfiguraciones." Next to his raging mother, the young narrator feels he is devoid of any rights in the eyes of this castrating maternal figure who also has succeeded in keeping her husband subdued. It is not surprising, therefore, that the narrator attempts to escape what he sees as maternal tyranny and defiantly seeks out women over whom he can exert some power in the darkened movie theater. [8]

Throughout *La Habana,* the narrator continuously expresses his fear of the "policía del sexo" whom he identifies early on as his mother: "y aunque había encontrado a Etelvina desnuda ... no dejaba de ser excitante, aun por encima de mi timidez, de mi miedo, de mi aprensión a la próxima llegada de mi madre que era entonces

---

[8] Perrone-Moisés writes: "La mère, par contre, est l'initiatrice de tous les plaisirs, c'est elle qui introduit l'enfant dans toutes les aires où sa libido va trouver une réalisation: cinéma, littérature, théâtre, musique.... Cette mère forte et fougueuse, intense dans son amour comme dans ses colères, déterminera un fantasme constant du narrateur: celui de la Femme-Géante," p. 52.

(con respecto a Etelvina) la policía del sexo ..." (p. 78).[9] The narrator's mother had assigned him the job of waking up Etelvina, a young prostitute who also lived in Zulueta 408. She had also instilled in him a fear of coming in contact with Etelvina, who might have had what the mother called an "enfermedad de mujer mala" (p. 76).

The narrator's earliest discoveries of feminine allure take place despite his mother's prohibitions. As an adolescent at the movies, he must also escape her watchful eye to initiate contact with female spectators (some of them older women like his mother). But in this situation the adolescent still shows his fear of authority, now transferred from the original enforcer, his mother, to the law's representatives at the movie theater: ushers, doormen, managers, etc.: "Yo, temeroso de la ley como siempre ... tengo miedo de que venga el acomodador incómodo ... el portero portátil, el malgenioso gerente del cine, acompañados por agentes del orden público, obvios y a la vez impenetrables policías que personifican la ley ..." (p. 231). Of course, the description "impenetrables policías" finds its maximum application to the narrator's mother, forbidden object of oedipal desire and harsh enforcer of the law — the Law that makes her "impenetrable" in the first place.

The narrator's link with his mother, represented as a metaphoric umbilical cord that carries their connection into the maternal world of Zulueta 408 and into the realm of the movies, must eventually be broken: "La etapa de Zulueta 408, más que un tiempo vivido, fue toda una vida y debió quedar detrás como la noche, pero en realidad era un cordón umbilical que, cortado de una vez, es siempre recordado en el ombligo" (p. 171). In an equally conscious manner, the narrator describes the process of breaking his adolescent attachment to his mother: "íbamos cada vez menos juntos a la filarmónica y al teatro porque salía con mis amigos artistas, estaba más envuelto en tareas culturales, escribiendo o porque por mi mayoría de edad real había roto el cordón umbilical afectivo adolescente ..." (p. 440). The narrator perceives in his outings with his mother during his teen years a prolongation of his infantile attachment to her and takes

---

[9] The expression "policía del sexo" also appears in *Tres tristes tigres* within the context of puns and jokes that characterizes that novel: "Te digo que la otra no es tía ni un carajo. Feroz lesbiana es lo que es y tiene a esta prisionera del miedo. ¡Prisionera del miedo! ¡Mierda! ¿Por qué no llama a la policía del sexo"? (p. 399).

steps to declare his (sexual) independence in the darkened movie theaters where he seeks out companionship with other females.

The recipients of the narrator's attentions at the movies never transcend their anonymity and remain in his mind as fragments of women which never form a whole being with whom a true relationship may be established: "A veces no hay más que un fragmento de mujer no de recuerdo, como la noche en el teatro Alkazar..." (p. 183). Cabrera Infante notes that for the narrator of *La Habana,* success "would have consisted of an assemblage of the various women he has met...." [10] His ideal, then, would be a collage of the memorable fragments of all his lovers. While the narrator relates the intricate details of his woman-stalking game, he nevertheless claims he is really searching for love in the dark: "una de las técnicas de rascabucheo (aunque no era eso, el simple contacto, lo que yo buscaba en lo oscuro sino amor, el amor, ese vencedor conquistado) en el cine era introducir un pie descalzo por la hendija de la luneta..." (p. 181). This humorous contrast between the idealistic, romantic notion of finding love at the movies and the reality of that pursuit leads the narrator to experience a great deception when the light of day reveals the true faces of his movie companions. He cruelly describes one such episode:

> El glamour existente en la sala semioscura... desapareció en cuanto estuvimos en la calle.... En la calle la nariz recortada de perfil y el pelado paje se mostraron como un conjunto de facciones de niña ñoña.... Hasta me pareció que cojeaba —¿o sería andar de retrasado? Fue una situación penosa y me curó de mi afición a las aventuras amorosas en el cine— pero sólo por un tiempo. ¿O debo decir unas noches? (pp. 191-92).

When the narrator of *La Habana* seeks to interact with female members of the movie audience, he ceases to function as a spectator, according to Christian Metz's definition of the latter:

> he has decided in advance to conduct himself as... a spectator and not an actor...; for the duration of the projection he puts off any plan of action. (Cinemas are of course also used for other purposes, but to the extent that they

---

10 "GCI: Three Islands," comp. Siemens, p. 11.

are, their occupants have ceased to be spectators and have
voluntarily abandoned the filmic state for a sort of behaviour
belonging to reality . . .). [11]

As an "occupant of the theater," the narrator performs the role of
an off-screen actor involved in his own romantic comedy. But, even
if his behavior belongs to reality, as Metz would argue, the pseudo-
spectator entertains fantasies and employs his imagination in assuming
an actor's role. Upon leaving the movie theater, the narrator emerges
from his fantasy world to re-enter the real world and often displays
surprise when he discovers the truth about his "leading lady": "Tengo
que decir, lamentablemente, que la princesa se volvió cenicienta: no
era una versión vertiginosa de Rita Hayworth: era todo menos
bella. . . . Su nariz no era, como creí en el cine, respingada a la manera de Judy Garland . . ." (p. 232). The narrator, who had constructed in his imagination a composite of Hollywood's stars, finds
out he has really acted in a performance with a cook whose hands
have been scarred by kitchen grease. His own intriguing adventures
as anti-hero comically rival those on the big screen. The movie theater
is transformed into a stage for another production, which in turn
becomes the basis for a third medium of entertainment — the novel.
We as readers then constitute a group similar to the spectators at
the movies, whom Metz characterizes as "an accumulation of indi-
viduals who, despite appearances, more closely resemble the fragmented group of readers of a novel." [12]

The narrator's conduct at the movies defies his mother's norms
and breaks the law enforced by the "policía del sexo," which by
now refers to both the outside authority and the internalized voice
of the conscience or super-ego. But in La Habana, another norm is
broken, as Cabrera himself recognized when he expressed the fear
that his work would be regarded as pornography. In fact, La Habana
para un infante difunto does border on pornographic literature in
many respects and could be considered "autobiopornography," to use
Tittler's term. [13] The fine line between literature and pornography

---

[11] Metz, p. 117.

[12] Metz, p. 64.

[13] Jonathan Tittler, "Cabrera Infante's Novels." Critics such as Gerald
Guinness see this side of the novel as a positive quality: "The play between
vulgarity and literary artifice in La Habana makes for much of the book's

may be as difficult to discern as is the division between autobiography and fiction. Modern critical theory allows for a blending of these demarcations into a gray area that incorporates characteristics from more than one genre. [14] Theoretical studies on pornography leave room for conflicting conclusions with respect to the nature of *La Habana*. For many of those writing about the subject, the classification of a work as pornography is at odds with its simultaneous designation as literature. Ernest van den Haag states that the aim of pornography is "to arouse the reader's lust so that, by sharing the fantasy manufactured for him, he may attain a vicarious sexual experience." [15] Kenneth Tynan opposes literature and pornography by defining the latter as "writing that is exclusively intended to cause sexual pleasure." [16] Anthony Burgess defines a pornographic work as "an instrument for procuring a sexual catharsis, but it rarely promotes the desire to achieve this through a social mode ... the book is, in a sense, a substitute for a sexual partner," whereas a work of literature's purpose is "to arouse emotions and discharge those emotions as part of the artistic experience." [17] Susan Sontag argues, however, that this particular definition fails to convince in view of the complex functions of literature, and the impossibility of ascertaining the author's intention to provoke a singular response in the reader. [18]

---

charm." Review of *La Habana, Revista de Estudios Hispánicos*, 7 (1980), 219. Further, autobiography and pornography are seen as interconnected by Stephen Spender: "the nature of the inner human personality is such that if they [autobiographers] tell what it is like to be themselves, they are immoralists, exhibitionists, pornographers." "Confessions and Autobiography," in *Autobiography*, ed. Olney, p. 118.

[14] Harry Levin, for example, states: "The quest for sensation has been approaching the line between serious literature and pornography, if indeed that borderline is still discernible." "The Unbanning of the Books," in *Perspectives on Pornography*, ed. Douglas A. Hughes (New York: St. Martin's Press, 1970), p. 17.

[15] Ernest van den Haag, "The Case for Pornography is the Case for Censorship and Vice Versa," in *Pornography*, ed. Hughes, p. 128.

[16] Kenneth Tynan, "Dirty Books Can Stay," in *Pornography*, ed. Hughes, p. 110.

[17] Anthony Burgess, "What Is Pornography?" in *Pornography*, ed. Hughes, pp. 5-6.

[18] Susan Sontag, "The Pornographic Imagination," in *Styles of Radical Will* (New York: Delta, 1970), p. 39. This problem which Sontag identifies may be extended to the difficulties inherent in determining an author's intention to write autobiography.

If pornography reaches the heights of literature, it represents an achievement which Peter Michelson describes as follows:

> a higher form of pornography which might be called *literary:* it is an exploration of human sexuality. This is real pornography .... Pornography on its lowest level exploits this rhythm [of human sexuality] by providing easy fantasy gratifications. On its highest level it *explores* this rhythm, its moral and psychic implications, and to the degree it does this it is poetic. [19]

Critics like George Steiner, though, do not find anything poetic about literary erotica, in which like its base counterpart, the "dirty book," "the same stimuli, the same contortions and fantasies, occur over and over with unutterable monotony." [20] The erotic scenes in Cabrera Infante's work may not easily be classified as monotonous. With the ironic perspective afforded by the viewpoint of the autobiographer writing about a past self, the narrator's exploits in the movie theater, in Julieta's apartment, or in the *posadas* he frequents, while often a repetition of the same activity, are never presented in the one-dimensional prose of a "dirty book." It is precisely the language of literature that shifts the focus from the act to the artifice, or from the story to the discourse.

Sontag makes an important point when she states:

> The emotional flatness of pornography is thus neither a failure of artistry nor an index of principled inhumanity. The arousal of a sexual response in the reader *requires* it. Only in the absence of directly stated emotions can the reader of pornography find room for his own responses. When the event narrated comes already festooned with the author's explicitly avowed sentiments, by which the reader may be stirred, it then becomes harder to be stirred by the event itself. [21]

To rephrase this in formalistic terms, we may say that the commentary provided by the first-person narrator and the irony facilitated

---

[19] Peter Michelson, "An Apology for Pornography," in *Pornography,* ed. Hughes, p. 69.

[20] George Steiner, "Night Words: High Pornography and Human Privacy," in *Pornography,* ed. Hughes, p. 101.

[21] Sontag, p. 54.

by the shift from story time to discourse time contribute to making *La Habana* a work of sexual fiction and not of pornography. For Sontag, the pornographic imagination "inhabits a universe that is . . . incomparably economical. The strictest possible criterion of relevance applies: everything must bear upon the erotic situation." [22] The narrator of *La Habana* continually tells us that his story is about his search for erotic love, yet the work ultimately offers a wide panorama of themes that acquire equal importance, such as the dilemma of deciding which story to tell, the problem of translating memories into words, the impossibility of maintaining true intimacy with another, the necessity of achieving independence, etc. The narration of the self's development becomes the chronicle of one's feelings as well as one's actions, and as such cannot do what pornography does by stripping the characters of their multi-faceted humanity. In the manner of Diderot's "paradoxe sur le comédien," the author who succeeds at pornography is the one whose characters, in their lack of stated feelings, allow for the reader to use his imagination to evoke what is absent from the text.

La Habana, then, while giving some evidence of the pornographic intention, surpasses the limits of that genre to emerge as a multidimensional portrait of a person in search of himself. Even though this search is related to the narrator's exploration of the erotic, he integrates this aspect of his development into his life as a whole and formulates an ironic, retrospective sexual picaresque work much along the lines of *Portnoy's Complaint* by Philip Roth. The "fragments of women" the narrator remembers from the movie theaters take their place in his memory and subsequently in his text, transformed from sexual objects into textual subjects that carry the narrator further along the road of self-exploration.

One fundamental difference between pornography and literary sexual fiction is the language employed in treating erotic themes. As Sontag points out: "Experiences aren't pornographic; only images and representations — structures of the imagination — are." [23] In true pornography, then, "language is a bothersome necessity, for its function . . . is to set going a series of non-verbal images, of fantasies, and if it could achieve this without the mediation of words it

---

[22] Sontag, p. 66.
[23] Sontag, p. 49.

would." [24] The medium that does achieve this is of course the pornographic film. The word, though, excites on a different level. In his analysis of the subject of sexual fiction, Maurice Charney attributes to Foucault, Barthes and Gass the notion that "sexuality only exists as a form of discourse, that without language sexuality as such would cease to be." [25] In fact, in both *La Habana* and *TTT* Cabrera Infante has shown a predilection for the theme of language as a magic instrument with the ability to create and excite, or with the maleficent power to destroy and to mask intimate feelings.

Cabrera's exploration into the language of the erotic in *La Habana* leads to a dichotomy that might be best summarized by the narrator's remark: "Ahora apenas atendía a lo que ella me decía entre los besos . . . sordo yo porque estaba más interesado en el beso en sí que en su literatura — en otra época podría haber dicho que atendía más a su lengua que a su lenguaje" (pp. 53-54). The narrator once would have used a play on words (like those typically found in *TTT*) to say that a moment of passion was more important than a discussion of literature. But he inverts the priorities at the level of the discourse in *La Habana*: he interrupts the story of his actions (*lengua*) to discuss his reactions to them (*lenguaje*), and thus he avoids turning into a pornographer. The focus rapidly shifts from explicit descriptions of erotic encounters to the reporting of mental activity in the form of commentary. Instead of the "play-by-play" narrative we expect in pornography, *La Habana* presents the "post-game analysis" complete with highlights and replays. The narrator claims to have paid more attention to *lengua* than *lenguaje*, but in signalling that dichotomy, he diverts the reader's attention from the action of the story to the language of its telling. [26]

---

[24] Steven Marcus, *The Other Victorians: A Study of Sexuality and Pornography in Mid-Nineteenth Century England* (1964; rpt. New York: Norton, 1985), p. 279.

[25] Charney, p. 10.

[26] Stephanie Merrim analyzes this process in a similar manner: "Al decirlo todo explícitamente, *La Habana* sacrifica mucho de su erotismo al mismo tiempo que su forma de expresarlo aleja el texto de la pornografía: el planteamiento topográfico implica una actitud hacia el sexo casi clínica y naturalista, más propia de un sexógrafo que de un pornógrafo. Pero el golpe final al erotismo y la pornografía lo da el humorismo de la narración; esto es, la ironía y los juegos de palabras." "*La Habana para un infante difunto* y su teoría topográfica de las formas," *Revista Iberoamericana*, 48 (January-June 1982), 410.

In *La Habana,* language is often shown to be a source of interference in the seduction game, as the narrator discovers that words become an obstacle to physical or emotional intimacy. While words may have the power to excite, the narrator clearly would prefer other forms of arousal in his early amorous adventures:

> esta mujer que había estado conmigo encerrada . . . semidesnuda, intimando, excitándome con su desnudez . . . pero también con su conversación (el hecho de que hablara sobre nada, naderías, mientras permanecía impasible en refajo era una forma de excitación verbal) . . . . (p. 70)

While the narrator shows great interest in the physical qualities — and defects — of his lovers, he also takes note of the manner in which they speak. Their conversational style often contrasts markedly with the uninhibited language they unleash during moments of passion. The narrator points out that he seems to choose women who speak a pseudo-literary language which he finds both amusing and distracting. His first love, Julieta Estévez, has no compunctions about her many adulterous affairs ("El amor no tiene moral," p. 382), even scheduling visits with her lovers immediately before her husband's expected arrival at lunchtime. She expresses realistic views concerning her sexual needs: "Vicente no es suficiente hombre para mí en la cama. Lo más natural es que busque mi satisfacción con otro" (p. 383), and considers the sexual act in itself the highest form of love. Her initial invitation to the narrator, "¿Quieres que hagamos el amor?" causes him to reflect: "Esas fueron sus exactas palabras y así era ella: nunca la oí referirse al sexo con palabras vulgares, como jamás dijo una vulgaridad . . ." (p. 367). Julieta's euphemistic language often produces a comic effect since it contrasts greatly with the situations in which she finds herself. On one occasion, for example, she and the narrator visit the famous *posada* at Second and Thirty-First, a *casa de citas* housing an array of couples who rent rooms by the hour. [27] Julieta nevertheless finds the place particularly laudable:

---

27 Perrone-Moisés applies the expression "casa de citas" to the whole work: "le livre est un immense montage de citations (en espagnol, un autre sens du mot *citas*); intersexe et intertexte," p. 48.

Me excita la idea de saber que este edificio está hecho exclusivamente para el acto de amor, que los que vienen aquí vienen nada más que a hacer el amor, que todo aquí está organizado para estar un rato haciendo el amor. ¡Es la arquitectura en función del amor! (p. 387)

While on the one hand Julieta employs romantic language to describe her erotic involvements, she also recognizes the banal realities that accompany a sexual relationship. She bluntly informs the narrator: "Querido, el amor es húmedo y no huele bien" (p. 378). But her words on the nature of love — free of vulgarity — contrast with the explicit, pornographic language the narrator adopts to recount his amorous initiation with Julieta, a style perhaps inspired by his having read "en novelitas pornográficas detalles minuciosos de esta operación..." (p. 377). While Julieta avoids the use of obscenities at all costs, the narrator's story is replete with them, perhaps an indication of how much distance really separated these lovers. Their parting may also be attributed to the fact that Julieta was seeking physical gratification without obligation, whereas the narrator claims to have been searching for love, or at least human warmth that would transcend an exclusively physical bond. [28] When Julieta refuses to make love with him after he has just eaten lunch, the narrator first believes that she was showing concern for his health, but instead she reveals her true feelings: " ¡Tú no te vas a acostar conmigo acabado de comer! ... No te me vas a quedar muerto en los brazos.... Yo no corro ese riesgo" (p. 392). Upon realizing the reason for her refusal, the narrator sadly reflects on her words: "Fue en esa frase fatal que vi que a ella le importaba poco que me muriera, con tal de que no lo hiciera en su cama: la verdad fue más brutal que sus palabras" (p. 392). He perceives himself as little more than Julieta's *Homo erectus* (p. 392), and perhaps attains the highest degree of revenge in vilifying the act she deems sacred with his string of obscenities that carry this tale toward the conventions of pornographic literature.

---

[28] Álvarez-Borland remarks: "The story becomes a dramatization of a relationship doomed to failure because it neglected any kind of spiritual closeness. The protagonists could only concentrate on their sexual desires, totally overlooking their spiritual needs." "*La Habana para un infante difunto*: Cabrera Infante's Self Conscious Narrative," *Hispania*, 68 (1985), 46.

This narrator who pens his "autobiopornography" finds great amusement in the pseudo-poetic language of his lovers, and notes that with these women, literature has gotten in the way:

> Además, yo no hablaba de literatura con las mujeres: en ese tiempo no había otra cosa que hacer con las mujeres que hablar de amor, tratar de hacerles el amor, de hecho singar —palabra que detestaba Julieta, que horrorizaría a Dulce. Pero he aquí que siempre venía a juntarme con mujeres que eran, de una manera o de otra, sacerdotisas de la literatura: la literatura fue culpable de que la relación con Julieta no fuera más profunda, más satisfactoria, ella loca por la poesía, viviendo una vida literaria por la demasiada lectura de la autobiografía de Isadora Duncan . . . . (p. 446)

Literature as these women read it creates a stumbling block that thwarts the narrator's objectives, such as attaining a more intimate relationship with Julieta, or achieving immediate physical gratification with Dulce.

If we view *La Habana* as sexual picaresque autobiography, we may note that whereas the classic *pícaro* ascends the hierarchy of society to better his lot in life, this narrator roams about the social scale in his search for amorous adventures. Thus he leaves Julieta, a colleague from the Bachillerato, to take up with Dulce, who works for a survey firm, and finally, to undertake a series of what he terms "casuales encuentros forzados" with any woman whom he could attract. It is among the maids, cooks, drivers, servants, etc. that he discovers an even greater gap between the language of romance and the vocabulary of sex. One such conquest, Lolita, a maid, demands of the narrator: "Júrame que me amas con todas las fuerzas de tu corazón" (p. 514), but later, at the height of passion, she utters obscenities:

> No gritaba como Julieta, mujer en celo, ni exclamaba como Dulce, pseudopoéticamente . . . pero sí se refería ella a . . . la unión de los dos, a la cópula con una variedad de nombres suficientes para componer un diccionario de malas palabras —si no fuera que luego, al tratar de enumerar lo que había dicho exactamente, me encontré que eran solamente una o dos palabras repetidas . . . . (p. 518)

Lolita's real language, like the language of pornography, tends to be repetitive, monotonous, and limited. [29]

But Lolita's deliberate pose, reflected in expressions such as "júrame que me amas," finds its origins in the romantic language employed in the radio soap opera that she avidly follows. The narrator comes to understand the dual nature of her speech: "mi amante actual, ese montón de carne y extrañas declaraciones de ahí al lado, pedía prestado a la radio no sólo su lenguaje sino sus sentimientos —o mejor, subordinaba sus sentimientos aparentes a un lenguaje que era para ella ideal" (p. 519). In Vargas Llosa's *La tía Julia y el escribidor,* a similar pattern develops when life imitates low forms of art, as the characters adopt Pedro Camacho's radio serial language to discuss their own soap opera like intrigues. Lolita imitates the exaggerated, sentimental language of her heroes from the "Novela del Aire" (p. 519) in the hopes that she, too, will become the ideal romantic lover. Her true being, however, emerges from the torrent of obscenities she releases when she discards the affected radio serial mask.

The notion that *La Habana* constitutes a type of sexual picaresque work may be further supported by the fact that the narrator acknowledges his inspiration in this genre:

> Rosita . . . componía en carne y cutis la imagen de un personaje que yo había tomado de una novela leída años atrás, lectura que empezó como pornografía pura y terminó por ser un libro mayor, al que volvía siempre para tomar nota. En esta historia el héroe . . . pasaba de la desgracia de la extrema pobreza (como la mía) a la gracia y la gloria gracias a las mujeres y por medio del periodismo (al que yo aspiraba). (p. 148)

La Habana may be considered a parody of the type of pornographic picaresque novel that had intrigued the narrator; but, as Sontag

---

[29] Steiner's claim that in erotic literature of all kinds the same stimuli and fantasies reccur with unutterable monotony implies that the vocabulary used to describe these sexual scenes also tends to be limited. One may argue, however, that new life can be breathed into even the most banal act, sexual or otherwise, when writing about it in literature. Tynan, in his criticism of Steiner, points out that only poor writers produce a boring, monotonous text, but that good writers often utilize standard scenes and language to create a work of erotic literature that transcends the traditional limitations of pornography (pp. 118-20).

points out, a true parody of the pornographic mode cannot be executed, since it still must succumb to the conventions of the genre it seeks to mock.[30] While metapornography remains in the realm of the pornographic, some of the best examples of sexual fiction — from the works of the Marquis de Sade to Roth's *Portnoy's Complaint* — rely heavily on parody and satire. *La Habana* may be included among those works that utilize the conventions of erotica within the overall context of satirical literature, and in so doing transcend the one-dimensional prose of pornography.

The narrator, who laments the ever-present *vulgaridad* in the expressions of feelings by the women with whom he is involved, nevertheless recognizes the human need for a language belonging to a lower order: "Carajo (usualmente destesto [sic] las obscenidades pero cuando las empleo es que las otras palabras no sirven para nada: donde mueren las palabras, nacen las malas palabras)" (p. 473). Ironically, the exclamation *carajo* hardly qualifies as an obscenity in Cuban Spanish, and it pales in comparison to the colorful erotic descriptions that fill the pages of *La Habana*. But the narrator brings out an important point here: that dirty words take the place of communicative language, and that their use covers an absence of verbal proficiency of another sort. Just as the narrator's pseudonyms mask his identity, his obscene language often serves as protection for the fragile inner self.

This "erotic disguise," as Eugenio Suárez-Galbán defines it,[31] is most appropriate in Cabrera Infante, whose timidity lurks behind the aggressive verbal front in *La Habana*. And the unabashedly pornographic language of the adolescent protagonist of *La Habana*, in contrast to the elliptical manner in which erotic themes are treated in *TTT*,[32] serves yet another purpose, as Suárez-Galbán points out: it creates a scandal — directed against the bourgeois — that approximates the work to other shocking literary confessions before it.

---

[30] Sontag, p. 51.

[31] Eugenio Suárez-Galbán Guerra comments: "Si el rebelde se aprovecha de una exposición chocante del tema vedado, el tímido no desperdiciará el disfraz que le brinda el tema erótico para, paradójicamente, desnudarse." "*La Habana para un infante difunto*: la falsa memoria verdadera de Guillermo Cabrera Infante," *Insula*, Nos. 404-405 (July-August 1980), p. 31.

[32] Suzanne Jill Levine notes this contrast in "Translation as (Sub) Version: On Translating *Infante's Inferno*," *SubStance*, 13, No. 1 (1984), 91.

The autobiographer finds that pornographic language may thus serve as the most effective vehicle for reaching one's intimate being. As Robert Adams notes, in the twentieth century "the obscene represents an act of deep choice, an affirmation, even a creation, of the self"; further, "through the obscene one declares one's independence of the rotten genteel tradition . . . ." [33] The uninhibited language of *La Habana* thus allows the narrator to liberate the repressed expressions of his sexual being, but may also alienate a large portion of his readership.

In writing the adventures of his youth, then, the narrator employs graphic language that appears to fit the mold of conventional pornography. Nevertheless, he claims to avoid obscenities in speech because they communicate very little. He does, however, employ another type of set language to attract women — the standard lines of a modern-day *burlador*:

> Momento que aproveché para iniciar una finta que con el tiempo se convertiría en toda una estocada y de ahí en maniobra, en técnica del duelo del amor —y si sueno como ese autor favorito de mi madre, M. Delly, es porque en el amor no queda más que repetir las palabras, como hacen Romeo y Julieta, o repetir frases hechas, ¿y quién mejor dictándolas que los autores de novelas baratas . . . ? (pp. 558-59)

To achieve his goals, the narrator depends on the effect of his words. He finds that for many of his intended conquests, the most successful lines come from the repertoire of ready-made words of love encountered in romantic novels.

Caught in this labyrinth of meaningless language, however, the narrator has trouble ascending to a higher level of communication. He discovers that the moments in life that should evoke expressions of deep feelings paradoxically bring forth in him a superficial, comic response such as the following, when Margarita reveals that she had been pregnant with the narrator's child. When she informs him: "Ese coágulo de sangre pudo haber sido tu hijo mío," he thinks: "No pude evitar recordar una canción que dice: 'Pensar que ese hijo tuyo / pudo haber sido mío,' a pesar de la seriedad de la situación"

---

[33] Adams, p. 87.

(p. 679). The narrator often is reminded of a *bolero* (a romantic pop ballad), a sentimental novel, a movie plot, etc., and partially lives life through the pervasive popular culture of his time. The narrator reports that he reacted to Margarita's announcement by remembering the words from a song, in effect retreating from the emotional impact that such news would surely bring. In a parallel manner, the subject of the discourse also uses mechanisms to turn a tragic scene into a comic one. When Margarita tells the narrator: "No fue mi hermana quien se hizo un aborto ese día sino yo," he remarks: "Hizo otra pausa que debiera llamar preñada pero no quiero ser brutal" (p. 679). The same technique that served well in the story also performs a function in the discourse; the text is interrupted by the intruding comic language of the eternal master of the pun, the one-liner, the opportune play on words (in this case based on the English expression "pregnant pause"). Tittler underscores the contrast between the language of *La Habana* and that of *TTT*:

> In that *Tres tristes tigres* thematizes the frailty of its language, it at once buttresses that frailty and shows that it, the novel, belongs, despite its jocular surface, to the world of tragedy. By repressing those disquieting impulses and focusing instead on what language *can* do — and not the least of those things is to incite sexual arousal — *La Habana para un infante difunto,* despite the rhetoric of failure it employs, offers a resolution which locates it within the domain of the comic. [34]

Despite the potential for tragedy, *La Habana* remains essentially comic because the narrator pokes fun at his own past humiliations and disappointments, or, more accurately, protects himself with a shield of words. Most applicable to Cabrera's *La Habana* are Robert Alter's comments on Laurence Sterne, creator of the prototypical self-conscious narrator-buffoon: "The comedy of *Tristram Shandy* is clearly of another order — not the affirmation of artifice as a means of constructing models of harmonious integration but the use of laughter as the defense-action of an embattled psyche, its chief means

---

[34] Tittler, "Cabrera Infante's Novels." Charney notes also that "humor is one of the safety valves in sexual fiction" (p. 165).

of confronting the terrors of loneliness, frustration, pain, of its own inevitable extinction." [35]

Ever aware of the power of language, the narrator of *La Habana* concludes that words, not acts, should be judged:

> estábamos en el cuarto de baño de una posada, dispuestos a dejarlo para acostarnos en la cama favorable y hacer el amor —ese galicismo que aprendí de Julieta como la única forma decente de decir singar. Ah, que las palabras, no los actos, sean sentenciados por la moral. (p. 567)

Claiming to despise euphemistic, romantic language as much as vulgarity, the narrator indicates that acts have little moralistic value attached to them. Words, on the other hand, can label an act and in so doing, charge it with negative or positive connotations. Here the narrator blurs the line between "hacer el amor" and "singar," in effect reducing human relations to the vulgar adolescent term.

Cabrera Infante has remarked that literature is no more than "words, words, words," and in keeping with this statement, the narrator of *La Habana* tells what his autobiography should be: "Es cierto que también pensé escribir una versión de *Mi vida* [by Isadora Duncan], pero mi vida sería un libro cerrado que al abrirse se vería lleno de actos inocentes escritos con palabras culpables" (p. 336). *La Habana* could thus be interpreted as the chronicle of adolescence with its typical, innocent, even standard scenes of growing up sexually. It is written with "guilty words" in several senses. First, the explicit language of the work may be classified as pornographic, and the obscenities used thus constitute "guilty words" which are generally forbidden. Second, the narrator often refers to his "censor" or to the "policía del sexo," an internal overseeing agent of parental origin that arouses guilt feelings that are consequently expressed with "guilty words." Further, the word is guilty in the sense that it cannot faithfully serve as a medium of communication, either between the narrator and his lovers or the narrator and his readers. [36] Lan-

---

[35] Robert Alter, *Partial Magic: The Novel as a Self-Conscious Genre* (Berkeley: Univ. of California Press, 1975), p. 42.

[36] Cabrera Infante comments in relation to *La Habana*: "I admit that within the sexual metaphor I am generating verbal texts. The book involves my erotic relationship with words." "GCI: Three Islands," comp. Siemens, p. 11.

guage turns traitor to those who attempt to manipulate it, a theme in Cabrera Infante which is clearly rooted in *TTT*.

La Habana ends with a fantastic episode that breaks with the autobiographical style of the rest of the work. In many respects, however, the epilogue, "Función continua" (the term for a continuous showing of a film), brings together several of the novel's themes in the form of a bizarre fantasy that occurs in a key place, the movie theater. By attaching this concluding chapter to a work of autobiography, Cabrera Infante moves closer to fiction, as does Mario Vargas Llosa by interpolating soap opera-inspired novelettes in the text of *La tía Julia y el escribidor*. The highly unreal scene in which the narrator of *La Habana* disappears inside a woman casts doubt over the entire autobiographical narration. Cabrera states: "The epilogue absolutely gives the lie to the rest of the book as reality — offers it to the reader as something totally unreal." If the epilogue is not to be believed, then how should we interpret the rest of *La Habana*? Cabrera recognizes what he calls a "fictional ambiguity at the close of the book: what really takes place?"[37] The same question is also then applicable to the first-person, dramatized narration that appears in the first eleven chapters of the work. What takes place: autobiographical writing or fictive invention?

The epilogue opens in the manner of Chapter Three, "Amor trompero," which chronicles the narrator's attemps to find erotic adventures at the movies. He seems to have caught a glimpse of a woman from those past days when he frequented Havana's many movie theaters, and naturally ascribes to her the characteristics of the type of woman he once pursued: "ahora estaba solamente devolviendo el vuelto a su monedero, el tique (así lo llamaría ella, habanera popular que debía ser) tomado, ticketeniente" (p. 689). He recalls: "antes sólo me mostró su espalda" (p. 689), so she may indeed be the anonymous woman (from Chapter Three) whose back he admired but never touched one day at the movies: "recuerdo esta espalda que aun en la penumbra gris del cine tenía un color canela y una lisura de la piel a la vista que casi se veía su olor en la oscuridad" (p. 183). This correspondence of a character from an earlier chapter to one in the epilogue further blurs the lines separat-

---

[37] "GCI: Three Islands," comp. Siemens, p. 11.

ing the autobiographical body of *La Habana* from its obviously fictitious conclusion.

Another tie between the epilogue and the rest of the work is the Anglicized warning sign the narrator notes upon entering the movie theater, "Infantes no admitidos" (p. 691). The narrator relentlessly continues to play his identity game by using a part of Cabrera Infante's name in the epilogue. The two main characters of the epilogue, though, remain a nameless *he* and *she* throughout. This reference to *Infante,* then, constitutes one final attempt to tease the audience with a hint at an extra-textual identity for the narrator.

The narrator finds that while the woman who sits beside him in the movie theater accepts his advances, she pays attention primarily to the action on the screen as if her body were dissociated from the viewing self. Metz notes that motor manifestations of movie spectators are few: "shifting around in the seat, more or less conscious modification of facial expression, occasional comment under the breath, laughing . . . ." [38] This woman seated next to the narrator performs several of these activities typical of the spectator, such as outbursts of laughter, which disconcert the narrator who pays no attention to the film in order to concentrate on other matters: "Ella se rió, no se sonrió, se rió a carcajadas que la sacudían, incluyendo a mi mano en su temblor de teta. Pero no se reía de mi acto sino de una acción que ocurría frente a ella allá en la pantalla" (p. 693). In this respect, she represents the ideal conquest in the movie theater: few tricks from the narrator's repertoire are called into play when the other party acquiesces so readily. His ideal is someone who, like the "fragments of women" he had admired before, consists of a body willing to submit to his advances.

Up to this point in the epilogue, the narrator has approached this woman using only tactile means, but a strange turn of events is initiated when he apparently loses his wedding ring during his explorations in the dark. He then finds it necessary to engage in conversation with her: "No habíamos hablado, yo no había tratado de hablar con ella antes (donde sobran los gestos, no nacen las palabras) pero en ese momento yo traté de hablarle . . ." (p. 696). Gestures take the place of words until spoken language becomes a

---

[38] Metz, p. 117.

necessity. When the narrator panics at having lost his ring, he expresses his fear of returning home empty-handed: "—¿Qué hago ahora? —dije en un lamento que expresaba la lástima de volver a casa sin mi anillo de bodas y enfrentar a mi mujer con mi afrenta. Además estaba mi madre, juez severo" (p. 697). This fantasy has its roots in several episodes recounted in the body of *La Habana,* such as the following incident when the narrator returns home very late to his waiting family after having been out with Margarita: "Fue mi madre, como siempre, quien me preguntó: '¿Dónde has estado hasta ahora?' Es evidente que era mi mujer quien debiera haber hecho esa pregunta, pero mi madre se ponía de su parte, como había hecho desde nuestro noviazgo..." (p. 601). As an adolescent, he was pursued by his mother who demanded explanations concerning his whereabouts. His mother then joins forces with his wife, and the two become linked in his mind as the enforcers of the moral code.

It is not surprising that in the epilogue this same fear should surface when the narrator loses the object that symbolizes his marital status: "Ni rastro de mi anillo y era el que me unía en sagrado matrimonio" (p. 698). The situation becomes worse when, in the search for his ring, the narrator also loses the watch his father gave him: "Ahora no sólo tenía que buscar mi anillo de bodas sino el reloj de mi padre. ¡Qué lata, los objetos de familia!" (p. 699). The narrator's guilt feelings about his activities at the movies are linked to the lost objects that represent his family ties. As this woman somehow devours his possessions, she also takes away his proof of identity as husband and son. The loss of the watch also signals the loss of the notion of time, a condition that characterizes the pre-conscious world to which the narrator returns in the epilogue.

Once dialogue is initiated with this passive spectator, the narrator discovers that she, like other women he has known, shows a preference for vulgar language. To her question "¿Qué carajo es ahora?" the narrator remarks to himself: "Detesto a las mujeres que dicen malas palabras pero no estaba en una posición para mostrarle mi aversión" (p. 700). This fantasy female shares many characteristics with the maids and cooks who were once the recipients of the narrator's attention at the movies. She also bears many of the negative traits attributed to his mother, and thus represents the eternal terrible woman:

Era ella . . . contra mí, furiosa, hecha una furia ahora. Mejor, era una hidra con todas estas cabezas vociferantes —megera, harpía, erinnia, Gorgona, Salomé, Mesalina, Agripina, bruja de Macbeth, Catalina de Médicis, Catalina Grandísima, Eva Perón, Ilse Koch y, finalmente, adelantada a su tiempo, Madame Mao —de mujeres múltiples inclinadas hacia mí terribles. (p. 702)

His fear of being annihilated by woman comes to realization in the epilogue. This woman, now presented as a furious monster, lends the narrator a light that she carries in her purse so he can continue his search for the missing objects. He proceeds inward: "En el momento que metí la cabeza toda sensación cesó — ruidos, texturas, olores, sabor amargo" (p. 703). This reentry into the womb brings to mind Alejo Carpentier's story "Viaje a la semilla" in which the protagonist lives his life in reverse, going from old age to a fetal state. Although Cabrera Infante does not execute an explicit parody on Carpentier's style here, as he does in *TTT,* for example, it nevertheless would be possible to interpret the epilogue of *La Habana* as a type of pastiche inspired in Carpentier's short story.

As the narrator loses his sense of orientation, he finds he also severs his connection with the city of Havana: "Me puse en pie de nuevo y traté de encontrar la rampa de entrada, a la que ya no podía llamar La Rampa, invisible ahora" (p. 704). The *infante* who bases his orientation on the topography of his city must now map out a new route in this foreign territory. [39] In the room that he describes as pear-shaped, he declares: "Mi éxito será mi salida" (p. 704), a play on words (éxito-exit) that reveals the narrator's wish to escape this world and reassume his being outside the womb. He then stumbles across a text, Jules Verne's *Voyage to the Center of the Earth.* Cabrera Infante's remarks on this discovery are relevant:

the only possible guide to a way out is literature, which he [the narrator] doesn't recognize as such. . . . That is, he

---

39 Perrone-Moisés remarks on the relationship between woman and city: "La Havana, qu'il appelle aussi 'la Vana' (la vaine), et qu'on pourrait appeler: 'la vaina' (le vagin), est ce vide féminin qui l'aspire et auquel il aspire, point de départ et d'arrivée de cet enfant qui doit dénaître pour devenir 'éternel' " (p. 55).

takes this work of pure fiction in an extremely literal manner, considering it a guide to the theater exit, and as such
the exit again into the book — the return to the *beginning*
of *La Habana*... which is what is implied by the ending:
"This is where we came in." Here there is not so much a
play on words; it is a pure phantasmagoric vision of the
possibilities within the feminine sex. [40]

Before the narrator discovers the exit, however, his guide book
comes to an abrupt end: "Aquí no pude seguir leyendo los frag-
mentos no porque fuera interrumpido por los elementos sino porque
el librito se acabó, *editio brevis*" (p. 710). Cabrera's preferred way
of ending a text also consists in putting an arbitrary halt to the
stream of words, such as the "Aquí llegamos" (p. 711) that signals
the point in the movie's projection at which the spectators had
arrived and that serves to close *La Habana*. Another case in point
is the epilogue of *TTT*, which stops in mid-sentence not because
Cabrera Infante originally planned it that way, but because the
Spanish censors suppressed the last lines of the text which were
considered to be religious slander. The ravings of the crazy woman
in *TTT* that appear on the last page consequently end in this manner: "ya no puedo más   registra y registra y registra   que viene
el mono con un cuchillo y me registra   me saca las tripas   el
mondongo para ver qué color tiene   ya no se puede más" (p. 451).
Cabrera decided that the final stroke of the censor's pen should not
be altered in future editions of the novel: "el libro estaba mejor así,
ya que acababa de una manera abrupta y curiosamente eficaz por
intervención de ese creativo censor." [41] The last two pages of *La
Habana*, like the ending of *TTT*, contain abrupt halts that leave
the novel *in medias res;* first, the novel that the narrator was reading stops in mid-sentence, and then his own story comes to an end
that really constitutes another beginning with the words "Aquí
llegamos."

The narrator finally finds the exit from the body that has im-
prisoned him when an earthquake-like tremor causes him to be
expelled:

---

[40] "GCI: Three Islands," comp. Siemens, p. 11.
[41] Interview with Cabrera Infante in *Siete voces,* ed. Guibert, p. 426.

Viajaba ahora a mayor velocidad sobre el suelo encharcado, a veces deslizándome como un trineo, otras navegaba sobre un colchón de aire como un hovercraft anacrónico, otras volaba en una alfombra mágica. Ahora rodaba, pegaba contra las paredes pálidas, dando nuevos tumbos contra columnas cálidas, contra muros muelles, para luego torcer una esquina redonda y volver a deslizarme, a correr, a volar a velocidad vertiginosa. (p. 711)

The narrator's description of the ordeal of his (re)birth fits in well with the burlesque tone of the rest of the work. It also takes us back to the beginning of La Habana where the narrator employs birth imagery to evoke the feelings he experienced upon arriving at his first residence in the city of Havana: "Enfrento . . . un pasillo largo, un túnel estrecho . . ." (p. 11). In the epilogue, the final words "Aquí llegamos" refer to both the topographic and the temporal points of entry. The birth canal constitutes the former, whereas the latter would be the moment in the film's projection when the spectators joined the action in progress.

In his own analysis of the epilogue, Cabrera Infante observes that "what the narrator achieves, in spite of himself, is a union with his dream, which is losing himself in the vagina. . . . I believe that if we have emerged from a woman there is always a certain need, however unconscious, to return . . . ." [42] In fact, this unconscious fantasy receives explicit treatment in La Habana, both in the epilogue and elsewhere in the text. When the narrator describes his sexual union with Julieta, he clearly associates the act with returning to the womb and being born: "los dos unidos por ese otro cordón umbilical, moviéndonos en unísono, como la madre con su hijo en el vientre, mi feto fanoso fundido a ella, y en esta fantasía estaba cuando . . . ella me daba finalmente a luz" (p. 379). [43] The narrator never completely escapes the maternal world, as Rodríguez Monegal points out, and therefore all his acts — including the sexual act — must be seen in this context. Rodríguez Monegal concludes: "Es de

---

[42] "GCI: Three Islands," comp. Siemens, p. 11.

[43] The instances in which the narrator mentions the umbilical cord may be divided into three categories: in relation to his mother; in reference to his connection with the city of Havana; as an emotional and sexual link with his lovers, as in the case of Julieta (p. 379) and Margarita: "Nuestro amor era un cordón umbilical y ella acababa de cortarlo con un clic" (p. 668).

esa madre, que certifica la conducta de infante del protagonista, y que lo sitúa en un tiempo ya difunto, de quien realmente se ocupa el libro." [44] The story of the narrator's life is overshadowed by the figure of his mother, who is perceived as dominant and sometimes terrible, and who intrudes into every aspect of her son's life, either directly or through the internalized mechanism the narrator calls his censor. [45]

If the themes in the fantasy that comprises the epilogue of *La Habana* may be viewed as a further development of some essential themes of the first eleven chapters, then it is not surprising that both the title of the epilogue, "Función continua," and the last words, "Aquí llegamos," should be found elsewhere in the text. Cabrera remarks: "Here 'Continuous Performance,' which is the title of the section, refers not only to the show, but to a possible interminable sexual experience. And what could be a more interminable sexual experience than to enter a woman and lose oneself inside her?" [46] The expression "función continua" indicates a type of movie that is projected over and over, with the spectators arriving and departing at different times throughout the showing. The narrator first attends this kind of show during his early days in Havana when a family friend, Eloy Santos, takes his brother and him to see "The Whole Town's Talking":

> En un momento la película se repetía, obsesiva, y Eloy Santos murmuró: "Aquí llegamos," y se levantó como si fuera el fin de la tanda. No entendíamos ni mi hermano ni yo. "Es una función continua," explicó Eloy Santos. "Hay que irse." "¿Por qué?", preguntó mi hermano casi fresco. "Porque la película se repite." "¿Y eso qué tiene de malo?", quiso saber mi hermano. "Son las reglas del juego," dijo Eloy Santos. "Hay que irse." (p. 29)

---

[44] Emir Rodríguez Monegal, p. 269. Levine remarks: "despite all the visible and naked women, the mother, always in the background, is the unifying chord, the ultimate Beatrice," p. 91.

[45] The narrator imagines that his mother is an intruder into the most intimate details of his sexual life:

> Al día siguiente... mi madre me preguntó qué le había pasado al pañuelo planchado (ella lo advertía todo) y tuve que inventar una complicada mentira ilógica de cómo llegó a ensuciarse tanto que daba grima lavarlo: yo lo había hecho para evitarle ese asco —lo que no estaba lejos de ser la verdad.... (p. 361)

[46] "GCI: "Three Islands," comp. Siemens, p. 11.

For the two children, the "rules of the game" seem to put an arbitrary end to their pleasure. But as they become more experienced spectators, they also play by the rules and learn when to leave at a continuous showing:

> una voz que se hizo familiar enseguida dijo a mi oído, gritando: "Aquí llegamos." Era, por supuesto, mi hermano, ojos y orejas oportunos, anunciándome que en esta parte de la película habíamos entrado al cine. Tuve que dejar mi labor de amor, ni ganada ni perdida pero inicial, y abandonar mi rincón romántico. (pp. 178-79)

The words "aquí llegamos," then, signal that an exit is imminent, and that the curtain must fall on the action of the movie or the text. This expression has been employed by the narrator as a play on words when it refers to the physical place of entry in the epilogue. The expression "función continua" also finds applicability in the language of the erotic. On several occasions the narrator finds himself executing a repeat performance with his lover of the moment, a kind of continuous showing that, like the films he sees, constitutes a mere repetition: "No hay cosa más parecida a un coito que otro coito — por lo que dispensaré al lector de la repetición" (p. 477). In effect, the narrator is stating "this is where we came in," and cuts the scene short. [47] He recognizes that sexual involvements resemble the on-going, never ending projection of a movie: "me tomó el tiempo de repetir o prolongar el beso húmedo, función continua ..." (p. 469). In many respects, the narrator telling the story of his past functions as a spectator at his own show as it replays in his mind. It is from this perspective that he can experience the effect of a "continuous showing" as one recollection leads to the next in a never ending cycle. Like Azorín, Cabrera Infante may conclude that "vivir es ver volver."

The ending of *La Habana*, then, takes us back to the beginning of the work, and in this manner, somewhat ironically reflects on the futile nature of this erotic autobiographer's task. He cannot tell the story of the past self without telling the story of another, and

---

[47] Antonio Prieto Taboada says of *La Habana*: "la obra se convierte en otro *show*, en una 'función continua' de la que hay que irse para evitar la repetición." Rev. of *La Habana*, *Hispamérica*, 30 (December 1981), 155.

to further complicate matters, his close bond with his mother prevents him from achieving independence at that particular stage of his life that serves as the story time. The text, therefore, centers on his condition as an *infante* (in the English sense) under his mother's domain. Yet this return to the womb may be seen as the maximum autobiographic illumination, according to Suárez-Galbán: "en la mujer, y especialmente ... dentro de una sala de cine, el narrador busca llenar el gran vacío de amor que define su personalidad de niño, adolescente y hombre que en el fondo se siente desamparado." [48] The cyclical ending of *La Habana* may also imply that there has been no progress in the text, and that its stuttering, tongue-tied structure in fact renders an autobiographic statement impossible to utter. [49]

I have mentioned another work of sexual fiction, Philip Roth's *Portnoy's Complaint,* with regard to *La Habana.* The end of Roth's novel also constitutes a mere beginning, thereby negating the character's purpose in telling his story on the pages of the text. Charney remarks:

> There is no holding back in Alex Portnoy's torrential confessions to his psychoanalyst, who listens patiently from the beginning of the book to the end and has only one line himself, the *punch line*: "So [said the doctor]. Now vee may perhaps to begin. Yes?" The whole book is only the worthless ravings of a neurotic patient, who must dispose of all his garbage before the serious business of psychotherapy can begin. [50]

Both the narrator of *La Habana* and Alex Portnoy unleash a stream of erotic language that tells their sexual life stories, and both works paradoxically end with the need to begin again. The narrators share another important characteristic:

> Portnoy ... can never enjoy sex for its own sake, juicy and non-meaningful. His elaborate and tormented language is a way of coping with the physical pleasure that slips out of

---

[48] Suárez-Galbán, p. 31.
[49] See Olney, "Autobiography and the Cultural Moment" in *Autobiography,* ed. Olney, p. 23, for a discussion of Renza's line of thought.
[50] Charney, p. 130.

his grasp. . . . Portnoy is a magnificent talker, and exhorter, and Dionysiac artist with words because the more direct reality eludes him. [51]

The narrator of *La Habana* devises elaborate word games and puns that reveal a comic, joyful attitude toward language, but the results are the same: both protagonists end up talking to themselves, deriving their greatest pleasure from their own voices, fulfilling themselves through what Cabrera has called *masturhablarse.*

The deepest level of eroticism, then, may be traced to the actual use of words in *La Habana,* as Cabrera Infante has pointed out: "hay un erotismo que comienza y termina en las palabras: la aliteración, el mecanismo retórico más usual en el libro, es una especie de enlace erótico dentro de la escritura, en que las palabras, comenzando por la misma letra o sílaba, parecen montarse unas a otras como en el más bestial de los coitos . . . ." [52] Suzanne Levine's comments further underscore this notion: "to alliterate is to mock conventions of propriety and to glorify words as mysterious objects: subverting the semantic, putting sound before sense, is a kind of liberation." [53] A liberation, as we have seen, that nevertheless traps the narrator in the prisonhouse of (erotic) language.

In *La Habana,* Cabrera Infante leads us through a world of popular culture that includes cinema, pornographic narrative, and many forms of fiction. The autobiographical exploration can paradoxically incorporate all of the above and, in so doing, produces a fusion of genres that typifies many modern autobiographical works. In the epilogue of *La Habana,* when the narrator takes the final plunge into his fantasy, he remarks: "Avancé decidido. A mi espalda rugió un león — o tal vez fueron tres leopardos al unísono" (p. 703). The Metro trademark, the roaring lion that appears at the beginning of their movies, is heard as the narrator retreats into his fantasy world. But the three leopards that produce a roar in unison clearly are a reference to Cabrera's three tigers of *TTT,* a novel whose title is encoded in several other places in *La Habana.* This final allusion to the novel *TTT* serves as a reminder that the autobiographer must always look over his shoulder, for fiction is never far behind him.

---

[51] Charney, p. 131.
[52] Álvarez-Borland, "Viaje verbal," p. 55.
[53] Levine, p. 87.

This last evocation of *TTT* also constitutes one more vital link between the two texts, whose interrelation should be fairly clear by now. *La Habana* may be seen as an explicit, elaborated and personalized version of *TTT*, a novel that exalted collectivity both in content (its gallery of characters) and in form (its collage-like structure). In fact, *TTT* may be viewed as a repressed autobiography in light of *La Habana,* Cabrera Infante's longest work to date. The two works share the same geographic setting and time period — the all-important Havana of Cabrera Infante's youth. The three tigers reconverge in *La Habana,* in which the solitary narrator sometimes speaks lines identical to those pronounced by characters in *TTT*. Characters whose names (or identities) correspond to real people make their appearance in both texts. The underlying themes of both works also bear similarities: nostalgia, the search for love, and the inability to communicate meaningfully with others.

In *La Habana,* the attention focuses on one individual whose "sexual *via crucis,*" to use Antonio Prieto's term,[54] determines all else in the work. If *TTT* concerned time, speed, and space, it also avoided direct confrontation with the voice of memory. In *La Habana,* the narrator (literally) takes himself into his own hands (a crucial chapter is, of course, "Amor propio") and allows the textual *I* to express "how real memories become self-conscious memoirs . . . ."[55] The repression of the individual self in *TTT* thus becomes reversed in *La Habana,* where all is *I* but *I* is no one.

Cabrera's first major work is often referred to with the initials *TTT*, both by the author himself and by critics. A parallel to the three t's might be the three c's of *La Habana para un infante difunto:* "El conocimiento carnal cansa" (p. 589). Perhaps this transmits the message of *La Habana* more than any other statement in the work. Carnal knowledge may eventually lose some of its excitement for the narrator who retells his search for that experience in all its erotic detail, but the language he employs in his text produces an arousal of its own. This "erotic relationship with words" culminates in the epilogue where one has the impression that the narrator could talk

---

[54] Prieto, p. 155.
[55] Levine, p. 88.

forever in a continuous showing of verbal prowess. For Cabrera Infante, then, the final page of a text must be an arbitrary cut-off point, invariably leading back to a new stream of words that reinitiates the whole cycle. Autobiographical enunciation in Cabrera Infante thus remains tantalizingly inconclusive, hopelessly evasive, which is exactly as he would wish.

CHAPTER III

MARIO VARGAS LLOSA'S *LA TÍA JULIA Y EL ESCRIBIDOR:* LIFE AS A FICTION

The publication of *La tía Julia y el escribidor* in 1977 marks the beginning of Mario Vargas Llosa's intensive literary study of the process of turning life into text. Far from a minor work, as some have viewed it, *La tía Julia* serves as the gateway to Vargas Llosa's exploration of two interrelated themes: the writer's role in the creation of a fictional work, and his intimate relationship with those who surround him. The author of a series of monumental novels including *La ciudad y los perros* (1963), *La casa verde* (1966), and *Conversación en La Catedral* (1969), Vargas Llosa intersperses autobiographical narration with fiction in *La tía Julia,* and follows this innovation with two dramatic works that treat the theme of the writer shaping life's material into words: *La señorita de Tacna* (1981) and *Kathie y el hipopótamo* (1983). To explore this subject, the Peruvian author returns to the genres with which he had first experimented at the initiation of his writing career, that is, the play and the short story. At the age of sixteen, Vargas Llosa had his first work for the theater, *La huida del inca,* staged in Piura. He also cultivated the short story as a young writer and in 1958 was awarded the "Leopoldo Alas" Prize for his collection *Los jefes.* While *La tía Julia* may be properly classified as a novel, it is in reality composed of nine short stories that parody the style of radio soap operas, and these alternate with eleven autobiographical episodes presented in serial fashion. These recent works of Vargas Llosa, then, show a mastery of the literary forms that originally attracted him, and serve to renew those genres by means of the innovative style the mature author now commands.

For Mario Vargas Llosa, literature is born from a spirit of nonconformism and rebellion:

> la literatura es fuego . . . y la razón de ser del escritor es la protesta, la contradicción y la crítica. . . . Nadie que esté satisfecho es capaz de escribir, nadie que esté de acuerdo, reconciliado con la realidad, cometería el ambicioso desatino de inventar realidades verbales.[1]

Vargas Llosa's autobiographical writings may be seen as his attempt to reconcile himself with the past which must be re-created with words to acquire the kind of textual reality that can satisfy the author. This idea in turn leads to the notion of an author's dual purpose as he writes: "Un hombre escribe novelas por una parte para rescatar y por la otra para exorcizar experiencias ya extintas, que lo obsesionan y torturan. Quiere liberarse de ellas y al mismo tiempo recobrarlas. . . ."[2] This apparent contradiction — to rescue the past while simultaneously casting it out — typifies the autobiographer's struggle as well as the novelist's. To write of one's life is both to recover past time and to release it in words, to create the textual figure of the *I* that both represents and replaces the self.

Vargas Llosa maintains that, as a writer, he bases his works on life's realities, but transforms them into something altogether different: "A la vez que expresa esa realidad, la obra de ficción la corrige, la modifica, la sustituye por una nueva realidad. . . ."[3] Reality here is understood as an author's particular perception of life, and his fictions therefore necessarily reflect his individual circumstances: "Poco a poco, uno va dándose cuenta de que las historias que cuenta,

---

[1] Mario Vargas Llosa, "La literatura es fuego," in *Homenaje a Mario Vargas Llosa,* ed. Helmy F. Giacoman and José Miguel Oviedo (Madrid: Anaya, 1971), p. 19. Vargas Llosa has reiterated this idea on several occasions: "creo que el novelista es ante todo aquél que no está satisfecho con la realidad, aquel hombre que tiene con el mundo una relación viciada." *La novela,* Conferencia pronunciada en el Paraninfo de la Universidad de Montevideo, 11 August 1966 (Argentina: América Nueva, 1974), p. 13; "el novelista . . . crea vida ilusoria, crea mundos verbales porque no acepta la vida y el mundo tal como son . . . . La raíz de su vocación es un sentimiento de insatisfacción contra la vida; cada novela es un deicidio secreto, un asesinato simbólico de la realidad." *García Márquez: Historia de un deicidio* (Barcelona: Barral, 1971), p. 85.

[2] Ricardo Cano Gaviria, *El buitre y el Ave Fénix: Conversaciones con Mario Vargas Llosa* (Barcelona: Anagrama, 1972), p. 16.

[3] Cano Gaviria, p. 51.

como hace todo novelista, son una proyección de su propia vida." [4]
Vargas Llosa believes that a writer does not freely elect a theme,
but rather is governed by what he has termed "demons": "un escritor
no elige sus temas sino que es elegido por ellos. El contenido —la
materia, el tema o el asunto— expresa ese sector de la personalidad
que es inconsciente y que aflora, en el momento de la creación, bajo
la forma de un tema determinado." [5] To the realistic content, though,
an author must add something of his own, what Vargas Llosa has
called the "elemento añadido": "Toda novela es un testimonio ci-
frado: constituye una representación del mundo, pero de un mundo
al que el novelista ha *añadido* algo: su sentimiento, su nostalgia, su
crítica." [6] But as Vargas Llosa observes, reality itself is chaotic: "It
has no order. But when translated into fictional terms it acquires one.
The stricter the construction of a novel the better will be the understanding of the world it evokes." [7] Literature thus becomes the shaper
of life's substance: "El cuento, la ficción, gozan de aquello [de] que
la vida vivida ... siempre carece: un orden, una coherencia, una
perspectiva, un tiempo cerrado...." [8]

Since texts develop from an author's own memories and percep-
tions, Vargas Llosa concludes:

> Yo creo que todas las novelas son autobiográficas y que sólo
> pueden ser autobiográficas ... y que la habilidad del escritor,

---

[4] María Ester Gilio, "Reportaje a Mario Vargas Llosa: Las claves del escribidor," *Clarín*: *Cultura y Nación* [Buenos Aires], 28 May 1981, p. 2.

[5] Cano Gaviria, p. 47. Vargas Llosa also remarks: "I can invent and fan-
tasize only with the support of memory. The basic raw material of images in
my memory is always the point of departure." Charles Ruas, "Talk With Mario
Vargas Llosa," *The New York Times Book Review,* 1 August 1982, p. 18.

[6] Vargas Llosa, *García Márquez,* p. 86.

[7] Luis Harss and Barbara Dohmann, *Into the Mainstream: Conversations
with Latin-American Writers* (New York: Harper and Row, 1967), p. 358.

[8] Vargas Llosa, "Las mentiras verdaderas," Prologue to *La señorita de Tacna*
(Barcelona: Seix Barral, 1981), p. 10. Vargas Llosa restates this idea in "El
teatro como ficción," Prologue to *Kathie y el hipopótamo* (Barcelona: Seix
Barral, 1983):

> La ficción no reproduce la vida: la contradice, cercenándole aquello
> que en la vida real nos sobra y añadiéndole lo que en la vida real nos
> falta, dando orden y lógica a lo que en nuestra experiencia es caos
> y absurdo, o, por el contrario, impregnando locura, misterio, riesgo,
> a lo que es sensatez, rutina, seguridad. (p. 11)

Further references to *La señorita* and *Kathie* will be given parenthetically in
the text.

del novelista, no está en crear propiamente sino en disimular, en enmascarar, en disfrazar lo que hay de personal en lo que escribe. [9]

This leads Vargas Llosa to compare the act of writing to that of the strip-tease:

> Lo que el novelista exhibe de sí mismo no son sus encantos secretos, como la desenvuelta muchacha, sino demonios que lo atormentan y obsesionan, la parte más fea de sí mismo: sus nostalgias, sus culpas, sus rencores. Otra diferencia es que en un strip-tease la muchacha está al principio vestida y al final desnuda. La trayectoria es la inversa en el caso de la novela: al comienzo el novelista está desnudo y al final vestido. [10]

The author starts with his intimate being and disguises it in his text: "el escritor parte de esa desnudez . . . y la va vistiendo, la va cubriendo, va superponiendo a ella toda clase de estratos, de capas, para ocultársela en [sic] los lectores y también, en muchos casos, para ocultársela a sí mismo." [11]

Fiction, then, emerges from an autobiographical reality, but disguises that reality (or nakedness) through its use of literary devices. Cabrera Infante has defined art as "a lie that becomes true in order to manufacture untruth," [12] but Vargas Llosa appears to be saying the opposite: art begins with truth that becomes a lie in order to turn into a different kind of reality or truth. Like Cabrera, Vargas Llosa sees the language of literature itself as the mechanism for carrying out this process of fictive invention: "La novela debe seducir, halagar, engañar, manipular el espíritu del lector hasta hacerle vivir la ficción como una historia real. Y eso sólo se consigue a través de la trampa, es decir de la forma." [13] What, then, takes place in autobiographical writing where the text supposedly transforms real events into words and renders a faithful account of a true life? Vargas

---

[9] Vargas Llosa, *La novela*, pp. 17-19.
[10] Vargas Llosa, *Historia secreta de una novela*, Conferencia pronunciada en Washington State Univ., 12 November 1968 (Barcelona: Tusquets, 1971), p. 7.
[11] Vargas Llosa, *La novela*, p. 27.
[12] "GCI: Three Islands," comp. Siemens, p. 8.
[13] Gilio, p. 2. See also Vargas Llosa's Prologue to *La señorita de Tacna*, where he applies to fiction Giambattista Vico's words: "El criterio de la verdad es haberla fabricado," (p. 11).

Llosa shows a deep awareness of the mechanisms of writing, and like Cabrera, recognizes that in autobiographical literature, even the correspondence of the narrator's and author's name does not indicate that these two figures are identical: "Pero después de Flaubert nosotros sabemos perfectamente que el narrador de una novela no es el mismo autor, que aún si narra en primera persona y con nombre y apellidos propios ese narrador es esencialmente distinto del autor." [14] Vargas Llosa goes on to say that a novel in reality contains two types of narrators: the hidden narrator who may be identified with the author, and the visible narrator who tells the story. In Wayne Booth's terms, the former would constitute the figure of the implied author, [15] who in *La tía Julia* takes the form of a disguised narrator in control of the machinery behind the visible narrator(s).

An autobiographical work for Vargas Llosa represents a contradiction in terms. For this author, all fiction is autobiographical; conversely, all autobiographies must be subjected to the mechanisms of fictive creation. In *La tía Julia y el escribidor,* Vargas Llosa consciously juxtaposes autobiography and fiction, ultimately causing the two modes to mix when fiction contaminates reality and vice versa. A review of some of Vargas Llosa's specific comments on the technique of his autobiographical novel will serve to elucidate the underlying structure of the work. Vargas Llosa states that his original intention in writing *La tía Julia* was to "do the story of a soap-opera writer based on a man I had known. My idea was to tell his story through little parodies of soap opera, through the mythology, the stereotypes and the impact of this kind of writing on large audiences." [16] Vargas Llosa identifies this writer as the Bolivian Raúl Salmón, who worked for Radio Central in Lima at the same time Vargas Llosa was employed at the sister station Radio Panamericana in the early 1950's. [17] However, fearing that the tale he had originally

---

[14] Cano Gaviria, p. 65. Concerning Flaubert, Vargas Llosa also comments: "Pero *L'éducation sentimentale* me provocó un entusiasmo infinitamente mayor que todos sus otros libros. Es todavía la novela que me llevaría a la isla desierta si me permitieran una sola." *Historia secreta,* p. 59.

[15] See Wayne Booth, *The Rhetoric of Fiction,* pp. 71-75.

[16] Ruas, p. 15.

[17] For Vargas Llosa's complete account of his inspiration for the structure of *La tía Julia,* see José Miguel Oviedo, "Conversación con Mario Vargas Llosa

planned would take the form of a totally unrealistic novel, Vargas Llosa developed the idea of intermixing autobiographical material with the fantastic stories.

The autobiographical act, then, serves as a balancing device for the inventive story teller who is afraid he might carry his fantastic tales beyond reader accessibility. The author discusses this technique of counter-balancing with relation to *La tía Julia*:

> Y entonces se me ocurrió que las historias delirantes del protagonista que escribe radioteatros y que tiene una imaginación perturbada, quizás podía mezclarse con una historia que fuera exactamente lo contrario, algo absolutamente objetivo y absolutamente cierto. . . . Intercalar esas dos historias era un poco como presentar el reverso y el anverso de una realidad, una parte objetiva y una parte subjetiva, una cara verídica y otra inventada. [18]

This blueprint for symmetry that Vargas Llosa outlines in his statements concerning the original dual structure he intended for his novel produces different results when the writer puts pen to paper and allows his themes to develop. Vargas Llosa discovers in the process of composing *La tía Julia* that this dissociation of autobiography and fiction is impossible, and instead he capitalizes on the natural intermingling of the two modes: "los episodios en los que yo quería no ser sino veraz y contar solamente cosas que estaba absolutamente seguro que habían ocurrido así, eran completamente imposibles, porque la memoria es engañosa, y se contamina de fantasía. . . ." [19] If autobiography becomes a fiction, then fiction also reflects autobiographical reality:

> en los capítulos que son supuestamente o síntesis o paráfrasis de los radioteatros del protagonista, la pura invención tampoco existe. Hay también unos ingredientes intrusos, diríamos, que proceden de la realidad objetiva, que se van infiltrando poco a poco. [20]

sobre *La tía Julia y el escribidor*," in *Mario Vargas Llosa: A Collection of Critical Essays*, ed. Charles Rossman and Alan Warren Friedman (Austin: Univ. of Texas Press, 1978), pp. 154-58.

[18] Oviedo, "Conversación con MVL," pp. 156-58. I have corrected two printing errors in the original.

[19] Oviedo, "Conversación con MVL," p. 158.

[20] Oviedo, "Conversación con MVL," p. 158. I have corrected a printing error in the original.

Vargas Llosa's ultimate dilemma, though, was which mode to stress in titling his work. His original title, *La tía Julia y el escribidor* seemed to him "demasiado jocoso y distorsionador de la historia." He thus invented what he calls "un título que es más... de novela picaresca: *Vida y milagros de Pedro Camacho*"[21] — a title that evokes the soap opera world of the hack writer. Vargas Llosa's final choice of *La tía Julia y el escribidor,* then, reflects the importance of the alternating structure of autobiography and fiction that characterizes the work.

If Guillermo Cabrera Infante refrains from making a commitment to the autobiographical pact in *La Habana para un infante difunto* by declining to reveal the narrator's identity, Mario Vargas Llosa apparently executes an explicit pact in *La tía Julia* by assigning versions of his own name to the narrator of the odd-numbered chapters. Yvette Miller affirms that *La tía Julia* is "una *autobiografía novelada* del autor-narrador-protagonista. Vargas Llosa, sin disfraces, relata con sus apelativos de Marito o Varguitas su amor de adolescente por su tía Julia...."[22] José Miguel Oviedo also determines that an explicit autobiographical pact is made in the work:

> The autobiographical episodes are noted for the lack of the most basic norms of novelistic discretion. Not the slightest attempt is made to veil the sharp focus on the private affairs of actual people; there are no (apparently) rhetorical disguises or even name changes. As never before in his previous novels, the protagonist, the narrator, and the author coincide perfectly and without the least ambiguity....[23]

By assigning his nicknames to the narrator of *La tía Julia,* the author performs an act of affiliation, if not one of complete identification, with his character. Cabrera Infante places emphasis on the search for an identity in *La Habana,* but Vargas Llosa bypasses that stage of the autobiographical exploration when relating the sentimental and

---

21 Oviedo, "Conversación con MVL," p. 158.

22 Yvette E. Miller, "Mario Vargas Llosa: Contexto y estructura de *La tía Julia y el escribidor*," in *Texto/Contexto en la literatura iberoamericana,* Memoria del XIX Congreso del Instituto Internacional de Literatura Iberoamericana, Pittsburgh, 1979 (Madrid: Artes Gráficas Benzal, 1980), p. 235.

23 Oviedo, "*La tía Julia y el escribidor,* or the Coded Self-Portrait," in *MVL: Critical Essays,* ed. Rossman and Friedman, p. 167.

literary education of the narrator of *La tía Julia* alongside the fantastic adventures inspired by the popular mode of the radio soap operas. It is appropriate to base this discussion of *La tía Julia* on an analysis of some of the rhetorical structures employed in Vargas Llosa's autobiographical writing and their relationship to the novel as a whole. Because of its highly structured system of narrative devices, in particular the alternation of autobiographical and fictional chapters, it will be helpful to follow essentially a chronological order in this study.

The novel begins with an autobiographical chapter in which the narrator sets his story in a past time frame: "En ese tiempo remoto, yo era muy joven y vivía con mis abuelos en una quinta de paredes blancas de la calle Ocharán, en Miraflores."[24] The narrator places these events in a distant past ("ese tiempo remoto"), thus accentuating the gap between the story time (*temps de l'énoncé*) and the discourse time (*temps de l'énonciation*). Whereas Cabrera Infante begins *La Habana* with a preterite verb form ("Subí"), Vargas Llosa employs the imperfect ("vivía") to initiate his tale. The difference in aspect may also be a difference in perspective. Cabrera's story is basically a compendium of erotic adventures in the form of often disconnected scenes. Vargas Llosa, however, tells the continuous serialized story of his courtship of Julia and his apprenticeship in the literary craft. The opening sentence of *La tía Julia* stands out in another respect. In reality, the temporal distance between story time and discourse time is only about twenty years. Thus, reference to the "remote past" highlights the emotional distance that separates the narrator from his younger self. From the start of *La tía Julia*, the narrator insinuates the enormous evolution that has taken place in his life since the time about which he writes.

This evolution has to do with two essential aspects of the narrator's life: his professional career as a writer and his amorous adventures that culminate in marriage to his Aunt Julia (in reality his uncle's sister-in-law). The desire to pursue a literary vocation is expressed in the second line of *La tía Julia*: "Estudiaba en San Marcos, Derecho, creo, resignado a ganarme más tarde la vida con una profesión liberal, aunque, en el fondo, me hubiera gustado más llegar

---

[24] Vargas Llosa, *La tía Julia y el escribidor* (Barcelona: Seix Barral, 1977), p. 11. Further references to *La tía Julia* will be given parenthetically in the text.

a ser un escritor" (p. 11). The adolescent on whom the story focuses has quite a distance to travel in terms of his emotional and professional development, and therefore the author perceives from his narrative present that the gap between his mature self and the way he was in the past is very large indeed. Nevertheless, as Jonathan Tittler points out, "the basic mode of the narration positions the two Marios as proximately as a face and its formfitting mask," so that "the primary values of the character are in accord with those of the narrator." At the same time, the narrator allows his greater wisdom to penetrate the story and thus "steps back and peeks out from behind his disguise." This process — the mature narrator (as a literary persona himself) poking fun at the adolescent Marito — opens up an ironic gap that is indispensable to the structure of autobiography. [25]

It is of interest to note that the narrator lives with his grandparents and that his parents are not mentioned until much later in the work. The absence of the immediately preceding generation from the household where Marito lives casts him as a type of orphan. This aspect of his being, along with the kind of job he holds ("un trabajo de título pomposo, sueldo modesto, apropiaciones ilícitas y horario elástico: director de Informaciones de Radio Panamericana," p. 11) contribute to the accumulation of characteristics that lead us to associate the protagonist with the literary model of the *pícaro*. Of the eight features Claudio Guillén lists as informing the generic picaresque code, the most important is that the *pícaro* is presented as an orphan, an unfortunate traveler, and an old adolescent. This is precisely the condition of Marito, who at the end of *La tía Julia* embarks on an obstacle-ridden course throughout a Peruvian province in search of a mayor to marry him to Aunt Julia.

The second most important characteristic of the picaresque mode consists in the work taking the form of a pseudo autobiography. Guillén also places emphasis on the *pícaro*'s status as an observer who moves horizontally through the geographic world and vertically through the social, and whose material level of existence is stressed. [26] To a greater or lesser degree, all of these features are applicable to

---

[25] Tittler, *Narrative Irony in the Contemporary Spanish-American Novel* (Ithaca: Cornell Univ. Press, 1984), pp. 140-42.

[26] Claudio Guillén, *Literature as System: Essays Toward the Theory of Literary History* (Princeton: Princeton Univ. Press, 1971), pp. 71-106, 135-58.

the narrator of *La tía Julia*. Robert Scholes points out that Guillén's scheme establishes the notion that the modern picaresque mode, which evolved from the early prototype of *Lazarillo,* allows for historical and literary shifts in the status of a particular feature or set of features. [27] Harry Sieber, in his discussion of the literary evolution of the *pícaro,* points to changes in the Spanish picaresque which are appropriate to the narrator of *La tía Julia.* The evolved *pícaro* had respectable parents, was more an adventurer than a rogue, and eventually became a satirist who finally achieved success and embraced virute at the end of his life. [28] We may thus speak of the picaresque elements in *La tía Julia* in the modern sense that they form part of a generic code and constitute an example of intertextuality.

The narrator's job as news director at Radio Panamericana may be seen as a modern-day equivalent of Lazarillo de Tormes' final occupation of *pregonero* (town crier). The profession of *pregonero,* while considered to be "el oficio más infame que hay," [29] is nevertheless an *oficio real.* Marito's job of disseminating via radio information illicitly extracted from the print medium makes him a type of dishonorable town crier. But at the same time, he holds a position that carries with it a pompous title — a modern *oficio real,* given the authoritative powers society accords to the news media. The narrator shares several traits of the *pícaro* with his ridiculed counterpart in the novel, the hack writer Pedro Camacho, an association corroborated by the other title Vargas Llosa had conceived for his work, *Vida y milagros de Pedro Camacho.* Like Cabrera Infante, then, Mario Vargas Llosa seems to find inspiration in the model of the picaresque genre, notably in the prototype of *Lazarillo de Tormes,* a key prose work in the autobiographical mode written in the Spanish language. [30] This relationship between the picaresque and Vargas

---

[27] Robert Scholes, *Structuralism in Literature* (New Haven: Yale Univ. Press, 1974), pp. 138-41.

[28] Harry Sieber, *The Picaresque* (London: Methuen, 1977), pp. 59-62.

[29] Francisco Rico, in his ed. of *Lazarillo de Tormes* (Barcelona: Planeta, 1976), p. 77.

[30] *La tía Julia y el escribidor* is not the first work by Vargas Llosa in which traces of the literary model of the picaresque may be found. See Jorge García Antezana, "Elementos de la picaresca en *Pantaleón y las visitadoras* de Mario Vargas Llosa," in *La picaresca: Orígenes, textos y estructuras.* Actas del I Congreso Internacional sobre la Picaresca, ed. Manuel Criado de Val (Madrid: Fundación Universitaria Española, 1979), pp. 1095-1116.

Llosa's autobiographical work becomes more explicit toward the end of *La tía Julia,* and I will return to it further ahead.

The narrator contrasts his place of employment, Radio Panamericana, with its sister station owned by the same family, Radio Central. Underneath its pompous exterior, Radio Panamericana conceals real deficiencies in its physical plant, such as the elevators that open between floors and the view of the garbage cans below. The narrator's pretentious job title hides the insubstantial nature of the work he performs, just as the pompous building that houses Radio Panamericana contains a run-down, faulty interior. Radio Central, home of the radio serials, merits the following description: "se apretaba en una vieja casa llena de patios y de vericuetos, y bastaba oír a sus locutores desenfadados y abusadores de la jerga, para reconocer su vocación multitudinaria, plebeya, criollísima" (p. 12). At Radio Central, appearances are also deceiving:

> me divertía mucho espiar a los intérpretes cuando estaban radiándolos [the serials]: actrices y actores declinantes, hambrientos, desastrados, cuyas voces juveniles, acariciadoras, cristalinas, diferían terriblemente de sus caras viejas, sus bocas amargas y sus ojos cansados. (p. 13)

The contrast established here is not so much between the radio stations themselves, but between two aspects of each, and the narrator, who goes back and forth from Radio Panamericana to Radio Central, only escapes this debased atmosphere when he occasionally attends a class at the University or steps out to a local café.

The narrator's interest in the production of the soap operas at Radio Central may be traced to his relatives' avid devotion to the serials:

> Siempre había tenido curiosidad por saber qué plumas manufacturaban esas seriales que entretenían las tardes de mi abuela, esas historias con las que solía darme de oídos donde mi tía Laura, mi tía Olga, mi tía Gaby o en las casas de mis numerosas primas, cuando iba a visitarlas. . . . (p. 13)

In relating his circuit of visits here, the narrator passes from his grandmother's generation to the next generation, his aunts, and finally arrives at his own, that of his cousins. This hierarchy symbolizes the narrator's sentimental evolution as well. He leaves his grandparents'

house to marry Aunt Julia and later abandons her to wed his cousin
Patricia, thus closing the distance that separated him from his own
generation and had caused him to feel like a child. Curiously, though,
this evolution does not remove him from the reduced circle of his
relatives, whom he describes as follows: "nuestra familia era bíblica,
miraflorina, muy unida" (p. 13). The narrator never really separates
from his extended family, but merely abandons one role to assume
another, thus changing from nephew to brother-in-law and finally to
son-in-law with respect to his Aunt Olga and Uncle Lucho, for
example.

The connection between the radio soap operas and the narrator's
relationship with his family, including his Aunt Julia, is sustained
throughout the whole work, and eventually transmits the notion that
Varguitas' life is itself a soap opera. [31] The figure of Pedro Camacho,
the prolific creator of Radio Central's serials, is related to Aunt Julia
when her name is first mentioned in the work: "Recuerdo muy bien
el día en que me habló [Genaro] del fenómeno radiofónico porque
ese mismo día, a la hora de almuerzo, vi a la tía Julia por primera
vez" (p. 16). Both Aunt Julia and Camacho are Bolivians and both
come into the narrator's life in Peru at the same time. The narrator's
fascination with these two Bolivians — and his eventual disenchant-
ment — function as the primary impetus for the autobiographical
exploration performed in *La tía Julia*.

But Marito's first encounter with Aunt Julia hardly qualifies as
love at first sight:

> —Así que tú eres el hijo de Dorita —me dijo, estam-
> pándome un beso en la mejilla—. ¿Ya terminaste el colegio,
> no?
> La odié a muerte. Mis leves choques con la familia, en
> ese entonces, se debían a que todos se empeñaban en tra-
> tarme todavía como un niño y no como lo que era, un
> hombre completo de dieciocho años. Nada me irritaba tanto
> como el *Marito;* tenía la sensación de que el diminutivo me
> regresaba al pantalón corto. (p. 16)

---

[31] Mario Vargas Llosa says: "I developed the idea of introducing a piece
of autobiography to mix in with the fantastic stories. In the 50's, I had worked
as a journalist in a radio station, and my personal life itself, my first marriage,
was a kind of soap opera." Ruas, p. 15. Oviedo discusses this idea in his
analysis of *La tía Julia*.

The narrator's initial reaction of hatred, expressed in the juvenile words "la odié a muerte," is provoked by Julia's treatment of him as a child. Her use of the diminutive *Marito* proves particularly annoying to the young man who is making every attempt to appear grown up, but instead receives the following verbal slap from the newcomer: "La verdad —me dio el puntillazo la tía Julia— es que pareces todavía una guagua, Marito" (p. 16). This encounter with Julia is the first incident which gives the narrator reason to mention his name in the text. Many statements in autobiography are a quotation of the words of another person, and, unlike what occurs in *La Habana,* this narrator actually records his hated name "Marito" in writing when he reports Julia's remark and his reaction to it. The autobiographical pact here involves the author's assigning to the narrator a juvenile nickname, that is, the symbol of a past self. Although the title *La tía Julia y el escribidor* does not make explicit mention of this child of the past (Cabrera's *infante difunto*) named Marito, the work essentially focuses on his life in relation to Aunt Julia and the scribbler, Pedro Camacho. But the author does evoke his own presence in the title, since the scribbler also points to Mario Vargas Llosa in the role of incipient writer in love with an older woman he calls Aunt Julia. [32]

Julia's initial treatment of the narrator as a child undergoes a change when she calls on him to take her to the movies in order to escape a dull evening with an older gentleman related to the family. On their way to the movie, significantly titled "Madre y amante," Julia tells Marito about the type of men a divorcee like herself meets: "No te enamoran, no te dicen galanterías finas, te proponen la cosa de buenas a primeras con la mayor vulgaridad. A mí me lleva la trampa. Para eso, en vez de que me saquen a bailar, prefiero venir al cine contigo" (p. 21). Marito, then, becomes the man who protects Julia from other men in that his company spares her from evenings with lecherous bores. In addition, he serves as a protector by accompanying her to the movies, a place where a correct young woman would not go alone. Julia reveals her vulnerability to Marito. She

---

[32] Rosario Ferré, among others, notes this: "En el título de la novela, el término *Escribidor,* se refiere no sólo a Pedro Camacho, autor de las radio-novelas, sino también al propio Vargas Llosa, entonces escritor en ciernes." "Mario Vargas Llosa o el escribidor," *Sin Nombre,* 9 (July-September 1978), 88.

acts in a manner typical of a woman living in a *machista* society who must seek male protection from other men, especially in situations such as walking at night or going into a darkened movie theater. [33] Marito thus occupies the position of a husband figure for this divorcee early on in their relationship, although neither one consciously acknowledges his assuming that powerful role.

When Marito meets Julia's fellow countryman Camacho for the first time, he notices both strengths and weaknesses in the scriptwriter:

> Era un ser pequeñito y menudo, en el límite mismo del hombre de baja estatura y el enano, con una nariz grande y unos ojos extraordinariamente vivos .... Pese a estar habituado a los contrastes entre voz y físico ... me asombró que de figurilla tan mínima, de hechura tan desvalida, pudiera brotar una voz tan firme y melodiosa, una dicción tan perfecta. (pp. 23-24)

Both Pedro Camacho and Aunt Julia are introduced in the first chapter of the work, and both figures arouse a conflicting reaction in the narrator, who feels an attraction to these exotic Bolivians but also experiences some resentment and envy. Julia at first incurs Marito's wrath because she treats him as if he were still a schoolboy, whereas the indefatigable Camacho bursts on the scene to take possession of the narrator's typewriter, thereby symbolically expropriating Marito's nascent literary talents. In the first chapter of *La tía Julia,* then, the three major characters are closely linked, an association that is sustained throughout the work.

The second chapter of *La tía Julia* begins in a manner that deviates from the autobiographical structure of the first chapter: "Era una de esas soleadas mañanas de la primavera limeña, en que los geranios amanecen más arrebatados, las rosas más fragantes ... cuando un famoso galeno de la ciudad, el doctor Alberto de Quinteros ... abrió los ojos ..." (p. 29). The even-numbered chapters are narrated in the third person, a clear break with the autobiographical

---

[33] According to Luis de Arrigoitia, Julia's behavior reflects *machista* society in that she later ridicules Marito's literary vocation and insinuates that a writer isn't a real man. "Machismo: Folklore y creación en Mario Vargas Llosa," *Sin Nombre,* 13 (July-September 1983), 22-23.

style that normally uses a dramatized, first-person narrator. [34] Further, the ornamental description of dawn in Lima clearly differs from the style of Chapter I. These even-numbered chapters, however, constitute a different type of autobiography. They supposedly are the product of Pedro Camacho's fantasies told in the form of short stories or novelettes that relay the content of his outlandish radio serials. Camacho produces his soap operas at a vertiginous rate and "transcribes the reality of his mental processes onto paper without sufficiently transposing it." [35] Pedro Camacho thus performs the unmediated autobiographical act:

> the free flow of Camacho's fantasies . . . is in reality a coded record of his perturbed mind. Camacho believes that he is imagining, that he is working with unreal and absurd material, that he is inventing and dreaming, but what he is actually doing, obliquely, is revealing himself. [36]

The radio serial parodies in *La tía Julia* may thus be interpreted as Pedro Camacho's naive autobiographical writings, or, to take it a step further, as a parody of autobiography composed by the real autobiographer himself.

Some fundamental differences between Camacho's and the narrator's autobiographies are apparent, however. While Vargas Llosa relates real incidents, he does not engage in much introspection in the text, so the interpretation and analysis of the facts of his life must be undertaken by the reader. In this way, the style of *La tía Julia* often borders on that of memoirs, which, according to Georges May, concern what one has seen, heard, done or said; in contrast,

---

[34] Of course, autobiography in the third person is possible, as Jean Starobinski points out, but "one must learn from external information that the narrator and the hero are one and the same person" (p. 288). Starobinski notes that this type of autobiography is usually historical or political. It may also be argued that the autobiographical novel in the third person represents a viable form of the autobiographical mode. I am thinking here of works such as Joyce's *A Portrait of the Artist as a Young Man* which, although written in the third person with a center of consciousness, has been traditionally categorized as autobiographical writing.

[35] Stephen M. Machen, " 'Pornoviolence' and Point of View in Mario Vargas Llosa's *La tía Julia y el escribidor*," *Latin American Literary Review*, 9 (Fall-Winter 1980), 12.

[36] Oviedo, "Coded Self-Portrait," p. 175.

true autobiography centers on what one has been. [37] Perhaps Vargas Llosa regards the external facts of his life at that time interesting enough to stand on their own since, as the author has remarked, they have all the appearances of soap opera material. The secretive Camacho, on the other hand, conceals his life and his past, so his stories provide the only immediate access to the workings of his mind. His novelettes directly transmit his crude fantasies and they lack any literary elaboration. The scribbler is not the writer, and his work takes the shape of "naked writing," seen by Vargas Llosa as a base form of literature which requires dressing and disguising.

But on another level, Pedro Camacho is merely a fictional creation of Vargas Llosa, and thus his fantasies in reality emerge from the imagination of the author who created him. Through his character Camacho, the narrator Marito's personality is completed and complemented. Vargas Llosa has remarked on this aspect of *La tía Julia:* "These soap operas are not only written out of the obsessions of Pedro Camacho, but out of my obsessions also. They are stories I wanted to write: incestuous love between brother and sister, a poor black man suddenly found in a port." [38] Pedro Camacho functions as a key element in the system of defenses the autobiographer constructs around his inner self and his fantasies. In addition, the medium that the narrator uses to express Pedro Camacho's fantasy world, the novelette as a prose rendition of the theatrical radio soap operas, converts these stories into a popular genre, thus integrating them into the collective human experience. [39] The intimate, personal style of the odd-numbered chapters gives way to the clichés of the hackwriter who nevertheless is able to penetrate into the countless households that tune in to his serials, including members of Varguitas' clan.

---

[37] Georges May, p. 123. It may be said that these categories are not mutually exclusive, however. Through the analysis of what one has done, the portrait of what one has been often emerges.

[38] Ruas, p. 15.

[39] Leslie Fiedler observes: "In ordinary street language, you know, a soap opera is called 'the story,' or even '*my story.*' You'll stand in line in a supermarket and a lady will push ahead of you. 'I gotta get home in time for my story,' she'll say." David Gates, "Fiedler's Utopian Vision," *Newsweek,* 9 January 1984, p. 11. This usage noted by Fiedler further supports the notion that radio soap operas generate a high degree of spectator identification. Also, the expression "my story" may connote that soap operas constitute "everybody's autobiography," so to speak.

The first radio serial chapter in *La tía Julia* concerns the incestuous relationship between Elianita and her brother Richard. A key figure in this story is their uncle, Dr. Alberto de Quinteros, whose description becomes the pattern after which subsequent characters in the even-numbered chapters are modeled: "frente ancha, nariz aguileña, mirada penetrante, rectitud y bondad en el espíritu . . ." (p. 29). His affections for Elianita surpass what may be considered normal in an uncle-niece relationship, and in this way, Quinteros' situation constitutes a parallel with the aunt-nephew love affair that the narrator of the autobiographical chapters relates. Elianita, as we later learn, is also the name of an aunt of the narrator's. Quinteros maintains his austere appearance and therefore does not permit himself to show his secret passions: "era un hombre al que ni el juego, ni las faldas ni el alcohol atraían más de lo debido . . ." (p. 30). Camacho, who projects himself in Quinteros, is also a fifty-year old man who espouses the ideal of maintaining a composed exterior that shows domination of one's inner passions. The privileged narrator of this soap opera, however, provides access to Quintero's feelings, and thus we learn that he cannot steer his thoughts from his niece even momentarily. He also shows jealousy toward the man she is about to marry: "No acabo de entender por qué se casa Elianita con el Pelirrojo Antúnez — se oyó decir a sí mismo, de pronto—. ¿Qué le ha visto?" (pp. 35-36). Quinteros' immediate attempt to suppress his thought ("Fue un acto fallido y se arrepintió al instante, pero Richard no pareció sorprenderse," p. 36) suggests that his guilt serves as a cover for his prohibited feelings.

Quinteros' age undergoes an interesting transition. The fifty-year old is presented as an aging old man by some of his friends at the gymnasium he frequents: "¿Todavía en pie, a pesar de los siglos?" (p. 31); "No se canse mucho, doctor, piense en sus nietos" (p. 31); " ¡Fuerza, tatarabuelo! ¡Más rápido, cadáver! " (p. 37). While some characters push Quinteros into the older generations of grandfather (which he is not) or even great-grandfather, in his own fantasy he steps down into the next generation through his repressed love for Elianita and his camaraderie with her brother Richard. Age thus constitutes an elastic category which is susceptible to dramatic increments or reductions. In this respect, it is interesting to note that Camacho is described by Marito as follows: "Podía tener cualquier edad entre treinta y cincuenta años . . ." (p. 24). Approximately

twenty years also come between the character Marito and Mario
Vargas Llosa at the time *La tía Julia* was written, twenty years
which have grown in his imagination ("un tiempo remoto"), and
have turned him into a figure we could also call "grandfather" or
even "great-grandfather." Or, to reverse the attraction between
nephew and aunt, Mario now with the passing of time may assume
the role of an uncle attracted to a potential niece, Julita, who has
remained fixed in story time. Of course, the other fundamental
relationship in Chapter II is the one between brother and sister,
which foreshadows the marriage of Marito and his cousin Patricia
at the end of *La tía Julia*. The uncle (aunt)-niece (nephew) attraction
dissolves into a co-generational one, even though it is always strictly
a family affair.

Quinteros clearly identifies with his nephew Richard, whom he
views as "el muchacho más apuesto de la tierra, un joven dios
bruñido por la intemperie . . ." (p. 32). His niece Elianita also receives the following praises: "una de esas bellezas que dignifican
a la especie . . ." (p. 33), and Quinteros tells that she always showed
"olímpico desdén" (p. 39) toward Pelirrojo Antúnez's affections.
These two Olympian-like siblings naturally are destined to be united.
Richard also represents a model of strength next to his weakened,
impotent uncle: "La pesa se le escapó de las manos al tercer intento
y tuvo que soportar las bromas de los pesistas . . . y ver, con muda
envidia, cómo Richard — siempre apurado, siempre furioso — com-
pletaba su rutina sin dificultad" (p. 37). In his incestuous love for
his sister, Richard dares to do what Quinteros could never bring
himself to admit consciously. The doctor never permits himself to
think of anything but his work, and projects his own past career
conflicts on the confused, unhappy Richard: "Y el doctor Quinteros
recordó cómo él también, a la edad de Richard, había pasado un
período difícil, dudando entre la medicina y la ingeniería aeronáutica"
(p. 41). The implied author's irony filters through here. By reducing
Richard's crisis to one of selecting a career, Quinteros excludes any
possibility of an inner sentimental life. Like Camacho, the doctor
has placed his professional activities above all other kinds of human
action or interaction.

Nevertheless, Quinteros, in his identification with his nephew, is
able to sympathize with him when he discovers that Richard and
Elianita have been involved in an incestuous relationship:

No pestañeó siquiera, ni se agitó su corazón, cuando en el incomprensible soliloquio de su sobrino, alcanzó a entender, dos o tres veces repetida, esa frase que sin dejar de ser atroz sonaba también hermosa y hasta pura: "Porque yo la quiero como hombre y no me importa nada de nada, tío." (p. 52)

This character with whom the imaginary Camacho identifies pronounces here an esthetic and moral justification for incest. Quinteros' identification with his nephew is completed when the doctor fantasizes that Richard, to forget his tragedy, leaves for London, Quinteros' own favorite city. If Elianita gave herself to another man, at least it was not the dullard Redhead, but a member of the distinguished Quinteros family. The female of the Quinteros clan, however, acquires an unsettling profile: "temeraria esposa"; "niña fraudulenta" (p. 53). She is thus attributed the primary responsibility for violating the incest taboo, and is also depicted as a dishonest girl who feigns innocence. The narrative point of view contributes greatly to this negative characterization. The story is told from Quinteros' and Richard's perspective, and Elianita, the object of the males' admiration and scorn, never speaks for herself. This distorted narrative perspective found in the first radio soap opera parody may be observed in the other even-numbered chapters and constitutes an essential part of their ironic structure.

Chapter III, second in the serialized autobiographical segments, begins with the following statement: "Volví a ver a Pedro Camacho pocos días después del incidente" (p. 55). Strictly speaking, the last incident narrated in the text was the catastrophic end to Elianita's wedding; therefore, the connection between Chapters I and III must be reestablished since the intervening radio serial episode has interrupted the continuity of the autobiographical sequence. The incident, then, is a reference to Pedro Camacho's having staked his claim to one of the typewriters belonging to Varguitas' news department. Camacho returns to tap Marito's knowledge of Lima for the purpose of marking off the various neighborhoods on a map. The scriptwriter classifies each section of the city with strange codes that supposedly denote their sociological composition: "MPZ" for "Marineros Pescadores Zambos" or "FOLI" for "Fámulas Operarios Labradores Indios" (pp. 64-65). Since the preceding radio serial concerning the Quinteros family is set in a precise section of Lima, it would appear, strangely enough, that this topographical orientation that Marito provides Camacho is posterior to the drafting of the soap opera episode. The author thus breaks the chronological rhythm in the odd and even numbered chapters and begins to manifest his domain over the other narrative voice in the work. As I have pointed out, the first radio soap opera comes as a surprise, since there has been no previous preparation for the dual levels of the work, that is, for the role of Camacho as supposed author of the radio soap opera chapters. This detail of the map-making, had it been included in Chapter I, would have at least explained how the foreigner Pedro Camacho had learned his way around town so quickly. Marito thus supplies key information used in the first radio drama, information which Camacho acquires further ahead in the novelistic sequence of events. This chronological alteration aside, it is also significant that Varguitas helps Camacho buy his map and provides him with the data he needs to construct his radio soap operas in and around Lima. Camacho is indebted to Marito for two of his basic instruments on the job: his typewriter and his topographical guide.

After describing some of Camacho's work habits, Marito gives an account of his own attempts at writing literature. The first of these is a plot for a short story based on a tale he heard from his Uncle Pedro (note that the name of this story teller is the same as Camacho's) about a group of peasants who dress up as "pishtacos" (devils). The narrator wants to alter the original story by introducing a real devil among the fakes: "Lo que yo quería contar no era tanto lo ocurrido en la hacienda de mi tío Pedro, como el final que se me ocurrió: que en un momento dado, entre tanto 'pishtaco' de mentiras, se deslizaba el diablo vivito y coleando" (p. 59). The title he selects, "El salto cualitativo," points to the gap between fiction and reality that his short story tries to bridge. [40] The short story's effect hinges on what is most likely an unreliable narrator: "Era un monólogo de cinco páginas; al final se descubría en el narrador al propio diablo" (p. 60). The narrator of "El salto cualitativo" thus assimilates himself into all the characters who adopt the role of "pishtacos."

---

[40] "El salto cualitativo" is one of the three major literary techniques that Vargas Llosa discusses in *La novela*. The others are: "los vasos comunicantes" and "las cajas chinas" (pp. 41-47).

Perhaps this attempt at a short story may be seen as a micro-structure that reflects the macrostructure of *La tía Julia*. Like the false devils, Camacho and the characters he supposedly creates eventually become confused with the narrator Marito's overriding voice; Marito in turn serves as a type of mask for his creator, Mario Vargas Llosa. It is the author himself who makes the qualitative leap from his real being to his fictional re-creation in the text. The narrator is one more fictive character in the work who assumes the form of devil, *pícaro,* author of cheap novelettes, short stories, and so forth. Thus he does not tell his own story directly, but rather his story is related by the other selves in the work, which justifies the existence of multiple narrators.

Of his short story "El salto cualitativo," Marito remarks: "quería que fuese frío, intelectual, condensado e irónico como un cuento de Borges . . ." (p. 59). This ideal style certainly differs greatly from that of Pedro Camacho, who, commenting on the fact that his office is located in a cubicle directly off the building's entrance, affirms: "Yo escribo sobre la vida y mis obras exigen el impacto de la realidad" (p. 58). In both theory and practice, Camacho is the anti-Borges and thus represents the prototype of the scribbler or hack-writer whose stories flow freely and effortlessly yet lack literary value. In *La tía Julia,* Vargas Llosa assimilates both styles, and overcomes the split between "scribbler" and "writer" that Oviedo summarizes as follows: "We have here, ironically, a 'scribbler' who does write, who does nothing else but write, and a 'writer' who can't write, who is distracted from his task, who spends his life on things other than literature." [41] In a way, *La tía Julia* serves as the proving ground for the mature author's talents. Vargas Llosa alludes to this when he remarks:

> Pedro Camacho is a natural storyteller without any kind of sophistication, a genius at that level, with a tremendous capacity to transform reality and fiction into his own form. The other, Varguitas, wants to be a writer but is self-critical. This rigor, in his case, is a kind of impotence. He wants to write a story, while Pedro is pouring out all kinds

---

41 Oviedo, "Coded Self-Portrait," p. 177.

of dramas and catastrophes. Pedro's dramas are not presented in scripts but are described by Varguitas, who transforms them. That is the apprenticeship he passes through. [42]

While the narrator supplies the details of his literary attempts in the second autobiographical chapter, including the development of another short story plot about an impotent senator distantly related to his family, he also provides clues to the evolution of his relationship with Julia. On the occasion of his Uncle Lucho's fiftieth birthday (also Pedro Camacho's age, which he shares with his characters), Marito and Julia accompany Lucho and Olga to celebrate at the Grill Bolívar. The unlikely pair, Marito and Julia, seem almost to belong together next to the older couple, and on the dance floor, Marito asserts his maturity in several ways:

> Cuando, entre la masa de parejas, el tío Lucho y la tía Olga quedaron distanciados, la estreché un poco contra mí y le junté la mejilla. La oí murmurar, confusa: "Oye, Marito...," pero la interrumpí diciéndole al oído: "Te prohíbo que me vuelvas a llamar Marito." Ella separó un poco la cara para mirarme e intentó sonreír, y entonces, en una acción casi mecánica, me incliné y la besé en los labios. (p. 75)

The chapter ends with Marito's query: "me pregunté cuántos años mayor que yo sería" (p. 75). He has already begun to cross the age barrier that evening at the Grill Bolívar. The narrator attempts to distance himself from his juvenile identity of *Marito* and orders Julia to discard that nickname as well. In the serial style that characterizes the autobiographical chapters of *La tía Julia,* this adventure ends on a suspenseful note: the kiss that starts the narrator on his romantic quest for Julia's hand in marriage. [43]

In the second interpolated radio serial-novelette, the distance between the various narrators is accentuated. The police officers in this story are presented as caricatures, which is apparent in their very names: Mocos Camacho and Manzanita Arévalo. The inclusion of a policeman named Camacho also signals a transformation of the

---

[42] Ruas, p. 15.

[43] For a discussion of the first kiss in *La tía Julia,* see Daniel R. Reedy, "Del beso de la mujer araña al de la tía Julia: estructura y dinámica interior," *Revista Iberoamericana,* 47 (July-December 1981), 109-16.

supposed narrator into one more character in the story, and thus uncovers the presence of a superseding narrator who provides the distance necessary for the irony that runs throughout this radio serial episode (and the others as well). Here, the mockery of the police officers, one of whom spends his time reading Donald Duck comics on the job, brings to mind the fierce satire of the military school "Leoncio Prado" in *La ciudad y los perros,* which reaffirms that the originating narrative source behind these soap opera parodies is a thinly disguised Mario Vargas Llosa.

One of the police officers relates an incident that he witnesses while on duty. He spots a man climbing through a window. The latter, when challenged, denies he is a burglar and instead claims to be a husband whose wife makes him play a game of robber: "Fíjese que verme entrar como ladrón la pone más cariñosa. Otras veces hace que la asuste con un cuchillo y hasta que me disfrace de diablo" (p. 92). This erotic fantasy is a variation of Marito's tale from the preceding autobiographical chapter in which a knife figures prominently in the robbery that left the Senator impotent. The facts, however, are reversed here: rather than a destructive, castrating instrument, the knife serves as an aid to sexual excitement. The disguise of a devil that appeals to the fake robber's wife also brings to mind Marito's first short story about the "pishtacos" in which real people assume the role of false demons but eventually are overcome by the real devil himself. The narrator of that short story thus reveals his true diabolic face at the end of the tale, proving that all is possible in the realm of fiction where reality by definition cannot exist.

But the real subject matter of this second radio soap opera is not the bungled burglary, but the capture of a naked, mute black man whose body is covered with scars. This latter tale is told by Sergeant Lituma, [44] who hardly believes his own eyes and has to

---

[44] Lituma is one of several of Vargas Llosa's characters that appear in more than one text. Lituma resurfaces in *Historia de Mayta* (Barcelona: Seix Barral, 1984). Of his recurring characters, Vargas Llosa remarks in an interview with José Miguel Oviedo: "Creo que en todo autor de ficciones esa tentación que Balzac maravillosamente concretó en *La comedia humana* borrando las fronteras entre sus novelas, está presente . . . . Bueno, yo siento esa tentación; indudablemente me doy cuenta que muchos de mis personajes los recuerdo con nostalgia y con una frustración por no haberlos continuado, por no haberlos prolongado."

check the jail cell to verify that this creature really exists. Shortly thereafter, Lituma sees the black man in his dreams: "Lo veía cercado de leones y víboras rojas, verdes y azules, en el corazón de Abisinia, con chistera, botas y una varita de domador" (p. 94). Is this version any less real than the flesh-and-blood man whom the police have incarcerated? In these stories, the intent is not to create the illusion of reality, as in the realistic mode of literature, but rather, to reveal the illusory nature of reality itself. [45] The supposed robber is a character in disguise; the "pishtacos" are characters dressed up as devils who eventually turn into the devil himself. All these stories within stories cannot be anchored to a verifiable reality or to a single narrative I: all the narrators themselves become the object of fiction when they reappear in the tales of others.

Lituma, in his attempt to make his story credible, conjectures with others about the black man's possible origins. An old woman contributes to the fictive quality of the tale by adding that he must have come from hell (another "pishtaco"). A fellow police officer ventures: "Es un salvaje del África que se vino de polizonte en un barco. Hizo el viaje escondido y al llegar al Callao se descolgó de nochecita al agua y se metió al Perú de contrabando" (p. 95). Lituma accepts this version and adds: "O sea que el cutato ni siquiera sabe dónde está . . . . O sea que esos ruidos no son de loco sino de salvaje, o sea que esos ruidos son su idioma . . ." and then exclaims: "Qué inteligentes somos . . . . Le descubrimos toda la vida al cutato"

"Mario Vargas Llosa: Maestro de las voces," in *Espejo de escritores,* ed. Reina Roffé (Hanover: Ediciones del Norte, 1985), p. 163. Further references to *Historia de Mayta* will be given parenthetically in the text.

[45] Intent is especially important in view of the manner in which Marvin A. Lewis interprets the character of the black man: "The artistic hand embellishes the scene with the physical description of a nappy-haired, frightened, scar-covered, blubber-lipped, saber-toothed, non-communicative, trapped beast. This anonymous creature is ordered killed by the authorities, but due to suspense the listener/reader never knows what his final destiny is. The destinies of his black predecessors are also in question." "From Cincha to Chimbote: Blacks in the Contemporary Peruvian Novel," *Afro-Hispanic Review,* 3 (May 1984), 7. Vargas Llosa's caricature, I think, has less to do with the question of race than with the interplay between fiction and reality. In the radio serial chapters, none of the characters — from all socio-economic, religious, and racial backgrounds — is exempt from an ironic, mocking treatment. And it is the Argentines who serve as the principal recipients of Pedro Camacho's scorn throughout the whole work. Lewis does, however, show that Vargas Llosa generally presents a non-positive depiction of blacks in his novels.

(p. 96). Or rather, they have invented for the mute man his life story. The lost man represents a defiance of the imagination because he does not fit into any of the categories of the policemen's world. Therefore, they decide to do away with him, and assign Lituma the job. But another officer suggests a different ending for the black man: "Dejémoslo que se escape. Diremos que lo matamos y, en fin, cualquier cuento para explicar la desaparición del cadáver..." (p. 103). As a literary creator, Lituma is free to choose the ending he wishes for his story, and if he allows the black man to flee, he will have to invent yet another tale ("cualquier cuento"). Appropriately, the tale is open-ended (as are all the radio serial chapters), and the destiny of the condemned man is left in suspense: "¿Estallaría el disparo? ¿Rodaría sobre las basuras indescifrables el misterioso inmigrante? ... ¿Cómo terminaría esa tragedia chalaca?" (p. 103). Just as the secondary narrator Lituma controls the outcome of his story, the overriding narrator becomes a potential creator or destroyer of his own characters, a trait that reaches culmination in the final radio drama cataclysms in *La tía Julia*.

"overriding" narrator is identified with Camacho

The radio soap opera in Chapter IV, with its multi-leveled narration and ironic structure, contrasts with the third autobiographical chapter which features melodramatic scenes between Marito and Julia more appropriate to the soap opera mode. Julia's original maternal pose ("Te parezco tu mamá y por eso te provoca hacerme confidencias ...," p. 109) gives way to the rites of an incipient courtship: "Después de tus atrevimientos de anoche, ya no puedo convidarte Coca-Colas .... Tengo que atenderte como a uno de mis pretendientes" (pp. 109-10). Marito thus finds himself in a type of no-man's land: in Julia's eyes, he is no longer a child but is not yet fully adult: "Me miraba con ironía y malicia, todavía no como a un hombre hecho y derecho, pero ya no como a un mocoso" (p. 109).

Julia resembles other women Varguitas has known in one aspect: "era (como todas las mujeres que había conocido hasta entonces) terriblemente aliteraria" (p. 110). She enjoys popular forms of literature, such as sentimental novelettes and now, in Peru, the radio serials that the women in Marito's family follow. Not surprisingly, Julia describes her relationship with Marito in terms borrowed from the afternoon soap operas, which recalls in *La Habana* the narrator's encounters with women whose speech reflected their devotion to the same medium of entertainment: "Los amores de un bebé y una anciana que además es algo así como su tía . . ." (p. 112). Julia often provides summaries of Camacho's radio adventures for Marito, who in turn informs her of his conversations with the hackwriter at the radio station. Varguitas thus recognizes that "Pedro Camacho pasó a ser un componente de nuestro romance" (p. 113). Their story resembles the type of plot that might be devised by Camacho, and Marito is attractive to Julia insofar as he represents an interesting character himself and also because he maintains contact with the author of the shows she enjoys. The radio serial mode brings Marito closer to Julia and to the family clan, whereas literature alienates him from the popular culture which his relatives embrace.

The world of the two radio stations is also a soap opera setting where the employees, including Pedro Camacho himself, resemble stock characters. One of these characters, "El Gran Pablito," is "uno de esos personajes pintorescos e indefinibles que atrae o fabrica el ambiente de la radio" (p. 115). The radio station not only produces the fictional characters of the soap operas, but actually transforms its own workers into characters. Camacho declares that he no longer wants Pablito to take charge of the sound effects for the shows, and threatens to do away with him through whatever means necessary. Marito summarizes Pablito's likely fate: "sería sacrificado sin misericordia" (p. 116). In his attitude toward Pablito, Camacho thus acts like his character Lituma from the preceding radio soap opera chapter. Further, like the black man whose fate was in Lituma's hands, Pablito is illiterate. Dismissed from Radio Central because there is no role that suits him there, Pablito becomes an assistant to Pascual, who works under Varguitas at Radio Panamericana, an assistant who "en realidad, se convirtió en esclavo de Pascual . . ." (p. 117). Like his counterpart in the radio serial, Pablito is assigned the role of a displaced slave, and the odd and even numbered chapters of *La tía Julia* develop another thematic link.

The radio station produces characters both within the context of the serials and outside it, and this in turn provides an ideal theme for a different level of fiction. Marito's friend Javier shows that he is cognizant of this when he remarks: "Radio Central es una mina para la literatura" (p. 118). Marito then proceeds to tell Javier about a short story he is writing that is based on an episode Aunt Julia had related to him, and discusses the transformation of this real incident into a fictive tale. The "mina de literatura" that Javier points to, then, does not become part of Vargas Llosa's work until much later. At the time of his close association with Javier, the narrator's efforts were concentrated on writing short stories and analyzing the results. When he relates his past literary struggles, the narrator performs an act that is essential to the autobiographical structure — writing about writing. Interestingly, this does not center on the primary task of composing the life story that is unfolding in the text of *La tía Julia* — the case in *La Habana,* for example — but instead concerns the series of unsuccessful attempts at writing short stories that, for the most part, end up in the waste basket. Vargas Llosa shows acute awareness, however, of the importance of writing about writing in autobiography when he cites Salvador Elizondo's words in the epigraph of *La tía Julia:* "Escribo. Escribo que escribo. Mentalmente me veo escribir que escribo y también puedo verme ver que escribo. Me recuerdo escribiendo ya y también viéndome que escribía" (p. 9). The process of writing about the self as a budding writer, then, is a labyrinth that entraps the author in his old writing.

The real story is not contained in the drafts that Marito sends out with the trash, but in their re-creation on the pages of *La tía Julia.* Vargas Llosa remarks: "la historia del propio Varguitas es una historia que está llena de cuentos que él quiere escribir o que no escribe o cuentos que ha escrito y que allá aparecen simplemente sintetizados como bosquejos de argumentos." [46] In addition to relating the plot of his short stories, Varguitas often tells of the style and tone he had attempted: "Quería que fuera un cuento cómico, y para aprender las técnicas del humor, leía en los colectivos ... todos los escritores risueños que se ponían a mi alcance ..." (p. 120). Perhaps he fails to achieve the humorous tone he desires in the discarded story, but the incident that Julia originally told, the basis for that short story, is indeed very comic in the "naked" form in which the narrator now relates it. Autobiography thus becomes a forum for overcoming past failures and rewriting one's life. For the narrator of *La Habana,* the triumph of memory and writing helped to soothe the pain of his search for love, whereas the narrator of

---

[46] Oviedo, "Maestro de las voces," p. 154.

La tía Julia successfully writes about his past difficulties in creating literature and in that way surmounts them.

In the third radio soap opera, the theme of how to tell a tale once again is dramatized, as it was in the story of the lost man and Lituma. Here, a fifty-year old judge, Dr. Pedro Barreda y Zaldívar, must adjudicate a case involving a Jehovah's Witness, Gumercindo Tello, accused of raping thirteen-year old Sarita Huanca Salaverría. A third-person omniscient narrative voice attributed to Pedro Barreda relates the alleged incident in a manner that resembles a police report, with some added commentary. The judge thus functions as a type of narrator (or co-narrator), another example of the elasticity of these radio serial characters who shun the simple role of actors in order to become authors who help determine the course of a story. When the witnesses appear before the judge, however, a different story than the one he had imagined develops, and doubt is cast on the veracity of the original report attributed to the impartial magistrate. Sarita's aging parents seem more concerned about marrying her off than seeking justice for the crime: "Sin dientes, con los ojos medio recubiertos por legañas, el padre, don Isaías Huanca, refrendó rápidamente el parte policial en lo que lo concernía y quiso saber después, con mucha urgencia, si Sarita contraería matrimonio con el señor Tello" (p. 137). The judge now feels like "un padre acrimonioso que se niega a autorizar la boda de su hijo" (p. 138), and even wonders if the parents could have fabricated the rape scenario to unburden themselves of their daughter. As potential inventors of fictions, the parents take the role of narrators or story tellers who offer their own conflicting version of the incident. Thus, each narrator uncovers another previous or underlying voice that alters the tale and underscores the impossibility of transmitting absolute truth in autobiography or fiction. At the same time, an authoritative voice (here the judge; Lituma in the preceding drama) is empowered to decide the outcome of the story by determining the characters' fate.

Sarita's appearance before the judge seriously challenges the facts as we know them. The Lolita-like creature of thirteen possesses characteristics of an adult: "parecía tener una experiencia dilatada, una sabiduría de siglos" (p. 139). Her description of the rape is closer to a reenactment, complete with gestures that cause her to resemble a seductress instead of a victim:

El mecánico siempre estaba tratando de tocarla, aquí: y las dos manitas, elevándose, se ahuecaron sobre los tiernos pechos y dedicaron a calentarlos amorosamente. Y también aquí: y las manitas caían sobre las rodillas y las repasaban, y subían, subían, arrugando la falda, por los (hasta hacía poco impúberes) muslitos. (p. 139)

The judge tries to repossess the scene which this child-turned-actress has taken over: "Le explicó que, aunque debía relatar con objetividad lo sucedido, no era imprescindible que se demorara en los detalles . . ." (p. 140). Barreda and his male secretary, however, obviously derive voyeuristic pleasure from the disquieting show which the magistrate nevertheless fears might become an unmitigated strip-tease if he allows Sarita to continue. His secret compliance with Sarita's mode of telling is revealed in his words to the accused, Gumercindo Tello: "Datos, datos —insistió—. Hechos, lugares, posiciones, palabras dichas, actos actuados. ¡Vamos, valor! " (p. 146). Tello proclaims his innocence and therefore fails to put on a show to match Sarita's. Instead, Tello seizes a letter opener and threatens to castrate himself in order to prove his innocence, thus changing the judge's chambers from the site of a burlesque show to a potential "sacrificial altar" (p. 148). All are actors before the judge, who becomes the real victim in this tragicomedy as he is manipulated by the witnesses and the accused. Both Dr. Barreda and the supposed narrator Camacho, then, lose control over the direction of their stories, while the hidden narrator Varguitas takes control of the characters and manipulates them much like puppets on a string.

But these radio soap operas also touch on the implied author's obsessions, as Vargas Llosa has affirmed, so that the final act of ridicule is directed toward himself. Gumercindo Tello remarks: "Yo soy puro, señor juez, yo no he conocido mujer. A mí, eso que otros usan para pecar, sólo me sirve para hacer pipí..." and then threatens to "cortarlo y botarlo a la basura . . ." (p. 148). Tello's explanation corresponds to the line Julia quoted when relating the impotent senator's story to Varguitas ("Porque a su hijo, eso que tienen los caballeros sólo le sirve para hacer pipí, señora," p. 61), an incident that then gives rise to a short story, which, like all of the narrator's early literary attempts, ends up in the waste basket. Further, the plot of this radio serial in turn reappears in the autobiographical Chapter IX when Aunt Olga gives her reaction to it as a listener: "ella decía que, a veces, a Pedro Camacho se le pasaba la mano y que a todas sus amigas la historia del pastor que se 'hería' con un cortapapeles delante del juez ... les parecía demasiado ..." (p. 189). Olga's critical remark helps to validate the alternating factual and fictional sequences in *La tía Julia* and anchors the imaginary chapters in the reality of the autobiographical narration (which of course should be seen as an illusional technique). But a deeper connection is also uncovered in Gumercindo Tello's story. The impotent young writer Marito repeatedly undergoes a type of psychological castration each time he tosses his creative works, such as the short story about the impotent senator, into the trash. He casts off the useless pieces of paper that, like Tello's "pene pecador" (p. 147), do not serve their intended purpose. This relationship between (phallic) potency and literature is far from casual, as will be proven by Camacho's fate; the theme also resurfaces in Vargas Llosa's works for the theater, as I will demonstrate later.

Varguitas uses the material provided by Julia, such as the senator's story, in three ways. First, Marito bases several short stories on the fantastic tales from life that Julia spins. Second, these attempts to transform life into text figure in the pages of *La tía Julia* when the narrator (as the *sujet de l'énonciation*) recounts his literary beginnings. And third, the same material is transposed and disguised, or even ridiculed, in the soap opera parodies attributed to Camacho. In the fourth autobiographical chapter, then, Marito tells of the first time he reads one of his stories to Julia:

> A medida que progresaba en la lectura, la tía Julia me iba interrumpiendo:
> —Pero si no fue así, pero si lo has puesto todo patas arriba —me decía, sorprendida y hasta enojada—, pero si no fue eso lo que dijo, pero si...
> Yo, angustiadísimo, hacía un alto para informarle que lo que escuchaba no era la relación fiel de la anécdota que me había contado, sino *un cuento, un cuento,* y que todas las cosas añadidas o suprimidas eran recursos para conseguir ciertos efectos. (pp. 151-52)

Julia, however, protests that Marito has stripped the tale of its humor: "con las cosas que has cambiado le quitaste toda la gracia" (p. 152). The story does not ring true to Julia. It started out as her tale, but in Varguitas' hands, it had become something quite different and did not reflect the events as she had witnessed them.

Julia represents the first in a series of narratees imbedded in the text to whom Marito reads his literary attempts. Her reactions, then, may be viewed as a gauge against which the readers outside the textual boundaries may measure their own readings of the work. Julia's protests that he has altered reality for the worse afford Varguitas the opportunity to defend his literary transformations; this episode in turn serves to caution the readers of *La tía Julia* that it, too, is *a story, a story.* The author extends his control from character to reader, and in effect forces the reader into compliance with his dictum on the nature of narrative. But, if we accept the negation of *La tía Julia* as anything but a story (that is, as autobiography), on one level, we must also discount it on a deeper level, as the interconnections between this text and others by Vargas Llosa will show.

Julia scorns the narrator in his role as writer, but reveres Pedro Camacho as a creator of fiction, and upon meeting her compatriot, tells him: "Soy una gran admiradora suya" (p. 160). Julia's attitude partially explains Marito's ambivalence toward Camacho's talents. On the one hand, Varguitas cannot contain his amazement at Camacho's methods of writing:

> ¿Cómo era posible que, a esa velocidad con que caían sus deditos sobre las teclas, estuviera nueve, diez horas al día, *inventando* las situaciones, las anécdotas, los diálogos, de varias historias distintas? Y, sin embargo, era posible: los libretos salían de esa cabecita tenaz y de esas manos infatigables. . . . (p. 158)

But he also scorns Julia's contention that Camacho is an intellectual: "Pedro Camacho es un intelectual entre comillas. ¿Te fijaste que no hay un solo libro en su cuarto?" (p. 165). If Marito truly hopes to fascinate Julia, he must emulate some of the hackwriter's positive qualities that she (and the public at large) admires. The ultimate forum for Mario Vargas Llosa's integration of high and low culture is precisely the alternating autobiographical sequences and radio soap opera parodies in *La tía Julia y el escribidor,* an achievement which demonstrates how well the narrator assimilated the lessons taught by Julia and Camacho. [47]

The evolution of the narrator in terms of his literary and sentimental development is further reflected in the changing names he assigns himself in the text. Once he prohibits Julia from calling him *Marito,* there is a void created by the lack of an acceptable name. At the café where the narrator reads one of his short stories to Julia, his friend Javier enters and discovers the pair holding hands, and remarks: "Vaya, vaya, Varguitas" (p. 152). The narrator reports: "Desde que se lo había oído a Javier, ella también me llamaba Varguitas" (p. 165). The new name, a creation of a peer, is a diminutive of the narrator's surname. *Marito,* a nickname belonging to his childhood, is employed by his relatives who still consider him immature. As the relationship between Julia and the narrator becomes more intimate, the need for an adult name to replace *Marito* becomes apparent. On the other hand, the narrator always refers to his first wife as "la tía Julia" in the text, which restores her to her original role of an older relative, thus reducing him to *Marito* once more. This usage of names constitutes an effective technique to allow the narrator to re-create lost time in a credible manner: it also opens up an ironic gap between the past self and the subject of the discourse.

In Chapter VII, the narrator mentions that at one time he used a pseudonym to sign book reviews and articles in cultural supplements. This pseudonym, which is not given, is in part created because of Julia: the narrator needed the extra income from his critical articles to meet their entertainment expenses. Vargas Llosa shares the use of a critical pseudonym with Cabrera Infante, who also declines to give his *nom de plume* in the pages of *La Habana.* In both cases, the autobiographical act entails name concealment and name transformation, although in Cabrera Infante's work this process has considerably more bearing on the protagonist's search for an identity.

---

[47] Ellen McCracken's study "Vargas Llosa's *La tía Julia y el escribidor: The New Novel and the Mass Media,*" *Ideologies and Literature,* 3 (June-August 1980), analyzes Vargas Llosa's adaptation of mass culture in his autobiographical novel. She remarks: "The technique of self-conscious adaptation through parody and exaggeration enables Vargas Llosa to criticize mass culture humorously while introducing it into the mainstream of high cultural production in the tradition of Leñero, Cortázar, and Puig," p. 61.

In the fifth autobiographical chapter, Varguitas finds that his relationship with Julia is at a standstill because she is being courted by " 'un buen partido': el doctor Guillermo Osores. Era un médico vagamente relacionado con la familia, un cincuentón muy presentable . . ." (p. 188). The narrator confides his troubles to Camacho during one of their tête-à-têtes in a café:

> Tengo una pena de amor, amigo Camacho —le confesé a boca de jarro, sorprendiéndome a mí mismo por la fórmula radioteatral; pero sentí que, hablándole así, me distanciaba de mi propia historia y al mismo tiempo conseguía desahogarme—. La mujer que quiero me engaña con otro hombre.
> (p 191)

In his confession, Varguitas discovers one of the useful aspects of radio serial language. It allows him to reveal his intimate feelings using the standard lines of soap opera characters, and thus to identify with mass cultural trivialization of sentiments while distancing himself from the intensity of his own feelings. The narrator experiences a need both to tell his tale and to put limits on it, to keep a part of it to himself. Camacho, however, is incapable of reacting to Marito's problems:

> Me alegré de haberle hecho confidencias. Sabía que, como para Pedro Camacho no existía nadie fuera de él mismo, mi problema ya ni lo recordaba, había sido un mero dispositivo para poner en acción su sistema teorizante. Oírlo me consolaría más (y con menos consecuencias) que una borrachera.
> (p. 191)

Pedro Camacho, after all, believes that a true artist like himself must shun any part of his life that does not relate directly to work: "la mujer y el arte son excluyentes, mi amigo. En cada vagina está enterrado un artista" (p. 193). Pedro Camacho thus functions more like a non-narratee for the narrator, the empty space that would normally be occupied by a true listener. The readers then become the audience outside the text who hears Varguitas' story in a way that Pedro Camacho cannot.

On the way to the café, Pedro Camacho stops at a pharmacy to buy rat poison to exterminate the rodents that have invaded his room at the squalid pension where he resides. This act provides a link to the previous soap opera (Chapter VIII), whose protagonist Federico Téllez Unzátegui was a fanatic rodent exterminator by profession. The obvious connection between Pedro Camacho's immediate reality and his lurid fantasies is highlighted in situations such as this throughout *La tía Julia*. For example, another incident concerning his pension that Camacho adapts and exaggerates is that of an unknown person who howls at the full moon. Camacho tells Varguitas about him in Chapter XI, and in the following radio serial episode, this screamer turns into a fifty-year old homicide victim in a pension setting. Also of interest in the exterminator's story is the surname Téllez, since an earlier soap opera parody concerned the accused rapist Gumercindo *Tello,* whose mother was called Gumercinda. One Camachian character gives rise to another, and they eventually become merged in the ensuing confusion.

When Julia and Varguitas arrive at a reconciliation after their disagreement over the physician, they hold their first discussion about their possible future together:

> Me lo sé con lujo de detalles, lo he visto en una bola de cristal —me dijo la tía Julia, sin la menor amargura—. En el mejor de los casos, lo nuestro duraría tres, tal vez unos cuatro años, es decir hasta que encuentres a la mocosita que será la mamá de tus hijos. Entonces me botarás y tendré que seducir a otro caballero. Y aparece la palabra fin.
> Le dije, mientras le besaba las manos, que le hacía mal oír radioteatros. (p. 206)

Their romance finds expression in the language of radio soap operas or sentimental movies, including the marker that graphically signals "The End." Julia, however, denies that her inspiration comes from the radio soap operas: [48]

> En los radioteatros de Pedro Camacho rara vez hay amores o cosas parecidas. Ahora, por ejemplo, Olga y yo estamos entretenidísimas con el de las tres. La tragedia de un muchacho que no puede dormir porque, apenas cierra los ojos, vuelve a apachurrar a una pobre niñita. (p. 206)

---

[48] Concerning Julia's negation of her soap opera-like speech, McCracken remarks: "We see in Julia ... both the media's formation of consciousness and the victim's inability to recognize it as such. Human understanding of an event is shaped not only by the content of mass culture but by its form ..." (p. 58).

This is an instance in *La tía Julia* in which an autobiographical character gives a preview of a Camachian radio serial episode. The following chapter treats the story of Lucho Abril, the tormented man who accidently strikes a child with his car. This preview technique further underscores the fictive nature of autobiography. When Julia and Marito arrive at a level of intimacy as they discuss their future together, the radio dramas that supposedly constitute the imaginary part of the work intervene. But we know that the soap opera parodies come from Vargas Llosa's pen, and not Camacho's, so that their presence in the autobiographical chapters is clearly a device that casts doubt on the validity of Marito's life story as he tells it in *La tía Julia*. The intrusion of the soap opera story lines serves as another constant reminder that the text is a fiction, and the assignation of real names to characters does not thereby rule out the creation of an imaginary life for them as well.

Chapter X, the tragicomedy of Lucho Abril, marks the halfway point in *La tía Julia* and significantly initiates the confusion of characters and story lines in the even-numbered chapters. The fifty-year old character who receives the standard description ("frente ancha, nariz aguileña, mirada penetrante, rectitud y bondad en el espíritu," p. 216) is Lucho Abril's therapist, Lucía Acémila. For the first time, the fifty-year old is not the male protagonist, but nevertheless continues to be the object of scorn, as the doctor's surname implies. The treatment she prescribes for Lucho's anxiety following the tragic accident is nothing short of absurd: she orders him to act on his supposed unconscious aggression toward children and reminds him: "Reflexione diariamente sobre las calamidades que causan los niños a la humanidad" (p. 222). When Lucho believes himself to be cured, he goes to thank the rodent exterminator, a character from a previous radio serial: "Corrió a besar las manos amazónicas de don Federico Téllez Unzátegui," who admonishes Lucho Abril to arrive on time at "Antirroedores S. A." (p. 228). Not only does this scene reintroduce a character who belongs to another story, but it also integrates elements of Camacho's life as told to Varguitas into the radio soap operas attributed to the hackwriter. Thus, in the preceding chapter when Varguitas accompanies Pedro Camacho to buy rat poison, we are given a clue to the tormented mind of the scribbler: "Si se contentaran con correr bajo mi cama, no me importaría, no son niños, a los animales no les tengo fobia..." (p. 191). The infanticidal character Lucho Abril, who indeed develops a phobia of children as a result of Dr. Acémila's treatment, shows his gratitude to the rat exterminator, who is transformed into his boss and also associated this way with the ridiculous Dr. Acémila. Camacho's fantasies are thus satirized as a demented transcription of life into text.

This confusion of characters that begins in a radio serial chapter projects into the next autobiographical sequence when Pedro Camacho, furiously typing away, says to Varguitas: "El ginecólogo Alberto de Quinteros está haciendo parir trillizos a una sobrina, y uno de los renacuajos se ha atravesado. ¿Puede esperarme cinco minutos? Hago una cesárea a la muchacha y nos tomamos una yerbaluisa con menta" (p. 232). In the first soap opera parody, Dr. Quinteros does have a triplet birth to attend: "Era sábado y, a menos de alguna complicación de último momento con la señora de los trillizos, no iría a la clínica..." (p. 29). The doctor also discovers his niece's pregnancy, but now Pedro Camacho merges the two story lines as he does with several other characters' lives. Varguitas remarks on Camacho's fast operation: "Para un parto de trillizos, con cesárea y todo, sólo necesita cinco minutos, qué más quiere. Yo me he demorado tres semanas para un cuento de tres muchachos que levitan aprovechando la presión de los aviones" (p. 233).

As seen in this comment, Varguitas both admires Camacho and scorns him. The scribbler, after all, is the closest example of a writer totally dedicated to his profession that Varguitas has observed:

> Cada vez me resultaba más evidente que lo único que quería ser en la vida era escritor y cada vez, también, me convencía más que la única manera de serlo era entregándose a la literatura en cuerpo y alma. No quería de ningún modo ser un escritor a medias y a poquitos, sino uno de verdad, como ¿quién? Lo más cercano a ese escritor a tiempo completo, obsesionado y apasionado con su vocación, que conocía, era el radionovelista boliviano: por eso me fascinaba tanto. (p. 236)

Camacho thus represents an ideal in that he is a productive, committed writer, and an object of mockery in that his product belongs to low popular culture. As Oviedo points out, "Camacho is the ludicrous portrait, the caricature, of Vargas Llosa's image of a writer

— the stubborn man-at-the-typewriter . . . ." [49] But the persistent hackwriter is nevertheless capable of turning out his product, whereas the incipient writer Varguitas, who later becomes a major figure in Spanish American literature, seems to have little success in his early writing endeavors.

La tía Julia is a chronicle of apprenticeship, both sentimental and literary. To a great extent, Marito's development as a writer takes precedence over his sentimental life in that he often reveals more intimate details of his frustrations and triumphs of writing than he does about his inner feelings concerning his relationship with Julia. After Marito and Julia see a play together, he confesses to her that he is attracted to the idea of becoming a playwright:

> De repente, cambio de género y en lugar de cuentos me pongo a escribir dramas —le dije, excitadísimo—. ¿Qué me aconsejas?
>
> En lo que a mí respecta, no hay inconveniente —me contestó la tía Julia, poniéndose de pie—. Pero ahora, Varguitas, sácame a bailar y dime cositas al oído. Entre pieza y pieza, si quieres, te doy permiso para que me hables de literatura. (p. 239)

The narrator presents himself as a writer in search of a genre. Autobiography may be seen as his medium for finding the ideal genre, be it drama, the short story, soap opera serials, satire, etc. This autobiographer uses various genres — often in parody — as a way to reveal parts of himself and ultimately creates a compendium of modes that somehow transmits a version of his life story. But Julia clearly wants to hear words belonging to the sentimental genre, a mode she thoroughly commands in her own autobiographical reply to her ex-husband, *Lo que Varguitas no dijo*. [50] Thus in *La tía Julia,* the model for female speech is derived from the empty talk of pseudo literature, whereas male speech, practiced by the subject of the discourse and the subject of the story, finds its roots in literary language. While Julia speaks of life, Varguitas speaks of words. They of course bridge the gap through non-verbal communication, an area in which Julia commands particular expertise.

---

[49] Oviedo, "Coded Self-Portrait," p. 175.
[50] Julia Urquidi Illanes, *Lo que Varguitas no dijo.* Biblioteca Popular Boliviana de Última Hora (La Paz: Khana Cruz, 1983).

The inexperienced young writer, then, also lacks wisdom in the matter of adult love. His adolescent feelings for Julia are expressed in terms of physical desire: "ésa fue la primera vez que . . . no disimulé el deseo que me provocaba: mientras bailábamos mis labios se hundían con morosidad en su cuello . . ." (p. 239). In a typically adolescent manner, Marito sees his desire as something prohibited, and thus all the more attractive to him. He is not yet independent of his family, and when his Uncle Jorge spots the couple on the dance floor, Marito fears the consequences of his relatives' certain negative reaction. But at the same time the narrator clearly relishes the suspense: "Saben todo y están planeando algo, le aseguraba yo a Javier, y él, harto de que no le hablara de otra cosa, respondía: En el fondo, estás muerto de ganas de que haya ese escándalo para tener de qué escribir" (p. 241). Ironically, the scandal to which Javier refers does not provide the basis for Marito's writing at the time of the story; rather, it becomes the very theme for *La tía Julia y el escribidor*, the autobiographical text that revives the scandal (and creates a few new ones). Javier underscores the importance of literary demons, as Vargas Llosa would call them, and implies that the narrator might be particularly attracted to this woman because of her potential as a literary character.

Clearly, though, Varguitas seeks more than a scandal or a story in his relationship with Julia. He views her as an adult woman ("una mujer hecha y derecha," p. 248) and hopes to become a fully grown man through his love for her. When Marito goes out on the town with his old schoolmates, he suffers a great disillusionment and fails to find pleasure in their adolescent activities: "yo no podía hablarles de las cosas que me importaban: la literatura y la tía Julia" (p. 248). Javier remarks: "Es que siguen siendo unos mocosos. Usted y yo ya somos hombres, Varguitas" (p. 249). Javier's solemn statement refers to the fact that, in their dedication to literature and their deep feelings toward the women they love, these two adolescents have taken decisive steps toward maturity. In Varguitas' case, however, those very steps put him in direct confrontation with other adults and thrust him prematurely into a complicated world that forces him to assume a grown-up stance.

Several of the interrelated themes that have already appeared in *La tía Julia* come together once more in the seventh autobiographical chapter. The first of these is the transformation of biographical material into text. When Marito reads his latest short story, "La tía Elianita," to an audience composed of Julia, Javier, and Varguitas' assistants Pascual and Gran Pablito, he discovers that his literary effort falls short of the enthusiastic response generated by an incident that occurred that morning, which he had previously related to the group: "Pero antes de hacerlo [reading "La tía Elianita"], en la tarde de ese lunes, les conté lo ocurrido con la damita mexicana y el hombre importante. Fue un error que pagué caro porque esta anécdota les pareció mucho más divertida que mi cuento" (p. 275). As with his other story "La humillación de la cruz," Julia finds Varguitas' current tale less captivating than the reality it attempts to transform.

"La tía Elianita" is "el monólogo de un niño que, tendido en su cama, trataba de descifrar el misterio de la desaparición de su tía . . . . Era un cuento 'social,' cargado de ira contra los parientes prejuiciosos" (p. 275). The story centers on the narrator's aunt, who was ostracized by the family when she married a Chinese bar owner. The relatives of the story are practically the same ones who now form a collective opposition to Varguitas' relationship with Julia. From Aunt Julia the narrator turns his attention to Aunt Elianita, and his story thus paves the way for the negative reaction that his own family shows toward what they consider a socially unacceptable romantic involvement. The characters in Varguitas' fictitious and real life stories become interchangeable and confused, including Marito himself as a character created by Vargas Llosa in *La tía Julia*. These multiple narrative planes at the autobiographical level interface with the confusion of characters and stories that surfaces on the other side of the text, in Pedro Camacho's radio dramas. In addition to the displacement of characters from one story to the next, Elianita, Marito's short story character, is also the name of the niece in the first radio soap opera parody. Elianita, like Marito, has an elastic familial identity: she changes from niece to aunt, just as Varguitas goes from nephew to husband in his relationship to Julia. By relating niece Elianita with Aunt Elianita, who is in turn associated with Aunt Julia, Vargas Llosa also symbolically equates his first wife with his second. The Elianita of the first radio serial does not become involved with her admiring uncle, but rather with her brother, a pattern similar to Vargas Llosa's marriages to his aunt and first cousin.

When Varguitas learns that two of his uncles have written to his father informing him of his son's involvement with Julia, the narrator's reaction elicits the following remark from Julia: "Te has puesto pálido, Varguitas. Ahora sí que tienes tema para un buen cuento" (p. 279). But it is decades later when the narrator finally utilizes this theme of his prohibited relationship with an older woman for a "good story," precisely the story told in *La tía Julia*. The narrative distance between the little boy who reflects on his lost Aunt Elianita and the adolescent composer of that story is comparable to the gap in the larger frame of the whole work which separates the mature writer from the subject of his story. Thus, much like the young narrator of "La tía Elianita" who thinks about the family's ostracism of his aunt, the adolescent Marito contemplates his present situation with Julia:

> Tumbado boca arriba en mi cama, en la oscuridad, pensé mucho en la tía Julia y en que . . . nos iban efectivamente a separar. Me daba mucha cólera y me parecía todo estúpido y mezquino y de repente se me venía a la cabeza la imagen de Pedro Camacho. Pensaba en las llamdas telefónicas de tíos y tías y primos y primas, sobre la tía Julia y sobre mí, y empezaba a escuchar las llamadas de los oyentes desorientados con esos personajes que cambiaban de nombre y saltaban del radioteatro de las tres al de las cinco. . . . (p. 285)

In Varguitas' imagination, his own complicated soap opera-like world becomes confused with the disorientation of Pedro Camacho's story-hopping characters. Ironically, Varguitas is sent by his boss to speak to Camacho precisely about the confusion of characters in the daily soap operas, and Camacho confesses to the narrator that he has lost control of his stories. Once more, the narrator and his alter ego, Pedro Camacho, find themselves on a similar course. Like a Camachian character, Varguitas is edging nearer to a break with the respectable role which society has assigned him, and like Camacho himself, comes closer to losing control of the events in his life. Varguitas' path certainly approximates Camacho's best plots when, in the face of parental opposition, he asks Julia to marry him.

Naturally, Varguitas encounters numerous obstacles in his effort to arrange his marriage with Julia. In the process, Varguitas comes even closer to performing acts worthy of Camacho's characters. Marito's best friend Javier listens to one of Camacho's cataclysmic soap operas for the first time and comments: "La verdad que tu compinche Camacho es capaz de cualquier cosa" (p. 318), and also says the same words to Varguitas after learning of his marriage plans: "Bueno, tú también eres capaz de cualquier cosa" (p. 319). Marito, lost in his own worried thoughts, fails to distinguish between soap opera and reality when he hears Gran Pablito and Pascual discussing a story: "Venían hablando de un incendio, muertos de risa con los ayes de las víctimas al ser achicharradas" (p. 322). Varguitas fears that this incident, which he presumes was reported in a newspaper, will become the basis for one of Pascual's infamous sadistic news bulletins. But as Gran Pablito clarifies: "No es una noticia, sino el radioteatro de las once" (p. 323). For Varguitas, life has taken on the qualities of an outlandish Camachian tale, and thus the narrator passes from one plane of reality to the next, as do the other employees at the radio station who seem to belong to the soap opera world themselves. This confusion of life and art is carried further when Varguitas fabricates stories in the Camachian mode to obtain the necessary papers for his marriage:

> Me echó una mano un profesor de la Universidad, asesor de la Cancillería, a quien tuve que inventar otro embrollado radioteatro: una señora cancerosa, en estado agónico, a la que había que casar cuanto antes, con el hombre que cohabitaba hacía años a fin de que muriera en paz con Dios. (p. 328)

But, similar to what occurs in Pedro Camacho's radio dramas, this fantasy is anchored in the events of its creator's life. In Marito's true story "La tía Elianita," the aunt with whom the narrator identifies dies of cancer after having married a man rejected by her family. As a character in his own soap opera, Varguitas patterns himself after the Camachian types whose demons always return to haunt them.

Marito further resembles a Camachian character in his destructive attitude that is brought to light in the face of the opposition to his relationship with Julia. The narrator derives a sense of power from the battle he must fight: "Llegué a la Radio exultante, sintiéndome capaz de pulverizar a todos los dragones que me salieran al encuentro" (p. 322). Marito wishes to conquer his own maturity through his marriage to Aunt Julia, and therefore feels a need to destroy his rivals (real or imaginary) from her generation in order to take his place as her husband: "le dije que ... íbamos a casarnos aunque tuviera que matar a un montón de gente" (p. 327). In his catastrophic imagination, Marito envisions himself as slayer of the paternal figures that stand in his way. He pays more attention to the external obstacles to his marriage, such as the legal problems, than to the difficulties inherent in maintaining the marriage itself. When Julia implores: "¿Cuánto duraría, Varguitas? . . . ¿Al cuánto tiempo te cansarías? ¿Al año, a los dos, a los tres?" (p. 327), Varguitas responds: "¿El embajador los podrá legalizar?", a reference to Julia's legal documents. The two seem not to hear each other and to be engaging in their own soliloquies. For Varguitas, love takes a secondary role to the immediate problem of finding a way to assemble the papers necessary for obtaining a certificate of marriage. He thinks that marrying Julia would promote him into full adulthood, even if the relationship failed to endure. Marriage thus would become Marito's passage to emancipation and would sever his dependence on his family.

If the episode in which Marito secures the required documents for his marriage has the makings of a Camachian script, then the account of his journey through the province of Chincha in search of a village mayor to marry the couple is fully played out in the exaggerated mode of Camacho's most memorable plots. Marito's age of eighteen constitutes the primary obstacle to a legal marriage, and the mayor of Chincha, who had originally agreed to perform the ceremony, subsequently refuses when he realizes that the bridegroom is a minor: "Me metería en un lío de padre y señor mío" (p. 366). This expression adequately captures the opposition to Julia's and Marito's marriage, which is an affront to paternal authority and to social order.

The mayor of Chincha, unwilling to marry the couple, suggests they enlist the aid of Martín the fisherman from the village of Tambo de Mora. Thus Marito and Julia (along with Javier and Pascual) initiate their difficult *via crucis* in which the picaresque and the mode of the sentimental novel intermingle. After the mayor of Tambo de Mora refuses to marry them ("Mi colega de Chincha se las sabe todas . . . . Cada vez que se le presenta algo podrido se lo manda de regalo al pescador Martín . . .", p. 368), the group combs the province in search of a willing mayor, and finally, the taxi driver recommends they travel to Grocio Prado, the village of the "Beata Melchorita." Marito's and Julia's *via crucis* appropriately ends in a town associated with the presence of a saint. The taxi driver who narrates the saint's story could easily be retelling one of Camacho's tales: "Había salvado agonizantes incurables, hablado con santos que se le aparecían, visto a Dios y hecho florecer una rosa en una piedra que se conservaba" (pp. 372-73). But, with the mayor of Grocio Prado absent, the search for an official to perform the marriage ceremony continues unsuccessfully. Entrapped in these frustrating circumstances, Marito truly feels like a Camachian character: "me había sentido viviendo uno de los cataclismos últimos de Pedro Camacho" (p. 376). Once more, the two planes of *La tía Julia* are fused. As Domingo Ynduráin points out, the climax of the fictitious level, that is, the cataclysms of Pedro Camacho, occurs at the same time Varguitas' relationship with Julia reaches its most dramatic moment. [51] More significantly, the two converging planes of fiction and reality cause the adventures of Marito and Julia to take on the appearance of a Pedro Camacho soap opera, and the protagonist feels himself possessed by the forces that move the hackwriter.

The mayor of Grocio Prado finally returns to town and agrees to marry the couple, but ironically, to legalize the union, he demands that the illegal act of altering Marito's birth certificate be performed. Thus, Varguitas comes of legal age through a falsification, as Javier remarks: "Ya está, ya eres mayor de edad" (p. 378). The story of the narrator's travels throughout provincial Peru may be read like a modern capsule version of *La vida de Lazarillo de Tormes y de sus fortunas y adversidades.* Marito's major *fortuna,* achieving his goal of marrying Aunt Julia, comes about through the use of trickery, consistent with the picaresque code. Satisfied with his new status as a married man, Marito ignores the social disapproval and legal complications that make this union a fraud. Aunt Julia's remark just before they are finally pronounced husband and wife is appropriate: "¿No te sientes como si estuvieras robando un banco y fuera a llegar la policía?" (p. 379). Significantly, Marito's status as a minor is emphasized at the close of the chapter when the narrator, victim of his own irony, confesses to the reader that his wedding day marked the first occasion on which he drank wine,

---

[51] Domingo Ynduráin, "Vargas Llosa y el escribidor," *Cuadernos Hispanoamericanos,* 370 (April 1981), 159-60. Arrigoitia also sees this interrelation: "podemos percibir que la lectura galopante del escribidor y sus desastrosas confusiones, corresponden a la desaforada pasión de Varguitas por 'la tía Julia' y al 'via crucis' que ambos padecen para poder unirse legalmente," p. 22.

though, so as to avoid appearing childlike, he had not dared to make Julia aware of this. Despite his illusions, Varguitas finds that the act of getting married itself does not automatically make a man out of him, even though he technically makes himself a man by altering his birth certificate.

The last radio soap opera that intervenes between the story of Varguitas' marriage and the book's conclusion brings together all of the protagonists from the even-numbered chapters while interchanging their identities and their relationships to one another. The two central characters, Crisanto Maravillas and Sor Fátima, eventually undergo radical identity changes that span the spectrum of possibilities. At first, Crisanto gives the appearance of being much younger than he is, which serves to his advantage at the convent where Fátima lives, until his true age is discovered:

> La segunda tragedia de su vida (después de su invalidez) ocurrió el día en que, por casualidad, la superiora de Las Descalzas lo descubrió vaciando la vejiga. La Madre Lituma cambió varias veces de color y tuvo un ataque de hipo. Corrió a preguntar a María Portal la edad de su hijo y la costurera confesó que, aunque su altura y formas eran de diez, había cumplido dieciocho años. La Madre Lituma, santiguándose, le prohibió la entrada al convento para siempre. (p. 391)

Like Marito, Crisanto is eighteen years of age, and his deceiving physical appearance brings to mind the description applied to Camacho: "Podía tener cualquier edad entre treinta y cincuenta años . . ." (p. 24). In the preceding chapter, Marito's basic problem was that of his age, the importance of which is somewhat minimized by its being indeterminable or elastic, like Camacho's and his characters'. Crisanto seems younger than his real age, as does Marito when he is symbolically given a more juvenile status by his lawyer:

> En cuanto a la tía Julia, sí era posible denunciarla como "corruptora de menores," sentar un parte en la policía y hacerla detener, por lo menos provisionalmente. Luego, habría un juicio, pero él [the lawyer] estaba seguro que, vistas las circunstancias — es decir, dado que yo tenía dieciocho y no doce años — era imposible que prosperara la acusación. . . . (p. 415)

Marito thus goes from twenty-one on his falsified birth certificate to an imaginary twelve years of age in the lawyer's illustration of the meaning of corruption of a minor.

The final radio soap opera ends in a typically catastrophic manner with an apocalyptic earthquake. Camacho's destructive fantasies go hand in hand with his erotic fantasies in which any type of love is permissible. Thus, Fátima, first described as the child of an incestuous brother and sister (presumably Richard and Elianita of Chapter II) who leave her in the care of the Descalzas, takes her religious vows, and becomes Sor Fátima. But her origin undergoes a radical change when she is called "esa muchachita milagrosamente salvada de las ruedas del automóvil conducido por el propagandista médico Lucho Abril . . ." (p. 396). Sor Fátima, in spite of her status as a nun, reciprocates the love Crisanto has felt for her since they were children: "había llegado, con el tiempo, en la soledad de su celda, a amar de amor sincero al aeda de los Barrios Altos" (p. 396). Since identity falls into an unstable category and one character may be changed into another, love between any of these changeable beings also falls into the range of the permissible.

With regards to elastic identities, it is interesting to note in this final radio drama the transformation of Fátima into Richard Quinteros' sister. The two become lovers, like Elianita and Richard in the first soap opera: "La muerte de Sor Fátima y Richard, ímpetu de amor que ni la sangre ni el hábito detienen, fue todavía más triste" (p. 400). Their relationship is not only incestuous but also sacrilegious. But, in her original role, Sor Fátima would be Richard's daughter, the child of his incestuous relationship with Elianita. This father-daughter incest, now added to brother-sister incest, finally gives way to the imaginary destruction of the most important taboo when the pair walk away from the earthquake's destruction: "Richard, entonces tomando de la cintura a la Madre Fátima, la arrastró hacia uno de los boquetes abiertos en los muros por la braveza del incendio" (p. 400). The incest now suggested involves mother and son, so that in the end man conquers the three women most closely related to him by blood (daughter, sister, mother) in the family constellation.

Richard and Fátima, like the other characters in this radio serial episode, also fall victim to Camacho's catastrophic bent:

Pero apenas habían dado unos pasos los amantes, cuando
— ¿infamia de la tierra carnívora?, ¿justicia celestial? —
se abrió el suelo a sus pies. . . .
    ¿Era el diablo quien se los llevaba? ¿Era el infierno
epílogo a sus amores? ¿0 era Dios, que, compadecido de
su azaroso padecer, los subía a los cielos? (pp. 400-01)

In the end, even heaven and hell are indistinguishable. Camacho
finds the only possible destiny for the characters he has confused
and transposed is to extinguish them arbitrarily.

The last radio soap opera in *La tía Julia* with its massive confusion of characters and holocaustic finale, lays the groundwork for
the conclusion of Pedro Camacho's personal life story. When Marito
returns to Lima after eloping with Julia and finally reappears at the
radio station, he is told: "A Pedro Camacho se lo han llevado al
manicomio . . ." (p. 410). The narrator comments on the events that
led to Camacho's downfall:

> Todo comenzó los mismos días en que yo andaba absorbido
> en mis trajines prematrimoniales. El principio del fin fueron
> las catástrofes, esos incendios, terremotos, choques, naufra-
> gios, descarrilamientos, que devastaban los radioteatros, aca-
> bando en pocos minutos con decenas de personajes. (pp.
> 410-11)

Thus, Marito's absence from Radio Panamericana coincides with
Camacho's disappearance from his job at Radio Central. Upon his
return, the narrator finds he must occupy both positions when his
boss assigns him Camacho's job: "Tienes que echarnos una mano.
Tú eres medio intelectual, para ti será un trabajo fácil" (p. 412).
Marito takes the place of Camacho by literally sitting in the hackwriter's place of work, the cubicle where the narrator now tries to
reconstruct radio dramas from old Cuban scripts that the station
had bought and used in the past. Marito's identification with Camacho culminates in this act of assuming the scribbler's work, which
allows the narrator to fulfill his goal of becoming a writer in a most
ironic manner. Marito's soap operas for Radio Central, however,
fail to generate enthusiasm in the listeners. Vargas Llosa's real success as a type of radio dramatist comes about in the pages of *La tía
Julia* where the even-numbered chapters, in their parody of a soap
opera writer's style, achieve a new status as literature. Vargas Llosa

thus assumes Camacho's role on the level of the discourse as well as the level of the story as he reveals himself to be the true narrator of the soap opera parodies in *La tía Julia* and the composer of Radio Central's post-Camachian radio serials.

As Varguitas' literary vocation takes the ironic turn that lands him in Camacho's cubicle to write soap operas, his personal life continues to resemble a Camachian plot with strains of the sentimental novel in the background. [52] Julia and Marito return to Lima to face the dozens of relatives whose reactions to their marriage range from the reluctant acceptance of Lucho and Olga to the homicidal rage of the narrator's father. Age again becomes an elastic category as the incongruous pair is received by different family relations. Marito's mother, for example, calls Julia "esa vieja," but his grandmother inquires: "¿Y la Julita está bien?" (p. 408). The diminutive, though commonly used in the colloquial speech of Lima, nevertheless serves to bring Julia closer in age to Marito, since from the oldest generation's perspective the disparity in age is not so great. At the same time, the grandmother treats Marito's mother as a little girl: "Había dejado de llorar y . . . la abuelita . . . sentada en el brazo del sillón, la acariciaba como si fuese una niña" (p. 409).

Marito, however, makes an attempt to pacify his mother by imprudently associating her with Julita: "pero, mamacita, deberías estar feliz, si me he casado con una gran amiga tuya" (p. 409). Varguitas inadvertently reveals his secret attraction for his mother's age group, and significantly, now finds his mother to be rejuvenated in appearance. She, on the other hand, exaggerates her son's tender age and considers him the victim of Aunt Julia's abusive behavior: "Hijito, cholito, amor mío, qué te han hecho, qué ha hecho contigo esa mujer" (p. 408). The narrator's mother acts in a manner that shows her jealousy toward the woman of her own generation who has the power to seduce her son. But his mother's tears and lamentations pale in comparison to his father's explosion of rage. In his

---

[52] On the connection between Camacho, Julia, and the young writer Varguitas, Saúl Sosnowski's remark is of interest: "A medida que Camacho se desplaza del texto se asienta aún más la relación literatura-Julia. Si bien Varguitas ha declarado reiteradamente esa secuencia, es la tía Julia la que condiciona y valora los textos." "Mario Vargas Llosa: entre radioteatros y escribidores," in *Latin American Fiction Today: A Symposium,* ed. Rose S. Minc (Tacoma Park and Montclair State College: Ediciones Hispamérica, 1980), p. 79.

threatening letter to Marito, his father interprets the secret marriage as a mockery of paternal authority: "quiero que sepas que ando
armado y que no permitiré que te burles de mí. Si no obedeces al
pie de la letra y esa mujer no sale del país en el plazo indicado, te
mataré de cinco balazos como a un perro, en plena calle" (p. 414).
In his extreme reaction, Marito's father proves that he views his
son not so much as a dependent minor, but as an equal, a rival. In
his letter, he addresses his son as *Mario,* and is thus the only character
in *La tía Julia* who does not use the diminutive in reference to the
narrator. This autobiographer who tries to make a name for himself
is nevertheless forced to accept the name assigned to him by his
father, the name which he later uses in adult life. His father literally
makes a man of the narrator in a way that marriage to Julia had not
yet accomplished. Both Varguitas' mother and Julia continue to use
the diminutive, and to treat the narrator essentially like a child. The
final words Julia speaks in the work reflect this basic attitude: "Vaya,
Varguitas .... Te estás haciendo un hombrecito. Ahora, para que
todo sea perfecto y se te quite esa cara de bebé, prométeme que te
dejarás crecer el bigote" (p. 428).

Varguitas has expressed a desire to be treated like "un hombre
hecho y derecho," that is, in adult terms. This is precisely the manner in which the narrator's father behaves toward his son. As he
signs the letter to his son with his two surnames and reaffirms his
intention to shoot Marito like "a dog in the street," the father acts
in the manner of a rival suitor challenging his opponent to a duel.
Marito's rebellion against paternal dictates poses a threat to his
father, who energetically reasserts his power over his minor child.
The narrator reacts in equally strong terms: "mientras caminaba por
las calles de Miraflores, hacia mi cuartito de soltero, en casa de los
abuelos, sentía amargura e impotencia, y me maldecía por no tener
ni siquiera con qué comprarme yo también un revólver" (p. 419).
His father's rage arouses in Marito a desire to arm himself in preparation for their imaginary shoot-out. The father's power highlights the
son's weakness, and conversely, the son's strength reveals the father's
debility. The two poles are intimately linked here and function in
a balance of opposites, just as they do in the case of the hackwriter
who harbors the conflict of impotence and strength within himself.

In the hopes of placating his father and eventually winning his
approval, Marito agrees to let Julia go to Chile while he attempts

to settle matters in Lima. To support himself and his wife, the narrator procures seven different jobs, in effect becoming a "mozo de muchos amos" in the traditional picaresque mold. After working at these various jobs for several weeks, Marito goes to see his father for the first time since the marriage to ask his permission to resume living with Julia. In reporting their conversation, the narrator initially employs formulas of direct discourse: "Pero se limitó a decirme, secamente: 'Como sabes, ese matrimonio no vale. Tú, menor de edad, no puedes casarte sin autorización' " (p. 426). He then shifts to indirect discourse: "Me explicó que la falsificación de un documento público era algo grave, penado por la ley" (p. 426). However, an important stylistic change takes place in this report of their meeting:

> Después de esa exposición legal, que profirió en tono helado, habló largamente, dejando transparentar, poco a poco, algo de emoción. Yo creía que él me odiaba, cuando la verdad era que siempre había querido mi bien, si se había mostrado alguna vez severo había sido a fin de corregir mis defectos y prepararme para el futuro. Mi rebeldía y mi espíritu de contradicción serían mi ruina. . . . Por lo demás, comprendía que me hubiera enamorado, eso no estaba mal, después de todo era un acto de hombría, más terrible hubiera sido, por ejemplo, que me hubiera dado por ser maricón. (p. 427)

The surprising statement, "yo creía que él me odiaba, cuando la verdad era que siempre había querido mi bien," initially creates the impression that Marito has finally come to acknowledge and accept his father's love and concern. But the comments that follow this statement, all formulated in the same style of free indirect discourse, clearly reveal that the narrator is merely reproducing his father's words without the introductory phrases "Me dijo que," etc. Gérard Genette discuses the rhetoric of "free indirect style": it entails confusion between uttered speech and inner speech, and especially, confusion between the speech of the character and that of the narrator. [53] We may then interpret the ambiguity created by the last

---

[53] Genette, p. 172. The critic also notes: "we know the remarkable advantage Flaubert derived from this ambiguity which permits him to make his own language speak this both loathsome and fascinating idiom of the 'other' without being wholly compromised or wholly innocent," p. 172. Vargas Llosa has of course acknowledged his great literary debt to Flaubert.

stylistic change, in which the narrator apparently places credence in his father's stated good intentions, as a case of wishful thinking. Marito's mockery of his father, transmitted by means of free indirect discourse weighted with irony, coexists with deep yearnings for paternal affection and approval, expressed in the initial comment "la verdad era que siempre había querido mi bien." When father and son embrace at the end of their meeting after a moment's hesitation, they show a strong mutual need for understanding and affection.

Once Varguitas and Julia are reunited, he announces his plans to read her a short story he has written in her absence, "La Beata y el Padre Nicolás," so that she may help him to select one of the two endings that he has devised for the protagonist, a priest named Padre Nicolás. The story is set in Grocio Prado, and it involves the Beata Melchorita. The plot would certainly have appealed to Camacho, who is now removed from the limelight of the novel. The two possible endings that Marito developed for Padre Nicolás are antithetical: in one, reminiscent of Camacho's catastrophic bent, the priest falls into disgrace and is lynched; in the other, he is named Archbishop of Lima. In a now familiar pattern, the real Archbishop of Lima appears in Chapter XX to authorize the Church's dispensation that allows Marito to marry his cousin (pp. 429-30). Padre Nicolás, like Camacho and Marito, oscillates between strength and impotence. His fate will be determined by Julia, so we may say woman is accorded the power to destroy or exalt man. This episode underscores the interrelation of the literary planes: that is, the radio soap operas, the short stories, and the autobiographical discourse. No genre, then, is shut off from the others. This is a primary example of Vargas Llosa's technique of the "vasos comunicantes" in that autobiography encompasses all of the modes found in La tía Julia, and conversely, any genre may contribute to the autobiographical tale. [54] Julia is thus transformed from character to co-narrator, just

---

[54] John M. Lipski's analysis is most appropriate: "The two types of embedded literature, Vargas Llosa's attempts and Camacho's stories, are both metacommentaries on literature, on Vargas Llosa's literary career; the entire novel is a metaphor, a metacommentary tracing the development of Mario Vargas Llosa as writer.... The most significant aspect of the text is ... the very fact of embedded self-parody: it is the reader of the novel reading Vargas Llosa the author, who is reading Vargas Llosa the character, who is reading both himself and Pedro Camacho, which is to say Vargas Llosa the author

as Marito functions as both narrator *(sujet de l'énonciation)* and character *(sujet de l'énoncé).*

see p. 109

The final chapter of *La tía Julia,* which serves as an epilogue and completes the autobiographical frame structure, breaks the perfect alternating rhythm of autobiography and fiction. This retrospective account of the outcome of Marito's marriage to his Aunt Julia also focuses on his reencounter with his old colleagues from the radio station, Gran Pablito, Pascual, and Pedro Camacho. The story time is now some twelve years after Marito has left Peru, and the evolution from "ese tiempo remoto" that opened the work to this new story time is apparent in the temporal shift to simply "ese tiempo" (p. 429). The narrator characterizes his first marriage: "El matrimonio con la tía Julia fue realmente un éxito . . ." (p. 429), and then informs us:

> Cuando la tía Julia y yo nos divorciamos hubo en mi dilatada familia copiosas lágrimas . . . . Y cuando, un año después, volví a casarme, esta vez con una prima (hija de la tía Olga y el tío Lucho, qué casualidad) el escándalo familiar fue menos ruidoso que la primera vez. . . . (p. 429)

Since the story told in *La tía Julia* centers exclusively on the narrator's first marriage, this new turn of events comes as a surprise.[55] Varguitas does not disclose very much of this new story line, but Julia Urquidi, in her *Lo que Varguitas no dijo,* provides the details of her ex-husband's attraction to her niece (his cousin and second wife). The publication of Vargas Llosa's autobiographical novel provokes Julia Urquidi's sequel in a continuous showing or striptease that Varguitas initiated when he set out to tell the story of his life with Aunt Julia. Ellen McCracken refers to the mass cultural aspects of autobiography that turn an author's private life into material for public consumption. The autobiography and the interview

---

once more." "Reading the Writers: Hidden Meta-Structures in the Modern Spanish American Novel," *Perspectives on Contemporary Literature,* 6 (1980), 122-23.

[55] As Julie Jones points out, "by refusing to allow his later knowledge to intrude in the autobiography, Vargas Llosa forces the reader to live in the contingent present and provides an element of suspense not usually present." "*La tía Julia y el escribidor:* Mario Vargas Llosa's Versions of Self," *Critique,* 21 (1979), 77.

serve to reveal parts of a writer-turned-star's life to a public who generally assumes that the hidden self equals the real artist. [56] Even though Vargas Llosa reassures Julia: "espero que la lectura de esta novela —pues, pese a todo, se trata de una novela y no de una autobiografía— no te cause irritación ni te ofendas," [57] she nevertheless reads the work primarily as the fictionalized (that is, falsified) chronicle of their intimate life together. [58] McCracken implies that the majority of readers will also react to this type of autobiographical work in the same manner. However, if we consider the work's value as literature, the biographical details and their distortion fade in light of what is revealed through the fictionalization itself. The reconstructed life as text takes on an autonomy that releases it from the bonds of biographical data, which Julia Urquidi recognizes in declaring that Vargas Llosa's work caused a favorable reaction in most people "as a book."

The epilogue of *La tía Julia* primarily serves to relate Camacho's tragic fate in life, which the narrator discovers on one of his return visits to Lima. Camacho is now employed at a sensationalist tabloid as a mere data collector. Pascual, Marito's former assistant at Radio Panamericana, serves as the editorial chief at this failing newspaper where Camacho is "la última rueda del coche" (p. 443). The narrator's description of Camacho is revealing:

> Poco a poco, no sin esfuerzo, fui relacionando, acercando, lo que recordaba de Pedro Camacho con lo que tenía presente. Los ojos saltones eran los mismos, pero habían perdido su fanatismo, la vibración obsesiva. . . . Y también los gestos

---

[56] McCracken, pp. 62-63.
[57] Urquidi, *Varguitas no dijo,* p. 293.
[58] Julia Urquidi remarks in *Lo que Varguitas no dijo:*

> El libro pasó de mano en mano. Gustó a la mayoría de las personas "como libro" pero ni una estuvo de acuerdo en lo que en él se dice de mí, en cuanto a las relaciones amorosas un poco "fogosas en la oscuridad de una boite". Mi fatal seducción no llegó a tanto. Lo único cierto de estas escenitas es que con el amor más puro, con el amor más grande, me entregué a él la noche antes de casarnos. (p. 295)

The last line shows Julia's talents as a writer of sentimental novels; her autobiography or memoirs thus fall into the genre of soap operas or novelettes. The narrator of *La tía Julia* could not have accomplished a better imitation of the language of Corín Tellado et al. than Julia's declaration, which seems totally free of parody on her part.

y ademanes, la manera de accionar cuando hablaba, ese mo-
vimiento antinatural del brazo y la mano que parecía el de
un *pregonero de feria,* eran los de antes, igual que su in-
comparable, cadenciosa, arrulladora voz. (p. 441) [emphasis
mine]

The associations that we have made between picaresque narrative
and *La tía Julia* culminate in the epilogue. If Marito was a modern-
day *pregonero* in his role as news director at Radio Panamericana,
then Camacho, explicitly designated with the archaic title of *pregonero,* assumes that role as a degraded assistant for a third-rate tabloid.
He is, in the narrator's words, "una caricatura de la caricatura que
era doce años atrás" (p. 442). Once the "town crier" of popular
culture at Radio Central where he created the famous serials, Camacho now has become the mute *pregonero* at *Extra.*

Like Lazarillo, Pedro Camacho has assumed the role of mute
pregonero in another crucial way: by turning a deaf ear to the
damaging accusations made against his wife.[59] We are told for the
first time that Camacho had a wife who abandoned him and now
has returned to support him in his moment of need: "Una gran
esposa, señor. Abnegada y buena como nadie. Estuvimos separados,
por circunstancias de la vida, pero, cuando necesité ayuda, ella volvió
para darme su apoyo" (p. 444). The reality of the situation, however,
is quite different, as Pascual's new boss explains: "Le tiene [Ca-
macho] ese agradecimiento de perro porque gracias a ella come
—lo rectificó el doctor Rebagliati—. ¿O tú crees que pueden vivir
con lo que gana Camacho trayendo datos policiales? Comen de la
putona . . ." (p. 445). Camacho's end in life is reminiscent of *Lazarillo de Tormes,* in which the picaresque hero also lives at his wife's
expense and chooses to silence in himself and others the voice of
the truth:

> Mayormente, si me quieren meter mal con mi mujer, que
> es la cosa del mundo que yo más quiero y la amo más que
> a mí, y me hace Dios con ella mil mercedes y más bien que

---

[59] Harry Sieber notes the important feature of the "mute *pregonero*" in
relation to Lazarillo: "the *pregonero* of Toledo becomes a mute in his own
home." *Language and Society in "La vida de Lazarillo de Tormes"* (Baltimore:
Johns Hopkins Univ. Press, 1978), p. 91.

yo merezco. Que yo juraré sobre la hostia consagrada que es
tan buena mujer como vive dentro de las puertas de
Toledo. [60]

Lazarillo sees himself at the height of grandeur at the novel's end
because he has prospered socially; he conspicuously excludes honor
from his hierarchy of values. This is not entirely Camacho's case,
since the former soap opera writer must close his eyes to all his
current misfortunes. We recall Vargas Llosa's alternate title for his
work, *Vida y milagros de Pedro Camacho,* and we may add: "y
de sus fortunas y adversidades."

The figure of the downtrodden Camacho contrasts sharply with
that of the narrator, who has become a legitimate writer and has
attained prosperity exclusively through literary activities. At the end
of *La tía Julia,* the narrator is about thirty years old and has already
produced two major novels, *La ciudad y los perros* and *La casa verde.*
His personal life also seems to have been successful, since he presents
his relationship with his first wife in favorable terms and apparently
finds satisfaction in his prompt remarriage within the family circle
after divorcing Julia. But throughout *La tía Julia,* each story has
the possibility of several endings, and each character has the potential
to triumph or to be destroyed. In his close identification with Camacho, Varguitas' life often seems to follow a path that runs parallel
to that of the characters that populate the hackwriter's soap operas.
Varguitas might have ended up like Camacho himself: that is, impotent in both the professional and personal spheres of his life. This
possible bad end for Marito is clearly implied when he and Julia
arrive in Madrid and the narrator announces: "Voy a tratar de ser
un escritor, sólo voy a aceptar trabajos que no me aparten de la
literatura," to which Julia responds: "¿Me rasgo la falda, me pongo
un turbante y salgo a la Gran Vía a buscar clientes desde hoy?"
(p. 430). Through this ironic and mocking remark, Julia suggests
that she may have to support her husband in the dishonorable way
that Camacho's and Lazarillo's wives earn their income. The distance
between the narrator as an accomplished author and as an unsuccessful writer is not so great after all, just as the gap between the
scribbler and the real writer is constantly being bridged in *La tía*

---

[60] *Lazarillo de Tormes,* ed. Rico, p. 80.

Julia y el escribidor. The title of the work also associates Aunt Julia with the scribbler who, as we have seen, is split into the figure of Camacho and Varguitas.

In his role as *escribidor,* Varguitas would be the up-and-coming writer who may never achieve success, a primary fear expressed by the narrator throughout the work. However, he does eventually win star status as an author, so we may say that *La tía Julia y el escribidor* becomes *Vida y milagros de Varguitas.* Harry Sieber's comments on the essence of Lazarillo's story are especially applicable to our discussion: "The *Lazarillo* is both the story of the 'fortunas y adversidades' experienced in becoming a dishonorable *pregonero* and the story of a *pregonero* who becomes an honorable author." [61] As we have stressed, the characters of Marito and Camacho function in a complementary fashion throughout *La tía Julia,* and their destinies are further linked when they are both associated with the figure of the *pícaro.* Thus, Camacho assumes the role of dishonorable *pregonero* at the end of the work when he lives "de la putona" and serves as news gatherer (crier) for a sensationalist paper. The other *pregonero,* Varguitas, who begins the story of his life at the moment when he occupies the position of news teller, transforms himself through his writing into a most honorable author. The structure that Sieber sees as basic to *Lazarillo de Tormes* also underlies the condition of the interrelated protagonists of the autobiographical and fictional segments of *La tía Julia,* but here the role of *pregonero* is divided between the two story tellers, Camacho and Varguitas.

The relationship of *La tía Julia* to the picaresque mode of autobiographical writing is firmly anchored in the particular narrative structure of story and discourse. According to Sieber, the meaning of the *Lazarillo* may be expressed in terms of the *pícaro*'s self-creation in words, which "is contained in that space between Lázaro as narrating subject (writing self) and the finalized product of his narration (written self)." [62] The gap that separates Lázaro from Lazarillo is comparable to the one between Mario and Marito (or Vargas and Varguitas). The mature autobiographer-narrator functions as a trickster or *pícaro* with respect to his own characters, as he outfoxes the (imaginary) Camacho by turning the stories against

---

[61] Sieber, *Language,* p. ix. See also his comments in *The Picaresque,* p. 14.
[62] Sieber, *Language,* pp. x–xi.

their supposed creator. The narrator performs a similar function vis-à-vis Marito, who also becomes the victim of the mature writer's mocking voice. As Claudio Guillén points out, "not only are the hero and his actions picaresque, but everything *else* in the story is colored by the sensibility, or filtered through the mind, of the *pícaro*-narrator. Both the hero and the principal point of view are picaresque." [63] It may be claimed, then, that the narrator of *La tía Julia* in his role as *pícaro* writes by his wits: his roguery lies in the double operation of self-concealment and self-revelation that his tale encompasses.

At the same time, the author often falls prey to his own picaresque narrative mode, [64] as underscored in the last paragraph of *La tía Julia*. Here, the possibility of an unplanned ending threatens the happy resolution of the autobiographical tale. When the narrator returns home after his lengthy visit with his former radio station colleagues, his new wife receives him angrily:

> Me dijo que era posible que con el cuento de documentarme para mis novelas, yo, a la tía Julia le hubiera metido el dedo a la boca . . . así que, la próxima vez que yo saliera a las ocho de la mañana con el cuento de ir a la Biblioteca Nacional a leerme los discursos del general Manuel Apolinario Odría y volviera a las ocho de la noche con los ojos colorados, apestando a cerveza, y seguramente con manchas de rouge en el pañuelo, ella me rasguñaría o me rompería un plato en la cabeza. La prima Patricia es una muchacha de mucho carácter, muy capaz de hacer lo que me prometía.
> (p. 447)

This ironic, Camachian ending suggests that Marito may have to face new obstacles in his life. Would Marito dare to defy his wife? Would cousin Patricia break a dish over his head someday? How will this soap opera that is the narrator's life finally end?

It should be reemphasized that the narrator's autobiography is written in serial form. The soap opera parodies in the even-numbered

---

[63] Guillén, p. 81.

[64] Sieber remarks: "the motif of the 'trickster-tricked,' one of the featured conventions of the genre from the *Lazarillo* onward, has been elevated in [Thomas Mann's] *Felix Krull* to express the relationship between the author and his narrator." *The Picaresque*, pp. 68-69. This motif receives similar treatment in *La tía Julia*.

chapters of *La tía Julia* are presented as short stories, so that the autobiography found in the odd-numbered chapters is the true serial which is continually interrupted by the Camachian radio dramas. The reader's response to the autobiographical narration is accordingly influenced by its peculiar structure:

> Most likely, the reader will relate to the continuing episodes of autobiography which chronicle this "impossible love" with the same responses he or she has learned from the mass media: eager to discover the outcome of the romance, some readers will be annoyed by the technique of serialization. . . . [65]

Through this technique, Vargas Llosa also executes a somewhat ironic tribute to Aunt Julia, to whom the soap opera serial mode was particularly dear. The narrator uses the radio drama style both to tell his story and at the same time to parody it, so that the homage to Julia, to whom the book is dedicated, also takes the form of a subtle mockery. [66]

Another mechanism that contributes to the ironic tone of *La tía Julia* is Vargas Llosa's choice of names for the characters. The narrator goes by the diminutives *Marito* or *Varguitas,* except to his father, thereby exposing his condition as an adolescent and contrasting him with the mature writer Mario Vargas Llosa. But the narrator also uses the childlike "tía" and "prima" in reference to his first and second wives. This technique serves several purposes. First, it creates a gap between the narrator and Julia, who, in her role as "la tía," remains an inaccessible, forbidden older relative. The relationship retains its element of scandal since the narrator persists in referring to his first wife as "la tía Julia." In addition, this consistent use of "Aunt" enhances the author's subtle mockery of his own situation and those involved in it. The "tía" he assigns to his first wife also reaffirms his family ties with her while at the same time dissociates her as lover and spouse.

---

[65] McCracken, p. 57.

[66] Oviedo sees this homage in more positive terms: "This novel is, simultaneously, the testimony that the narrator is, to some extent, her [Julia's] own creation and the late but mature homage that she receives from the adolescent he once was." "Coded Self-Portrait," p. 170.

Similarly, the narrator's second wife is called "la prima Patricia," another way of underscoring the blood relationship while eschewing the amorous one. The terms "la prima" and "la tía" are interconnected in another important way. Julia was not Varguitas' real aunt; in fact, she was his Uncle Lucho's wife's sister. But by marrying Julia's niece, "la prima Patricia," Varguitas now comes much closer to making Julia the aunt that he has always called her: Julia is aunt to Varguitas' wife and, through that marriage, to him. In his insistence on calling his first wife "la tía Julia," the narrator also reasserts his place in his own generation with his new wife. But in her designation as "cousin Patricia," she equally lacks an identity outside the one of a family relation. The labels assigned to both females thus reduce them to the status of relatives and ultimately, to the role of characters in a novel. [67]

Amusingly enough, the story told in La tía Julia as autobiographical fiction continues outside the text, not only in Julia Urquidi's Lo que Varguitas no dijo, but also through other modes of story telling, such as the real soap opera serial on Colombian television that was based on Vargas Llosa's novel. Julia Urquidi lets her sentiments be known concerning this television exploitation of her life with the Peruvian author: "Advertí a Vargas Llosa, a través de una carta dirigida a mi sobrina, o sea, a su esposa, que no daba mi autorización a filmar dicha telenovela —de lo cual me enteré por la Prensa— porque pienso que no se puede comerciar con la vida privada de una persona." [68] Fact and fiction once more become joined as an autobiographical novel is made into a television soap opera, which in turn provokes a reaction from a real life counterpart of one of the characters, who thinks her privacy is being invaded and her life story distorted. Mario Vargas Llosa probably could not have imagined a more fitting end to La tía Julia than the television adaptation that turned his text into a mass cultural spectacle much like the radio serials of Pedro Camacho.

---

[67] In La tía Julia, the narrator dedicates one of his short stories: "Al femenino de Julio" (p. 207), a further instance of woman being reduced to a grammatical function or label.

[68] El País [Madrid], 16 July 1981, p. 47. Urquidi's letter was originally published in El Espectador [Bogotá].

Julia Urquidi is not the only character from *La tía Julia* to prolong the story line of the work beyond the text. Two other major figures, Vargas Llosa's father, and the man who inspired the character of Pedro Camacho, also react in a manner consistent with their exaggerated depiction in the novel. Julia Urquidi exposes the author's father's reaction to *La tía Julia y el escribidor*: "El libro produjo una reacción bastante fuerte en mi ex-suegro, que envió a todos sus amigos y familiares una especie de circular dando su opinión sobre la novela y su hijo, que según tengo entendido fastidió mucho a Mario." [69] Once again, the father becomes enraged at his son's rebellious act of indiscretion, and the son, still dependent on parental approval, responds to his father's anger with strong feelings of his own. Raúl Salmón, the colleague from Radio Central after whom Vargas Llosa claims to have molded his character Pedro Camacho, also apparently had an extreme negative reaction to the autobiographical novel, as Vargas Llosa tells Julia in a letter:

> No sabes cuánto lamento todo el lío de Raúl Salmón. La culpa inicial es mía, por cierto, pues cometí el gravísimo error de decir . . . que el personaje estaba inspirado en él. Lo hice porque me imaginaba que el Raúl Salmón de la realidad se había muerto, o seguía loco o perdido por el mundo. ¿Quién me iba a decir que era todo un señor de la radio (¡justamente!) y que leería el reportaje? He tratado de darle explicaciones en múltiples reportajes . . . . Pero veo que nada lo calma y que sigue haciendo amenazas a diestra y siniestra. [70]

Will Raúl Salmón appear at Vargas Llosa's doorstep to challenge him to a duel? Will Julia Urquidi win her lawsuit against her ex-husband and the Colombian television station? Will Vargas Llosa's father seek a publisher for his retaliations, as his ex-daughter-in-law did? Curiously, Mario Vargas Llosa's text has given rise to a series of events that seem extremely close to his autobiographical fiction and that would not be out of place on the pages of *La tía Julia*. Life, then, has ended up imitating fiction, in a manner of speaking. Vargas Llosa's mock autobiography, in its juxtaposition and eventual fusion of

---

[69] Urquidi, *Varguitas no dijo*, p. 295.

[70] Urquidi, *Varguitas no dijo*, p. 293. I have corrected two printing errors in the original.

(supposed) reality and fantasy, demonstrates that to write of oneself is to write a fiction and ultimately, it is to perform the act of writing about (fiction) writing ("Escribo que escribo . . .").

Vargas Llosa continues his exploration of writing about writing and the adaptation of life into text in two dramatic works that follow *La tía Julia*: *La señorita de Tacna* and *Kathie y el hipopótamo*. A brief analysis of these plays will confirm their link to *La tía Julia* and deepen our understanding of the autobiographical mode in Vargas Llosa. Reference has already been made to the prologues of both works where the author expounds his theories on "Las mentiras verdaderas" and "El teatro como ficción," titles which already establish the relationship that Vargas Llosa sees between life and literature. Inspired in a relative of the author, "la señorita de Tacna" is an elderly woman known familiarly as Mamaé, who lives with her cousin, Abuela Carmen. The grandson, Belisario, is the writer who tells Mamaé's story and at the same time carries on a monologue on the nature of creating fiction from reality. Belisario, a typical Vargas Llosian character, resembles Marito in *La tía Julia* and Santiago in *Conversación en La Catedral* in that he declares himself to be a poet (or writer) who is pursuing legal studies only to please his relatives who consider him the hope of the family.

Vargas Llosa reaffirms in his prologue to *La señorita* what he consistently has demonstrated in *La tía Julia*:

> Para conocer lo que somos, como individuos y como pueblos, no tenemos otro recurso que salir de nosotros mismos y, ayudados por la memoria y la imaginación, proyectarnos en esas "ficciones" que hacen de lo que somos algo paradójicamente semejante y distinto de nosotros. La ficción es el hombre "completo," en su verdad y en su mentira confundidas. (p. 10)

To know ourselves, we must project ourselves in fiction, and the total person is thus the sum of his reality and his lies, according to Vargas Llosa. In his autobiographical work *La tía Julia*, Vargas Llosa presents data from his own life together with fiction to re-create a period of his youth. Only through that fusion can the true self be both unveiled and cloaked in the reverse strip-tease that underlies Vargas Llosa's texts.

This process also receives explicit treatment in *Historia de Mayta* (1984), in which a novelist-character collects data on a purportedly real revolutionary figure (much in the mold of a Pedro Camacho). The narrator blatantly admits to having resorted to lies, inventions, and fantasies in telling Mayta's story: "Le explico una vez más que no pretendo escribir 'la verdadera historia' de Mayta. Sólo recopilar la mayor cantidad de datos y opiniones sobre él, para, luego, añadiendo copiosas dosis de invención a esos materiales, construir algo que será una versión irreconocible de lo sucedido" (p. 93). At the core of the novel is the figure of the writer as liar, also an essential structure in picaresque narrative, as we have seen. *Historia de Mayta* presents itself as a fluid work-in-progress in which the writer-narrator pursues the elusive truth only to alter it once it has been captured.

As a story that is being continuously re-written, *Historia de Mayta* flaunts its own contradictions and falsehoods. After exposing Mayta's homosexuality throughout the entire text, the novelist-narrator finally interviews the real Mayta and informs him: "El personaje de mi novela es maricón" and further explains that he has re-created him this way "para acentuar su marginalidad, su condición de hombre lleno de contradicciones." But Mayta surprises us with his response: "Nunca tuve prejuicios sobre nada . . . . Pero, sobre los maricas, creo que tengo. Después de haberlos visto" (pp. 335-36). Once again, Vargas Llosa insists that the literary text is always a fiction, and that a lie may nevertheless transmit other truths.

In *La señorita de Tacna*, Belisario, like Marito in *La tía Julia*, plays a dual role. He is both the middle-aged writer who struggles with the story he is attempting to tell, and the young law student who fights his family's opposition to his decisions, in this case the choice of a literary career. As the mature writer, Belisario returns in fantasy to Mamaé's past world to re-create her story, which is dramatized on the stage. In the process, Belisario finds himself grappling with the problem of what story to tell as he speaks to himself: "¿Vas a escribir una historia de amor, o qué? Voy a escribir o qué (*se ríe de sí mismo, se deprime*)" (p. 23). The story he sets out to tell, the love story, takes a minor role to the "o qué," the other tale that interferes and demands to be written. Belisario finds that the theme chooses the writer and not vice versa. Thus he defines the writer: "aquel que escribe, no lo que quiere escribir —ése es el hombre normal— sino lo que sus demonios quieren" (p. 114). As in autobiography, Belisario's attempts to tell the story of a life are instead transformed into a chronicle of the problems involved in writing about that life.

This meta-theatrical structure —the mature author on stage who provides commentary on the story he attempts to write — has led to problems in staging the work before an audience. Wolfgang Luchting comments on the 1981 triumph of the edited version of *La señorita* in Lima: "For understandable reasons, the text's references to its own melodramatic essence were cut." [71] But Sharon Magnarelli reports a very different reaction to the 1983 Mexican performance: "the Mexican audience was clearly uncomfortable and confused. The abrubt changes of time and place, although essential to the message of the work, are nearly impossible to follow on stage without the visual clues of the written text and/or without some indication that such has occurred." [72] Its staging difficulties aside, the play's focus on a theoretical investigation into the problems of fiction writing makes for a successful reading of the work, especially in relation to Vargas Llosa's recent literary production.

Belisario's role in *La señorita* is extremely complex, as C. Lucía Garavito has shown in her analysis of characters and spectators in the work. [73] He simultaneously functions as protagonist, as the supposed author and reader of the story that is being written, and as the spectator of his own recollections that other characters dramatize. More importantly, Belisario disguises himself as one of his own characters — as does Pedro Camacho in the radio soap operas of *La tía Julia* — in order to "get inside" his literary creations. Belisario thus takes over the role of the priest who hears Mamaé's confessions, Padre Venancio. This disguise may be seen as a mechanism to cloak the fragile figure of the writer, who always feels himself at the brink of failure; but it also serves as a (mock) glorification of the author as character. He becomes, so to speak, a high priest of literature, a role that corresponds well to modern society's attitude toward a writer of the stature of Mario Vargas Llosa.

---

[71] Wolfgang A. Luchting, "The Usual and Some Better Shows: Peruvian Theatre in 1981," *Latin American Theatre Review*, 15 (Spring 1982), 59-60.

[72] Magnarelli, "The Spring 1983 Theatre Season in Mexico," *Latin American Theatre Review*, 17 (Fall 1983), 72.

[73] C. Lucía Garavito, "*La señorita de Tacna* o la escritura de una lectura," *Latin American Theatre Review*, 16 (Fall 1982), 3-14.

Belisario also plays the role of the young man who confesses his literary vocation to his family. His Uncle Agustín asks him: "¿Y para qué crees que has nacido, Belisario?", and he answers, "para ser poeta, tío." Uncle Agustín laughs: "No me río de ti, sobrino, no te enojes. Sino de mí. Creí que me ibas a decir que eras maricón . . ." (p. 124), a remark similar to the one Marito's father made to the young newlywed in *La tía Julia*. Belisario incarnates the figure of the poet (his youthful aspiration), the novelist (his efforts to turn Mamaé's story into fiction) and the actor in a play that dramatizes the process of becoming a writer. While success in his artistic endeavors would accord Belisario a feeling of personal satisfaction, the fear of failure causes him to experience doubts about his worth as a writer and a man. To a large extent, his family — in particular the paternal figure — contributes to his insecurities which result in his compelling need to prove himself. Marito, in his oscillation between strength and impotence, suffers the same condition.

Another important connection between *La señorita* and *La tía Julia* is Pedro Camacho, who appears in the play as the creator of the radio soap operas that entertain Mamaé. Mamaé lives in a fantasy world populated by characters from her past as well as Camacho's fictional creatures in her present. The elderly woman, in recounting the story of her youth, performs the autobiographical act, but speaks of herself as another, as a character in a type of serial. That is, her primary activity consists in narrating and inventing. In so doing, she bridges the gap between herself as the young Elvira and the old Mamaé, much as Belisario moves between the mature writer and the adolescent.[74] To tell their stories, the characters enter into mutual dependence. Mamaé needs Belisario, the shaper of the raw material, the writer who transforms acts into words. He, on the other hand, cannot perform this transformation without Mamaé's verbal recollections and her inspiring presence.

A similar process takes place in *Kathie y el hipopótamo*, a play about the creation of fictions and the writer's search for success. The protagonists are Santiago Zavala, a character from *Conversación en*

---

[74] Magnarelli discusses Mamaé's role in this manner in "Mario Vargas Llosa's *La señorita de Tacna:* Autobiography and/as Theatre," Autobiography and Fiction in Hispanic Literature, NEMLA Convention, Hartford, 30 March 1985.

La Catedral, and Kathie Kennety, a rich Peruvian residing in Paris who hires Santiago to ghost write her travel memoirs. [75] Santiago and Kathie try to compose an adventure book together, but they instead allow their personal fantasies to take over. The dramatization of these fantasies overshadows the trivial story of Kathie's trip around the world, so that the play centers on the upstaging that occurs when a writer's demons overthrow the conscious story he had originally set out to tell.

In their fantasy world, Kathie and Santiago converse with Juan, Kathie's imaginary husband, and Ana, Santiago's wife, characters described as follows: "A diferencia de Kathie y de Santiago, personajes de carne y hueso, que existen contemporáneamente a la acción, ellos son personajes entre recordados e inventados, presentes sólo en la memoria y en la fantasía de los dos protagonistas" (p. 20). In addition, Kathie at times assumes the role of Adèle, Santiago's lover in his role as Victor Hugo. And to further complicate matters, Kathie (and occasionally Ana) addresses Santiago as Mark Griffen, and Kathie Kennety itself is a pseudonym which she has invented because "los nombres peruanos no parecen de escritores" (p. 35).

In the prologue, Vargas Llosa states: "el asunto profundo de *Kathie y el hipopótamo* es, acaso, la naturaleza del teatro en particular y la de la ficción en general" (p. 21). Through fiction, we may accomplish the following: "tramposamente completar las insuficiencias de la vida, ensanchar las fronteras asfixiantes de nuestra condición y acceder a mundos más ricos o más sórdidos o más intensos" (p. 10). Yet, paradoxically, the dramatic structure of *Kathie* impedes this process of submerging oneself in fiction, since the play constitutes an anatomy of the creation of a literary work. In fact, the play centers entirely on the figure of the writer who, like Camacho, is called *escribidor* (p. 12). Santiago Zavala transforms Kathie's simple spoken language into formulas that belong to the sub-literary sentimental

---

[75] Concerning the revival of Santiago Zavala, Vargas Llosa remarks to Oviedo: "yo necesitaba un personaje que de pronto descubrí tenía las características de Santiago Zavala, que era lo que bien podía ser Santiago Zavala diez o quince años después de la historia ésa, un hombre que además había elegido la frustración . . . ." "Maestro de las voces," p. 163. In her book, Julia Urquidi makes reference to a job Vargas Llosa held as a ghost writer in Paris for a wealthy woman, which would give the play an autobiographical base in the classic sense.

novel. Kathie says: "En eso, quién sabe de dónde, se me apareció un tipo. No pude ni gritar. ¡Qué miedo!" Santiago writes: "Una figura masculina, de chilaba roja y turbante blanco, surge repentinamente ante mí, como segregada por el aire caliente del desierto o por la historia egipcia.... ¿Debo correr, pedir auxilio, llorar?" (p. 29). Kathie functions as the originator of the text and as the narratee of that same story once Santiago has transformed it into his own words. Santiago, originally the receptor of Kathie's verbal tales, becomes a scribe — and an author in his own right — as he turns her words to (his) text.

On another level, however, the work-in-progress (Kathie's travel memoirs) takes a secondary role to the imaginary world the two protagonists convoke. A crucial figure is Juan, Kathie's imaginary husband, who is a champion surfer and an incorrigible pursuer of women. His triumphs on his (phallic) surfboard represent his desire to conquer the waves so as not to loose himself in them: "Entro al agua despacito, deslizándome, burlando las olas.... Me monto sobre la tabla ... me encojo, me estiro ... ¡A mí no me tumbas tú, olita!" (pp. 58-59). Juan also exalts his sexual freedom and torments his wife: "Te mueres de celos de todas las chicas que se me acercan. Porque las tengo aquí, por decenas, por centenas. En Lima, en Hawai, en Australia, en Sudáfrica." Kathie responds: "Es verdad. Pierden la cabeza porque un estúpido sabe hacer equilibrio sobre una tabla" (p. 112). The triumphs on the surfboard may also symbolize the writer's success in the modern world, where an adoring public embraces the famous author and expects certain behavior from him.

But if on the one hand the surfing champion is glorified, on the other he suffers degradation — which he brings upon himself — when Kathie informs him that she has been unfaithful with Juan's friends and even his brother Abel. In his mono-dialogue, Juan shows awareness of his real failure: "Puedes ganar todos los campeonatos de tabla, bajar las olas más asesinas. ¿De qué te servirá? Estos cuernos seguirán aquí, firmes como rocas, hasta que te mueras. Y después de muerto seguirás siendo cornudo, Johnny" (p. 131). He implores Kathie to pull the trigger on his gun and execute the *coup de grâce*. Juan's status as champion (of surfing, women, or literature) matters little in view of the humiliation he suffers when his wife violates the (masculine) code of values. What constitutes Juan's sense of freedom and masculinity is ultimately turned against him by the woman whom he has scorned. Her power, in the final analysis, surpasses his: his condition of *cornudo* will haunt him even in death.

Santiago, the ghost writer, also harbors similar conflicts about his masculinity. On the one hand, Santiago proclaims to his wife, Ana, the values of passionless love: "el sexo es apenas un ingrediente entre los otros y ni siquiera el más importante. El amor-solidaridad se basa en la comprensión mutua . . . en la identidad espiritual, intelectual y moral" (p. 66). However, on the other hand he turns into a type of mythical Victor Hugo in his fantasy world. His lover Adèle tells of his sexual prowess: " ¡Eres una maravilla de la naturaleza! . . . ¡Eres insaciable, incansable, insuperable! " (pp. 98-99). In his role as supermale, Santiago requires a harem to satisfy his sexual appetite. But like Juan, he meets with woman's vengeance and scorn. Kathie (in her role as Adèle) chides him: "Te pasas el día diciéndome que me quieres, que te mueres por mí, pero a la hora de la verdad . . . psst... te desinflas como un globo con huecos" (p. 107). Now woman proves to be the empassioned lover and accuses man of failing to satisfy her.

Santiago's impotence, however, is clearly related to his being a writer. He vents his frustration on himself: " ¿Qué pasó con esos libros que no escribiste? . . . ¿Qué pasó con esas proezas intelectuales, sociales, sexuales que nunca realizaste?" (pp. 125-26). Adèle and Ana join in to heap more insults upon him, to which he responds: "Me casé con la mujer que no debía. . . . Me casé con una infeliz que me frustró, que me fregó, que me castró" (p. 126). Woman not only has the power to deprive man of his intimate satisfactions as sexual master, but she also may frustrate his artistic destiny. The three furies, Adèle, Kathie, and Ana, evoke the figures of Marito's and Camacho's wives at the end of *La tía Julia*, who as spouses of *pícaros* potentially or actually further the degradation of the writer-males, victims of real or imagined failures.

In *Kathie,* Santiago projects his literary failures not only on Ana and Adèle, but also on Kathie, the woman who pays him to pen her memoirs: "no he olvidado que eres la patrona . . . escribidora imaginaria, cacógrafa. Te odio" (p. 76). These recriminating words are directed more to Santiago himself than to his listener. Thus, the autobiography contained in *La tía Julia y el escribidor* leads to the "cacography" of *Kathie y el hipopótamo,* whose title is a parodic reflection of the novel's: woman-muse-fury in her relationship to the (degraded) writer. As Kathie says to Santiago: "Eres puro bluff . . . pura pinta, un hipopótamo que parece terrorífico pero que sólo come pajaritos" (p. 107). The writer — be it Santiago, Marito or Belisario — reveals his fears that he will never amount to more than a scribbler, impotent in all spheres of his life, like Camacho at the end of *La tía Julia*. At the same time, the writer expresses the urgent need to be a champion, a conqueror of women and words. Like Mamaé in *La señorita de Tacna,* Kathie facilitates the transition from scribbler to writer, not through the travel book they compose but by means of the fantasy world she (with the aid of other female characters) brings to life. At the end of both plays, the writer reconciles with his muse and acknowledges her inspiration. Belisario says to Mamaé: "¿Por qué me dio por contar tu historia? Pues has de saber que, en vez de abogado, diplomático o poeta, resulté dedicándome a este oficio que a lo mejor aprendí de ti: contar cuentos. Mira, tal vez sea por eso: para pagar una deuda" (p. 146). And Santiago's feelings toward Kathie evolve from initial ridicule to gratitude: "Me reía y creía venir aquí cada día, ese par de horas, por los soles que me pagaba. Pero ya no es verdad. La verdad es que desde hace tiempo el juego también me gusta y que estas dos horitas, de mentiras que se vuelven verdades, de verdades que son mentiras, también me ayudan a soportar mejor las demás horas del día" (p. 141). Similarly, Vargas Llosa dedicates *La tía Julia* to his first wife: "A Julia Urquidi Illanes, a quien tanto debemos yo y esta novela" (p. 7), the writer's extra-textual acknowledgement of woman's vital role in the creation of his literature.

As always with metafiction, an author destroys some artistic conventions merely to create others in their place. Thus in laying bare the anatomy of the creative process in *La señorita de Tacna* and *Kathie y el hipopótamo,* Vargas Llosa naturally fails to uncover the man behind the onstage writer's mask. The plays serve as a mirror in which the protagonist-writer contemplates his changing image — at times he sees a champion, and at others he glimpses a cuckold, a Camacho. The dramatic exploration of the writer's relation to his craft and to his muses provides a necessary dimension to the understanding of *La tía Julia y el escribidor,* where similar problems are treated. In his autobiographical trilogy, then, Vargas Llosa's characters find that the truth leads to the telling of lies. Paradoxically, it is only through these lies that the writer can capture his past in words as he knowingly forges his signature on the autobiographical pact.

CONCLUSION

While the narrative structure of Guillermo Cabrera Infante's *La Habana para un infante difunto* differs greatly from that of Mario Vargas Llosa's *La tía Julia y el escribidor*, an examination of the autobiographical rhetoric in both works uncovers a host of common features essential to that mode. The authors' use of their names on the pages of their autobiographical texts reveals much information concerning the type of literary pact they have explicitly executed and their concept of the past self. I have discussed Cabrera Infante's reluctance to assign his name to the narrator of *La Habana* and the latter's stated hatred of his given name, a hatred also felt by the narrator of *La tía Julia,* who despised the childlike diminutive "Marito." The narrator of *La Habana* adopts his critical pseudonym (presumably G. Caín) to hide his true name from the ladies he meets. Similarly, his identity is also concealed from the reader for whom he remains anonymous despite numerous coded hints at a name. The identity game in *La Habana* is played by several female characters as well, so that the unwillingness to share one's true name signals the inability to sustain a meaningful level of intimacy with another.

Mario Vargas Llosa assigns his juvenile nicknames "Marito" and "Varguitas" to the narrator of the odd-numbered chapters of *La tía Julia,* but these explicit references to the narrator's identity function essentially as a mask. Even though the factual data in the work correspond to events in the author's life, that fictive radio soap opera parodies alternate with the autobiographical chapters in *La tía Julia* casts a shadow of doubt over the authenticity of the text as a whole. Marito, a past self, becomes one more character in the gallery of fictitious creatures. Like the narrator of *La Habana,* Marito is also a character in search of a name. This involves both seeking an identity as an adult, that is, transcending the diminutive given to him by his family, and making a name for himself as a writer. The narrator of *La tía Julia* thus undergoes a literary and sentimental education on the road to adulthood.

The problem of the name in both works also entails the identity of the *I* who narrates the autobiographical story. Since the *I* stands for both the subject of the discourse and the subject of the story in autobiography, it undergoes a split as the *I* of the narrator's present attempts to tell the life of his past *I*. In Cabrera Infante, this condition leads to the wide spectrum of rhetorical devices that permit the narrator of *La Habana* to tell his story while simultaneously struggling with the problem of how to translate his memories into words. Vargas Llosa approaches the challenge of writing autobiography in a different manner. Unlike Cabrera Infante, he does not ascribe to the narrator of *La tía Julia* the acute degree of self-consciousness of an author struggling to tell his past life from his present perspective (*temps de l'énonciation*), but instead gives the autobiographical chapters the structure of memoirs. The narrator's awareness of the self as writer of his past in *La tía Julia* is manifested in two primary ways. First, the mature author tells of Marito's early attempts at transforming life into text in his short stories, most of which were discarded. Their mention in the autobiographical chapters, however, turns these early failures into objects of the narrator's scrutiny, and in this way they exhibit the anatomy of story telling. Autobiography becomes an exercise in writing about writing which, after all, constitutes a valid portrait of the essence of the young author's life.

The second way in which Vargas Llosa manipulates the technical difficulties inherent in autobiographical writing is through the confusion of narrative voices that pervades the even-numbered soap opera chapters of *La tía Julia* and eventually the autobiographical chapters as well. Throughout the work, stories are attributed to many narrators, ranging from the primary or overriding narrator, Varguitas, to the supposed author of the radio serial chapters, Pedro Camacho, in reality a disguise for the autobiographer himself. In addition, Camacho's authority is constantly being challenged in the even-numbered chapters by a series of characters who try to usurp the role of narrator for themselves. Behind these multiple textual voices ultimately stands the subject of the discourse who controls the outcome of each character's story, including Marito's. This hybrid autobiographical novel continually poses the problem of how to tell a story, a theme which is essential to *La Habana para un infante difunto*. In *La tía Julia,* the problem is encoded in the work's very structure: the alternating autobiographical and fictional chapters, the disguised narrators who compete as authoritative story tellers, the open-ended quality of the characters' fates and, finally, the presentation of life as a fiction. Vargas Llosa continues the exploration of these themes in his plays *La señorita de Tacna* and *Kathie y el hipopótamo,* in which the author-protagonists on stage attempt to illuminate the process of transforming reality into literature. Their struggles to become accomplished authors go hand in hand with the need to prove themselves as men; both aspects of their development are intimately linked to the women who inspire or frustrate them.

The narrator of *La Habana* deals with the problem of how to tell his life story in a more direct way. The rhetorical devices he employs cause the focus of the text to shift continuously from the *énoncé* to the *énonciation,* so that the autobiographical work centers on both the events of the past and the actual unfolding of those events in writing. As he attempts to tell his past, the narrator performs constant textual interruptions by means of specific techniques, some of which I have identified as self-editing, negation as a means of assertion, and the correction of remembrances. In addition, the inclusion of references to other works by Cabrera Infante within the pages of *La Habana* points to the notion that the autobiographical act encompasses more than the stories recounted by the narrator and his reflections on their telling, and extends into the realm of other written words which constitute an essential part of the author's identity.

The literary autobiographies of Cabrera Infante and Vargas Llosa distinguish themselves in several important ways from objective, depersonalized autobiographies that are often classified as historical. The autobiographers' focus on the act of writing itself in literary autobiography constitutes the major difference. In *La tía Julia* and *La Habana,* the facts concerning the authors' lives take a secondary role to the expression of the development of their inner selves, as writers and as men. In Cabrera Infante's case, the term "pornographer" may be applicable when the narrator of *La Habana* uses the conventions of erotic literature to relate his amorous adventures in explicit detail. However, the "guilty words" that the narrator employs instead serve as a mask, much like the pseudonyms he adopts, and in reality they impede full expression of the love and loss that the narrator claims to feel.

In their literary autobiographies Vargas Llosa and Cabrera Infante place emphasis on the manifestations of mass culture that they observed first-hand as urban adolescents. Vargas Llosa parodies the conventions of radio soap opera in his sensationalistic short stories that alternate with the autobiographical material in *La tía Julia.* The female members of Marito's family were particularly devoted to radio soap operas, movies, and sentimental novels, and so his incorporation of popular culture into a work of literature may be interpreted as both a homage to and a criticism of those values and those who embrace them, particularly Aunt Julia. Marito feels himself surrounded by the ever-present radio serials which kept his first wife entertained; the mature author makes good use of their literary possibilities, especially by exploiting the interrelationship between life and mass-produced forms of popular culture.

Cabrera Infante also underscores the importance of these forms of popular culture to his youth and adolescence, particularly the role of the movies as a medium of entertainment and as a means of meeting women. In addition, the narrator's occupation as movie reviewer affords him the opportunity to view films in the line of duty as well as for pleasure. Like Marito, the narrator of *La Habana* finds that the language of popular culture intrudes into his intimate relationships with women. In *La Habana,* female characters often speak a pseudo-literary language, or use expressions from radio soap operas, movies, and so forth. The narrator also finds himself quoting lyrics from *boleros,* remembering erotic literature he read as a youth, or comparing scenes from his life to the action on the movie screen. In this way, autobiographies of this type assume the characteristics of fiction, since a life is recounted in terms of other forms of story telling.

In theory, autobiography treats the span of an author's life from birth to death, and literary autobiographies often depict these events symbolically. Cabrera Infante employs birth imagery to evoke his symbolic rebirth as an urban adolescent which occurred as he ascended the staircase of his first place of residence in Havana. While Vargas Llosa does not begin his autobiographical novel with the traditional introduction "I was born," he nevertheless constructs his text around the development or birth of the mature self. In *La tía Julia,* the closure of the autobiographical episodes illustrates one of the possibilities for a symbolic end to the narrator's life: the arrival at a vocation. The discourse time in the last chapter of *La tía Julia* allows the narrator to signal his success as a writer and to provide a happy outcome to his story, a story which often suggested the potential for failure as well. The repetitive, obsessive question found in the soap opera parodies, "how would this story end?" may also be applied to the autobiographical chapters, for the outcome of the characters' fate is presented as open-ended. In Vargas Llosa's work, then, the unutterable "I died" is replaced by a metaphorical ending, that is, "I have achieved success."

Cabrera Infante, on the other hand, illustrates other possibilities for closure in autobiography: leaving the work open, "to be continued," or returning it to its starting point. In the epilogue of *La Habana,* "Continuous Showing," the idea of picking up the action *in medias res* ("aquí llegamos") suggests that the story of one's life can have no true ending on the written page, and that the narrator's symbolic return to the womb best approximates a living death. This epilogue also functions much like Vargas Llosa's soap opera parodies in *La tía Julia:* by including a fantastic, unreal episode in a supposed autobiography, the author reaffirms the notion that to write of the self is to create a fiction, to invent an ending.

An essential aspect of both narrators' achieving maturity and ending childhood is their break with parental authority. In *La Habana,* the narrator needs to sever his close relationship with his oppressive mother who closely monitors his adolescent activities and is depicted as an enforcer of the law ("policía del sexo"). The narrator asserts his independence by seeking female companionship, primarily at the movies, and by marrying his first wife, who is hardly mentioned in the work except as an ally of the narrator's mother. The ending of *La Habana,* however, underscores the futility of attempting to sever completely the maternal attachment and suggests the power of woman to engulf and annihilate man. In *La tía Julia,* Marito does battle with the paternal figure who becomes a type of rival when the narrator takes daring steps to win his independence. By marrying a woman of his mother's generation who is also related to the family, the narrator paradoxically achieves adult status but also reconfirm his position as a nephew tied to the family circle. This is further exaggerated by the juvenile title "la tía Julia" which Varguitas persists in assigning to his first wife throughout the text.

Varguitas and the narrator of *La Habana* also share some specific characteristics of the picaresque anti-hero. *La Habana* may be termed a type of sexual picaresque work in that the protagonist moves about the social scale in search of erotic adventures and makes use of his cleverness to seduce women. The youthful rogue must extricate himself from the traps into which he falls as he experiments with his Donjuanesque style. Vargas Llosa finds inspiration for *La tía Julia y el escribidor,* once titled *Vida y milagros de Pedro Camacho,* in the picaresque novel. The two primary characters, Marito and the scriptwriter Pedro Camacho, are both ascribed several key features of the *pícaro.* At the close of *La tía Julia,* Camacho is explicitly associated with Lazarillo when Marito refers to him with the title *pregonero,* and when we are informed of his wife's dishonorable occupation.

The narrator Varguitas, an older adolescent separated from his parents, sets out at a young age to search for a vocation and to marry his Aunt Julia. The obstacle-ridden path Marito follows to accomplish his goals leads him to commit acts of trickery (the falsifying of documents, the enlisting of accomplices, etc.) in what may be seen as a capsule version of the "fortunas y adversidades" of Lazarillo de Tormes. Both story tellers, Camacho and Varguitas, are intimately linked in the work. Thus, it is suggested that Varguitas' own life story may end like his counterpart's, the downtrodden Camacho who fell in disgrace from his position of soap opera king, and turned into a dishonorable *pregonero.* Marito, however, triumphs over adversity, and ultimately writes himself a happy conclusion to his autobiographical exploration by assuming the role of successful author. The picaresque point of view from which *La tía Julia* is written allows for the interplay between author and narrator, separated by the ironic gap that often pits one against the other in a new variation of the "trickster-tricked" motif.

The success of *La Habana* and *La tía Julia* may be largely attributed to the authors' previous literary triumphs that accorded them a salient position among modern novelists. Cabrera Infante and Vargas Llosa have won their prominent standing within the modern tradition with highly acclaimed works such as *Tres tristes tigres* and *La ciudad*

y los perros, and their recent achievements in the exploration of
the self now place them alongside other major writers who have
also attempted the literary autobiographical act. It seems that only
after a writer has made the arduous climb to the top may he
laughingly and convincincly capture through autobiographical expression the long journey upward. More than anything else, perhaps
it is the self-mockery and laughter in Cabrera Infante's and Vargas
Llosa's fictional autobiographies that cause us to wonder about their
place within the Hispanic literary tradition. Many have noted the
lack of a well-developed secular confessional mode in Hispanic letters,
which has been attributed to everything from the self-effacing modesty
of the Spanish character to the absence of literary salons and their
feminine inspiration. [1]

Speculations of this sort aside, what commands our attention is
the way in which Hispanic autobiography appears to be evolving.
Having practically bypassed the important phase of the confessional
novel in the mold of Rousseau, the type of fictional autobiography
emerging in Spanish America (and Spain) never claims to be a sincere
literary portrait of the writer, but instead flaunts its condition as
artifice and invention. Not only do Cabrera Infante and Vargas Llosa
cross the "modesty barrier," but they take great delight in baring
themselves for the reading public. At the same time, however, they
cloak the self-as-character in fictive garb, as if to disclaim their
literary creature and deny his status as anything except words on a
page.

In this study, I have been compelled to take seriously works
that show off their own frivolity, and I have tried to extract from
the self-mockery some of the weighty reflections these autobiographers
make as they examine what they have been. My discussion of the
narrative structure of *La tía Julia* and *La Habana* may lead to the
conclusion that these works, like others that deviate from the traditional autobiographical mode, have broken down into an incoherent
form of stuttering or a fragmented text with no legitimate beginning
or ending. However, along with James Olney, I do not feel that

---

[1] See especially Juan Marichal, who discusses the "barrera de pudor" and
the man-to-man confessional mode with relation to Unamuno: "La originalidad
de Unamuno y la literatura de confesión," in his *La voluntad de estilo* (Barcelona: Seix Barral, 1957), pp. 233-58.

the structural analysis of the modern autobiographical novel must necessarily become an act of "babbling about stuttering." Rather, it must remain an attempt to decipher the mechanisms of self-creation and ultimately to show how autobiographies like *La Habana para un infante difunto* and *La tía Julia y el escribidor,* though forged with the devices of fiction, do capture a version of the self in the text. I think that through my study of two authors who write about their past selves writing, I have also come to experience the phenomenon of "closet autobiography," as Olney calls it: [2] that vicarious and immensely enjoyable critical activity performed by students of the genre.

---

[2] Olney, "Autobiography and the Cultural Moment," p. 5.

WORKS CITED

Adams, Robert M. *Bad Mouth: Fugitive Papers on the Dark Side.* Berkeley: Univ. of California Press, 1977.

Alter, Robert. *Partial Magic: The Novel as a Self-Conscious Genre.* Berkeley: Univ. of California Press, 1975.

Álvarez-Borland, Isabel. "*La Habana para un infante difunto:* Cabrera Infante's Self Conscious Narrative." *Hispania,* 68 (1985), 44-48.

————. "Viaje verbal a La Habana, ¡Ah Vana! " *Hispamérica,* 11 (April 1982), 51-68.

Arrigoitia, Luis de. "Machismo: Folklore y creación en Mario Vargas Llosa." *Sin Nombre,* 13 (July-September 1983), 7-24.

Bates, E. Stuart. *Inside Out: An Introduction to Autobiography.* New York: Sheridan House, 1937.

Benveniste, Émile. *Problèmes de linguistique générale.* Paris: Gallimard, 1966.

Booth, Wayne C. *The Rhetoric of Fiction.* Chicago: Univ. of Chicago Press, 1961.

Bruss, Elizabeth W. *Autobiographical Acts: The Changing Situation of a Literary Genre.* Baltimore: Johns Hopkins Univ. Press, 1976.

Burgess, Anthony. "What Is Pornography?" In *Perspectives on Pornography.* Ed. Douglas A. Hughes. New York: St. Martin's Press, 1970, pp. 4-8.

Cabrera Infante, Guillermo. *Arcadia todas las noches.* Barcelona: Seix Barral, 1978.

————. *Así en la paz como en la guerra.* Barcelona: Seix Barral, 1971.

————. *Exorcismos de esti(l)o.* Barcelona: Seix Barral, 1976.

————. *La Habana para un infante difunto.* Barcelona: Seix Barral, 1979.

————. Lecture at Cornell University, Ithaca, New York. 25 February 1982.

————. *Un oficio del siglo XX.* Barcelona: Seix Barral, 1973.

————. "Orígenes." In *Guillermo Cabrera Infante.* Julio Ortega et al. Madrid: Espiral/Fundamentos, 1974, pp. 5-18.

————. *Tres tristes tigres.* Barcelona: Seix Barral, 1970.

————. *Vista del amanecer en el trópico.* Barcelona: Seix Barral, 1974.

Cano Gaviria, Ricardo. *El buitre y el Ave Fénix: Conversaciones con Mario Vargas Llosa.* Barcelona: Anagrama, 1972.

Carpentier, Alejo. "Viaje a la semilla." In *Guerra del tiempo.* 5th ed. Barcelona: Barral, 1975.

Charney, Maurice. *Sexual Fiction.* New Accents. New York: Methuen, 1981.

Chatman, Seymour. *Story and Discourse: Narrative Structure in Fiction and Film.* Ithaca: Cornell Univ. Press, 1978.

de Man, Paul. "Autobiography as De-Facement." *Modern Language Notes*, 94 (1979), 919-30.

Downing, Christine. "Re-Visioning Autobiography: The Bequest of Freud and Jung." *Soundings*, 60 (1977), 210-28.

Earle, William. *The Autobiographical Consciousness.* Chicago: Quadrangle Books, 1972.

Federman, Raymond, ed. *Surfiction: Fiction Now... and Tomorrow.* 2nd ed. Chicago: Swallow Press, 1981.

Ferré, Rosario. "Mario Vargas Llosa o el escribidor." *Sin Nombre*, 9 (July-September 1978), 86-90.

Fowler, Alastair. *Kinds of Literature: An Introduction to the Theory of Genres and Modes.* Cambridge: Harvard Univ. Press, 1982.

Frye, Northrop. *Anatomy of Criticism: Four Essays.* 1957; rpt. New York: Atheneum, 1968.

Garavito, C. Lucía. "*La señorita de Tacna* o la escritura de una lectura." *Latin American Theatre Review*, 16 (Fall 1982), 3-14.

García Antezana, Jorge. "Elementos de la picaresca en *Pantaleón y las visitadoras* de Mario Vargas Llosa." In *La picaresca: Orígenes, textos y estructuras.* Actas del I Congreso Internacional sobre la Picaresca. Ed. Manuel Criado de Val. Madrid: Fundación Universitaria Española, 1979, pp. 1095-1116.

Garma, Ángel. *The Psychoanalysis of Dreams.* New York: Dell Publishing, 1966.

Gates, David. "Fiedler's Utopian Vision." *Newsweek*, 9 January 1984, p. 11.

Gedo, Mary Mathews. *Picasso: Art as Autobiography.* Chicago: Univ. of Chicago Press, 1980.

Genette, Gérard. *Narrative Discourse: An Essay in Method.* Trans. Jane E. Lewin. Ithaca: Cornell Univ. Press, 1980.

Gilio, María Ester. "Reportaje a Mario Vargas Llosa: Las claves del escribidor." *Clarín: Cultura y Nación* [Buenos Aires], 28 May 1981, pp. 1-3.

Grossman, Lionel. "The Innocent Art of Confession and Reverie." *Daedalus*, 107 (1978), 59-77.

Guibert, Rita, ed. "Guillermo Cabrera Infante." In *Siete voces.* Mexico: Alfred A. Knopf, 1972, pp. 351-446.

Guillén, Claudio. *Literature as System: Essays Toward the Theory of Literary History.* Princeton: Princeton Univ. Press, 1971.

Guinness, Gerald. Review of *La Habana para un infante difunto. Revista de Estudios Hispánicos* (Puerto Rico), 7 (1980), 216-19.

Gusdorf, Georges. "Conditions and Limits of Autobiography." Trans. James Olney. In *Autobiography: Essays Theoretical and Critical.* Ed. Olney. Princeton: Princeton Univ. Press, 1980, pp. 28-48.

Haag, Ernest van den. "The Case for Pornography is the Case for Censorship and Vice Versa." In *Perspectives on Pornography.* Ed. Douglas A. Hughes. New York: St. Martin's Press, 1970, pp. 122-30.

Harss, Luis, and Barbara Dohmann. *Into the Mainstream: Conversations with Latin-American Writers.* New York: Harper and Row, 1967.

Howarth, William L. "Some Principles of Autobiography." In *Autobiography: Essays Theoretical and Critical.* Ed. James Olney. Princeton: Princeton Univ. Press, 1980, pp. 84-114.

Jay, Paul. *Being in the Text: Self-Representation from Wordsworth to Roland Barthes.* Ithaca: Cornell Univ. Press, 1984.

Jones, Julie. "*La tía Julia y el escribidor:* Mario Vargas Llosa's Versions of Self." *Critique,* 21 (1979), 73-82.

Kazin, Alfred. "Autobiography as Narrative." *Michigan Quarterly Review,* 3 (1964), 210-16.

Kellman, Steven G. *The Self-Begetting Novel.* New York: Columbia Univ. Press, 1980.

Kellogg, Robert, and Robert Scholes. *The Nature of Narrative.* New York: Oxford Univ. Press, 1966.

Lacan, Jacques. "Le Stade du miroir comme formateur de la fonction du Je." In *Écrits I.* Collection Points. Paris: Éditions du Seuil, 1966, pp. 89-97.

Lazarillo de Tormes. Ed. Francisco Rico. Barcelona: Planeta, 1976.

Lejeune, Philippe. *Je est un autre: L'autobiographie de la littérature aux médias.* Paris: Éditions du Seuil, 1980.

——. *Le Pacte autobiographique.* Paris: Éditions du Seuil, 1975.

——. "Le Pacte autobiographique (bis)." In *L'Autobiographie en Espagne: Actes du IIe Colloque International de la Baume-les-Aix.* 23-25 May 1981. Études Hispaniques 5. Aix-en-Provence: Université de Provence, 1982, pp. 7-26.

Levin, Harry. "The Unbanning of the Books." In *Perspectives on Pornography.* Ed. Douglas A. Hughes. New York: St. Martin's Press, 1970, pp. 9-20.

Levine, Suzanne Jill. "Translation as (Sub) Version: On Translating *Infante's Inferno.*" *SubStance,* 13, No. 1 (1984), 85-94.

Lewis, Marvin A. "From Chincha to Chimbote: Blacks in the Contemporary Peruvian Novel." *Afro-Hispanic Review,* 3 (May 1984), 5-10.

Lipski, John M. "Reading the Writers: Hidden Meta-Structures in the Modern Spanish American Novel." *Perspectives on Contemporary Literature,* 6 (1980), 117-24.

Luchting, Wolfgang A. "The Usual and Some Better Shows: Peruvian Theatre in 1981." *Latin American Theatre Review,* 15 (Spring 1982), 59-63.

Machen, Stephen M. " 'Pornoviolence' and Point of View in Mario Vargas Llosa's *La tía Julia y el escribidor.*" *Latin American Literary Review,* 9 (Fall-Winter 1980), 9-16.

Magnarelli, Sharon. "Mario Vargas Llosa's *La señorita de Tacna:* Autobiography and/as Theatre." Autobiography and Fiction in Hispanic Literature, NEMLA Convention, Hartford. 30 March 1985.

——. "The Spring 1983 Theatre Season in Mexico." *Latin American Theatre Review,* 17 (Fall 1983), 69-75.

——. "21 en el 21: Una entrevista de larga distancia con Guillermo Cabrera Infante." *Prismal/Cabral,* No. 5 (Fall 1979), pp. 23-42.

——. "The 'Writerly' in *Tres tristes tigres.*" In *The Analysis of Hispanic Texts: Current Trends in Methodology.* Proc. of the Second York College Colloquium on Hispanic Texts, 23 April 1976. Ed. Lisa E. Davis and Isabel C. Tarán. New York: Bilingual Press/Editorial Bilingüe, 1976, pp. 320-35.

Mandel, Barrett J. "Full of Life Now." In *Autobiography: Essays Theoretical and Critical.* Ed. James Olney. Princeton: Princeton Univ. Press, 1980, pp. 49-72.

Marcus, Steven. *The Other Victorians: A Study of Sexuality and Pornography in Mid-Nineteenth Century England.* 1964; rpt. New York: Norton, 1985.

Marichal, Juan. *La voluntad de estilo.* Barcelona: Seix Barral, 1957.

Marin, Louis. "The Autobiographical Interruption: About Stendhal's *Life of Henry Brulard.*" *Modern Language Notes,* 93 (1978), 597-617.

"Mario Vargas Llosa." *El País* [Madrid], 16 July 1981, p. 48.

Matas, Julio. "Guillermo Cabrera Infante: Autobiografía y novela," In *La cuestión del género literario: Casos de las letras hispánicas.* Madrid: Gredos, 1979, pp. 207-31.

May, Georges. *L'Autobiographie.* Paris: Presses Universitaires de France, 1979.

McCracken, Ellen. "Vargas Llosa's *La tía Julia y el escribidor:* The New Novel and the Mass Media." *Ideologies and Literature,* 3 (June-August 1980), 54-69.

Merrim, Stephanie. "*La Habana para un infante difunto* y su teoría topográfica de las formas." *Revista Iberoamericana,* 48 (January-June 1982), 403-13.

Metz, Christian. *The Imaginary Signifier: Psychoanalysis and the Cinema.* Trans. Celia Britton, Annwyl Williams, Ben Brewster and Alfred Guzzetti. Bloomington: Indiana Univ. Press, 1982.

Michelson, Peter. "An Apology for Pornography." In *Perspectives on Pornography.* Ed. Douglas A. Hughes. New York: St. Martin's Press, 1970, pp. 61-71.

Miller, Yvette E. "Mario Vargas Llosa: Contexto y estructura de *La tía Julia y el escribidor.*" In *Texto/Contexto en la literatura iberoamericana.* Memoria del XIX Congreso del Instituto Internacional de Literatura Iberoamericana, Pittsburgh, 1979. Madrid: Artes Gráficas Benzal, 1980, pp. 235-40.

Mitchell, Phyllis. "The Reel against the Real: Cinema in the Novels of Guillermo Cabrera Infante and Manuel Puig." *Latin American Literary Review,* 6 (Fall-Winter 1977), 22-29.

Montes-Huidobro, Matías. Review of *La Habana para un infante difunto. Chasqui,* 8 (May 1979), 90-91.

Morris, John N. *Versions of the Self: Studies in English Autobiography from John Bunyan to John Stuart Mill.* New York: Basic Books, 1966.

Nelson, Ardis L. *Cabrera Infante in the Menippean Tradition.* Newark, Delaware: Juan de la Cuesta, 1983.

———. "Cabrera Infante's 'Continuous Showing.' " Review of *La Habana para un infante difunto. Revista Canadiense de Estudios Hispánicos,* 5 (1981), 216-18.

———. "*Tres tristes tigres* y el cine." *Kentucky Romance Quarterly,* 29 (1982), 391-404.

Olney, James. "Autobiography and the Cultural Moment: A Thematic, Historical, and Bibliographical Introduction." In *Autobiography: Essays Theoretical and Critical.* Ed. Olney. Princeton: Princeton Univ. Press, 1980, pp. 3-27.

———. *Metaphors of Self: The Meaning of Autobiography.* Princeton: Princeton Univ. Press, 1972.

———. "Some Versions of Memory/Some Versions of *Bios:* The Ontology of Autobiography." In *Autobiography: Essays Theoretical and Critical.* Ed. Olney. Princeton: Princeton Univ. Press, 1980, pp. 236-67.

Oviedo, José Miguel. "Conversación con Mario Vargas Llosa sobre *La tía Julia y el escribidor.*" In *Mario Vargas Llosa: A Collection of Critical Essays.* Ed. Charles Rossman and Alan Warren Friedman. Austin: Univ. of Texas Press, 1978, pp. 152-65.

———. "Mario Vargas Llosa: Maestro de las voces."In *Espejo de escritores.* Ed. Reina Roffé. Hanover: Ediciones del Norte, 1985, pp. 147-72.

———. "*La tía Julia y el escribidor,* or the Coded Self-Portrait." In *Mario Vargas Llosa: A Collection of Critical Essays.* Ed. Charles Rossman and Alan Warren Friedman. Austin: Univ. of Texas Press, 1978, pp. 166-81.

Pascal, Roy. *Design and Truth in Autobiography*. Cambridge: Harvard Univ. Press, 1960.

Pereda, Rosa María. *Guillermo Cabrera Infante*. Escritores de todos los tiempos, No. 3. Madrid: EDAF, 1978.

Perrone-Moisés, Leyla. "L'Enfant dans la glace ou Don Juan en Amérique latine." *Cahiers Confrontation*, No. 6 (1981), pp. 47-55.

Pike, Burton. "Time in Autobiography." *Comparative Literature*, 28 (1976), 326-42.

Pilling, John. *Autobiography and Imagination: Studies in Self-Scrutiny*. London: Routledge and Kegan Paul, 1981.

Prieto Taboada, Antonio. Review of *La Habana para un infante difunto*. *Hispamérica*, 30 (December 1981), 154-56.

Prince, Gerald. "Introduction to the Study of the Narratee." In *Reader-Response Criticism: From Formalism to Post-Structuralism*. Ed. Jane P. Tompkins. Baltimore: Johns Hopkins Univ. Press, 1980, pp. 7-25.

Reedy, Daniel R. "Del beso de la mujer araña al de la tía Julia: estructura y dinámica interior." *Revista Iberoamericana*, 47 (July-December 1981), 190-16.

Renza, Louis A. "The Veto of the Imagination: A Theory of Autobiography." In *Autobiography: Essays Theoretical and Critical*. Ed. James Olney. Princeton: Princeton Univ. Press, 1980, pp. 268-95.

Rodríguez Monegal, Emir. "Cabrera Infante: La novela como autobiografía total." *Revista Iberoamericana*, 47 (July-December 1981), 265-71.

Romberg, Bertil. *Studies in the Narrative Technique of the First-Person Novel*. Trans. Michael Taylor and Harold H. Borland. Lund, Sweden: Almquist and Wiksell, 1962.

Rosenblatt, Roger. "Black Autobiography: Life as the Death Weapon." In *Autobiography: Essays Theoretical and Critical*. Ed. James Olney. Princeton: Princeton Univ. Press, 1980, pp. 169-80.

Roth, Philip. *Portnoy's Complaint*. New York: Bantam, 1970.

Rousset, Jean. *Narcisse romancier: Essai sur la première personne dans le roman*. Paris: Librairie José Corti, 1973.

Ruas, Charles. "Talk with Mario Vargas Llosa." *The New York Times Book Review*, 1 August 1982, pp. 15, 18.

Scholes, Robert. *Structuralism in Literature*. New Haven: Yale Univ. Press, 1974.

Shapiro, Stephen A. "The Dark Continent of Literature: Autobiography." *Comparative Literature Studies*, 5 (1968), 421-54.

Sieber, Harry. *Language and Society in "La vida de Lazarillo de Tormes."* Baltimore: Johns Hopkins Univ. Press, 1978.

———. *The Picaresque*. London: Methuen, 1977.

Siemens, William L., comp. "Guillermo Cabrera Infante: Man of Three Islands." *Review*, 28 (January-April 1981), 8-11.

Sontag, Susan. "The Pornographic Imagination." In *Styles of Radical Will*. New York: Delta, 1970, pp. 35-73.

Sosnowski, Saúl. "Mario Vargas Llosa: entre radioteatros y escribidores." In *Latin American Fiction Today: A Symposium*. Ed. Rose S. Minc. Tacoma Park and Montclair State College: Ediciones Hispamérica, 1980, pp. 75-82.

Spacks, Patricia Meyer. *Imagining a Self: Autobiography and Novel in Eighteenth-Century England*. Cambridge: Harvard Univ. Press, 1976.

Spender, Stephen. "Confessions and Autobiography." In *Autobiography: Essays Theoretical and Critical*. Ed. James Olney. Princeton: Princeton Univ. Press, 1980, pp. 115-22.

Spengemann, William C. *The Forms of Autobiography: Episodes in the History of a Literary Genre*. New Haven: Yale Univ. Press, 1980.

Spires, Robert C. *Beyond the Metafictional Mode: Directions in the Modern Spanish Novel*. Lexington: Kentucky Univ. Press, 1984.

Starobinski, Jean. "The Style of Autobiography." Trans. Seymour Chatman. In *Literary Style: A Symposium*. Ed. Chatman. New York: Oxford Univ. Press, 1971, pp. 285-94.

Steiner, George. "Night Words: High Pornography and Human Privacy." In *Perspectives on Pornography*. Ed. Douglas A. Hughes. New York: St. Martin's Press, 1970, pp. 96-108.

Suárez-Galbán Guerra, Eugenio. "*La Habana para un infante difunto:* la falsa memoria verdadera de Guillermo Cabrera Infante." *Insula*, Nos. 404-405 (July-August 1980), p. 31.

Suleiman, Susan R., and Inge Crosman, eds. *The Reader in the Text: Essays on Audience and Interpretation*. Princeton: Princeton Univ. Press, 1980.

Tittler, Jonathan. "Cabrera Infante's Novels: From the Failure of Language to the Language of Failure." Lecture at Cornell University, Ithaca, New York. 25 February 1982.

———. *Narrative Irony in the Contemporary Spanish-American Novel*. Ithaca: Cornell Univ. Press, 1984.

Tynan, Kenneth. "Dirty Books Can Stay." In *Perspectives on Pornography*. Ed. Douglas A. Hughes. New York: St. Martin's Press, 1970, pp. 109-21.

Unamuno, Miguel de. *Abel Sánchez*. In *Obras completas*, II. Madrid: Escelicer, 1967.

Updike, John. "The Astronomer." In *Pigeon Feathers and Other Stories*. New York: Crest, 1963.

Urquidi Illanes, Julia. *Lo que Varguitas no dijo*. Biblioteca Popular Boliviana de Última Hora. La Paz: Khana Cruz, 1983.

Valle-Inclán, Ramón del. *Luces de Bohemia*. 4th ed. Madrid: Espasa-Calpe, 1973.

Vargas Llosa, Mario. *La casa verde*. Barcelona: Seix Barral, 1966.

———. *La ciudad y los perros*. 7th ed. Barcelona: Seix Barral, 1966.

———. *Conversación en La Catedral*. 12th ed. Barcelona: Seix Barral, 1980.

———. *García Márquez: Historia de un deicidio*. Barcelona: Barral, 1971.

———. *Historia de Mayta*. Barcelona: Seix Barral, 1984.

———. *Historia secreta de una novela*. Conferencia pronunciada en Washington State Univ., 12 November 1968. Barcelona: Tusquets, 1971.

———. *Kathie y el hipopótamo*. Barcelona: Seix Barral, 1983.

———. "La literatura es fuego." In *Homenaje a Mario Vargas Llosa*. Ed. Helmy F. Giacoman and José Miguel Oviedo. Madrid: Anaya, 1971, pp. 17-21.

———. *La novela*. Conferencia pronunciada en el Paraninfo de la Universidad de Montevideo, 11 August 1966. Argentina: América Nueva, 1974.

———. *La orgía perpetua: Flaubert y "Madame Bovary."* Barcelona: Seix Barral, 1975.

———. *Pantaleón y las visitadoras*. Barcelona: Seix Barral, 1973.

———. *La señorita de Tacna*. Barcelona: Seix Barral, 1981.

———. *La tía Julia y el escribidor*. Barcelona: Seix Barral, 1977.

Wyers, Frances. "Manuel Puig at the Movies." *Hispanic Review*, 49 (1981), 163-81.

Ynduráin, Domingo. "Vargas Llosa y el escribidor." *Cuadernos Hispanoamericanos*, 370 (April 1981), 150-72.